KU-574-767

MUSEUMS
OF
INDIA

Shobita Punja was born in south India. Travelling with her parents she attended several schools in India, Beirut and London. Her first university degree was in the history of art, which still remains her prime passion. Later she read history at the Jawaharlal Nehru University in New Delhi and went on to study art education at Stanford University in California. Her doctoral thesis was in the area of cultural education for Indian schools. She has travelled to several countries including Cuba and England to study innovative educational practices. She has been engaged in teaching both teachers and students about art and in creating an appreciation for the rich cultural heritage of India. She has had the privilege of working under several eminent art historians and educationalists whom she recognises as her gurus.

Dr Punja is the author of several books: *Museums of India* was first published in 1990 in Hong Kong by Odyssey Guides. *Divine Ecstasy: The Story of Khajuraho,* published by Viking-Penguin, Delhi in 1992, is an innovative analysis and interpretation of the sculptures and architecture of the tenth century temples at Khajuraho in central India. Her other books include *Khajuraho* and *Benaras* in Our World in Colour series, Hong Kong, 1990; *Great Monuments of India, Bhutan, Nepal, Pakistan and Sri Lanka,* published by the Guidebook Company, Hong Kong in 1994; *Listen to the Animals* and *Stories about This and That,* Puffin Books, India, 1994; *Daughters of the Ocean. Discovering the Goddess Within,* Viking-Penguin, 1996; and *This is India* for New Holland Publishers, London, 1997.

At present she is working on several conservation projects for the preservation of Indian's cultural heritage.

She lives in Delhi with her daughter, Samiha.

MUSEUMS
OF
INDIA

Shobita Punja

Photography by Jean-Louis Nou

LOCAL COLOUR

Copyright © 1998, 1991 Local Colour Limited, Hong Kong

The moral right of the author has been asserted

All rights reserved. Without limiting the rights under copyright reserved above, no part of this publication may be reproduced into a retrieval system, or transmitted in any form or by any means (electronic, mechanical, photocopying, recording or otherwise), without the prior written permission of both the copyright owner and the above publisher of this book

Although the Publisher and the Author have made every effort to ensure the information was correct at the time of going to press, the Publishers and the Author do not assume and hereby disclaim any liability to any party for the loss or damage by errors, ommissions, misleading information, or any potential travel disruption due to labour or financial difficulty, whether such errors or ommissions result from negligence, accident or by any other cause

A CIP catalogue record for this is available from the British Library

ISBN 962–217–385–3

Editors: Aruna Ghose and Wendy de Veer

Map Artwork: Bai Yiliang

Design: Gulmohur Press (Pvt) Limited

Photo Credits: Kamal Sahai: half title, 22–23, 34, 46–47, 138, 155, 160, 164, 177, 225, 232, 238, 239

Printed and bound in Hong Kong

Padmapani Bodhisattva, *State Museum, Patna*

Contents

Preface   12

Introduction   16

How to Use this Guidebook   16
A Brief History of Indian Museums   21
Towards an Appreciation of Indian Art   25

Some Aspects of the Cultural History of India   36

Setting the Stage   36
The Indus Valley or Harappan Civilization (2500-1500 BC)   37
The Iron Age and the Evolution of Vedic Literature (1500-1000 BC)   38
The Birth of Buddhism and Jainism (1000-500 BC)   40
The Spread of Buddhism (500 BC-AD 1)   43
The Rise of Empires (AD 1-500)   50
The Age of Experimentation (AD 500-1000)   56
The Maturation of Hindu Art and the Introduction of Islam (AD 1000-1500)   60
The Last Five Hundred Years (AD 1500-2000)   64

Museums   75

New Delhi   75

The National Museum   75
    The Indus Valley Civilization Gallery   75
    Mauryan, Sunga and Satavahana Art   80
    The Art of Gandhara and Mathura   80
    The Art of the Gupta Period   82
    Medieval Sculpture Galleries   85
    The Indian Bronze Gallery   88
    The Gallery of Manuscripts and Paintings   90
    Central Asian Antiquities   98
    Other Important Galleries   99
    Museum Services   101
The National Gallery of Modern Art   102
    Museum Services   110
The Crafts Museum   110
    Museum Services   112
The Archaeological Museum at the Red Fort   113
The Gandhi Memorial Museum at Raj Ghat   116
The Gandhi Smriti Museum on Tees January Marg   116
    Museum Services   117
The Nehru Memorial Museum and Library   118
    Museum Services   120

Mumbai	121
The Prince of Wales Museum	121
The Natural History Section	132

Calcutta	135
The Indian Museum	135
The Bharhut Room	135
Gandhara Sculptures	139
The Numismatic Galllery	140
Indian Sculpture of Different Regions	141
The Zoological Section	143
The Ashutosh Museum of Indian Art	144
The Collection of Crafts	146
The Victoria Memorial Museum	150

Chennai	156
The Government State Museum and National Art Gallery	156
The Amaravati Collection	156
The Bronze Gallery	159
The Fort St George Museum	165

Ahmedabad (Gujarat)	170
The Calico Museum of Textiles	170
The Utensils Museum	175

| Alwar (Rajasthan) | 180 |
| The Government Museum | 180 |

| Vadodara (Gujarat) | 181 |
| The Baroda Museum and Picture Gallery | 181 |

| Bhopal (Madhya Pradesh) | 183 |
| The Bharat Bhavan | 183 |

| Bhubaneswar (Orissa) | 186 |
| The Orissa State Museum | 186 |

| Goa | 189 |
| The Archaeological Museum, Old Goa | 189 |

| Guwahati (Assam) | 191 |
| The Assam State Museum | 191 |

| Hyderabad (Andhra Pradesh) | 193 |
| The Salar Jung Museum | 193 |

Jaipur (Rajasthan)   202
  The Maharaja Sawai Madho Singh Museum 202

Khajuraho (Madhya Pradesh)   209
  The Archaeological Museum   209

Mathura (Uttar Pradesh)   215
  The Government Museum   215

Patna (Bihar)   224
  The State Museum   224

Pune (Maharashtra)   227
  The Raja Dinkar Kelkar Museum   227

Sanchi (Madhya Pradesh)   231
  The Archaeological Museum   231

Sarnath (Uttar Pradesh)   234
  The Archaeological Museum   234

Srirangapatnam (Karnataka)   237
  The Tipu Sultan Museum   237

Thanjavur (Tamil Nadu)   240
  The Thanjavur Art Gallery   240

Thiruvananthapuram (Kerala)   243
  The Government Museum   243

Varanasi (Uttar Pradesh)   245
  The Bharat Kala Bhavan   245

Reference Section   260
  A Statewise List of Museums   260
  Indian Iconography and Glossary of Terms   271
  Chronology, Historical Sites and Related Museums   289

Recommended Reading   296

Index   298

Jain Manuscript illustration, western India style, 15th century;
National Museum, New Delhi

Acknowledgements

The author would like to thank her grandparents and parents, Naomi Meadows and Ramesh and Premalata Punja, for introducing her to the world of art; her teachers and those with whom she has had the privilege to work, Dr D B Desai, Dr Elliot Eisner, Dr M C Joshi, Dr Kapila Vatsyayan, Prof Mrs S Mutakar, Ms Premlata Puri, the late Kamladevi Chattopadhyay and the late B K Thapar. Her gratitude extends to all those whose untiring help made this guidebook possible, in particular the directors of all the museums, Carolyn Watts and everyone at Local Colour. The late Jean-Louis Nou, whose captivating photographs illustrate this book, and whose love for India will always be missed.

Devi, detail of Chola Bronze, 11th century; Thanjavur Art Gallery, Thanjavur

Preface

India's museums house many of the greatest artistic treasures ever produced in the sub-continent. Some of them are well-known; others are favourite haunts of the well-informed; all deserve much greater attention.

The history of these museums, like those in other parts of the world, reflects a pattern of changing concerns with the past, the present and the future. In India two sets of attitudes to time confront each other, the one indigenous, the other introduced. The idea of the museum is in some way alien to India, but there had of course always been royal treasuries, storehouses of works of art, that serviced courtly ceremonies. Temples, too, large and small, owned collections of textiles, manuscripts, images of deities, and ritual appurtenances for use in their daily rites and their annual cycle of festivals. But these treasured items, whether of great antiquity or of recent manufacture, were an integral part of a living tradition. It was the British who established India's first 'museum' at the turn of the 18th and 19th centuries. As the Western concept of time as a linear sequence gained ground in India, and Britain recognised the importance of documenting India's natural resources, museums began to gradually establish themselves as centres for the safe-keeping of items of cultural, historical and scientific importance, and their number grew steadily through the 19th and early 20th centuries. Since Independence, as the pace of economic change has accelerated, India's museums have become even more important as guardians of valuable cultural traditions.

There are, however, striking differences between museums in India and those in the West. In India, for many of the museum-going public, the items on display are still part of their living tradition. Images of deities — their iconography readily recognisable — may even be viewed as objects of reverence rather than examples of high art. Kings and emperors depicted in miniature paintings are familiar — the heroes of a continuing, popular, oral tradition. The shapes and styles of more utilitarian objects evoke childhood memories among the older generation.

The strength of this cultural continuity, which obviates some of the local visitor's need or wish for extensive verbal explanation has, however, clear disadvantages for the foreign visitor who has come to expect didactic aids even when confronting his own cultural past. That is perhaps why, India's museums have hitherto received little attention in general guides for tourists. They have certainly never been the sole focus of interest. This new guide, the first of its kind, is thus an invaluable addition to the literature. It provides not only an introduction to the most important of India's museums, but also, by means of a general essay on Indian cultural history and aesthetic philosophy, a simple route through the complex maze of India's cultural traditions. Descriptions of particular museums both survey the range of their collections and highlight important artifacts for close attention.

India's museums are a microcosm of her rich history and varied traditions. The buildings that house them reflect, too, the diversity of her architecture. Archaeological site museums allow the visitor to examine artifacts in relation to the total site. A museum like the Crafts Museum in New Delhi, with its village-style layout, gives the visitor a preview of India's rural traditions. The museums housed in the City Palace at Jaipur and the Fort at Jodhpur evoke the former glories of the Rajput courts. The Salar Jung Museum in Hyderabad and other later 19th- and early 20th-century princely collections demonstrate the eclectic taste of the maharajas of the period. The Prince of Wales Museum, its central range built in 1914, is an accomplished example of the so-called Indo-Saracenic style of architecture which became important in the late 19th century. Teen Murti House in New Delhi, built in a European classical style, and now the Nehru Memorial Museum, offers revealing insights into India's 20th-century history in a setting that highlights the ironies of the complex relationships that developed between Britain and India. Charles Correa's design for the new Bharat Bhavan in Bhopal, itself an experimental form of museum, exemplifies the achievements of India's contemporary architects.

Some of the great works of art from India's museum collections have been shown over the past decade in festivals of India throughout the world. Many more can be seen on their home ground. This richly illustrated volume will be an enjoyable companion and indispensable guide on the road to their discovery.

Dr D A Swallow
Curator of the Indian Collection, Victoria and Albert Museum, London.

The external boundaries of the following map are neither authentic nor correct

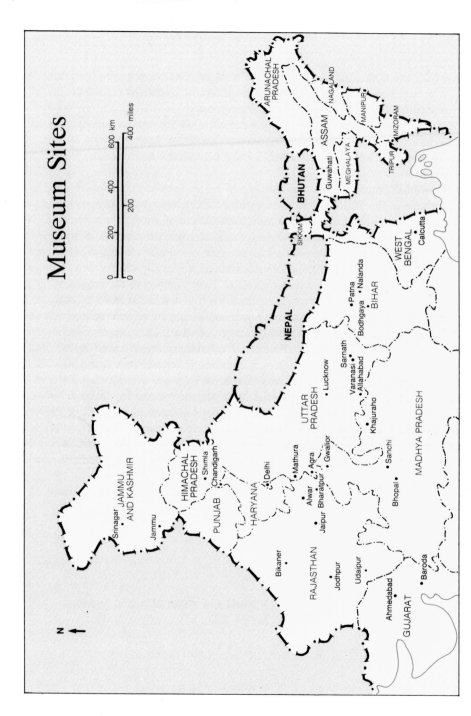

Museum Sites

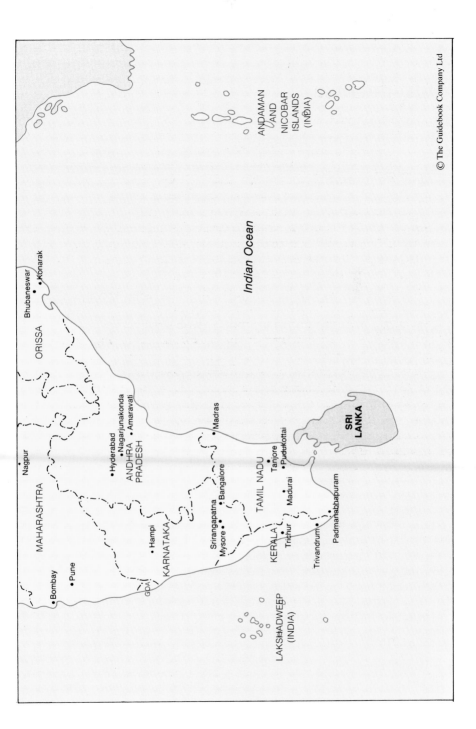

© The Guidebook Company Ltd

Introduction

How to Use this Guidebook

In recent years there has been growing interest in India's art and her ancient culture. Thousands of tourists, visitors and scholars come to India each year, and for their use several guidebooks are now available. However, an area of interest that has been neglected so far is that of Indian museums, where a great part of India's artistic heritage is now housed and exhibited. This guidebook hopes to serve as a handy introduction to some of India's finest museums, and to the wealth and richness of Indian art and history.

The guide has been divided into three major sections, as follows:

SOME ASPECTS OF THE CULTURAL HISTORY OF INDIA

This section of the book describes the evolution of India's artistic traditions and the major turning points in this evolution, painted on a broad historical canvas. The whole section is subdivided into nine short parts, so that the reader can refer to the appropriate part before he visits a museum, or while he is studying an object of interest in the museum. The exhibit labelling provided in the museums themselves usually refers to a historical period, or a date, and the reader can therefore use this dating to find the most suitable part of the book for the relevant section of India's cultural history.

MUSEUMS

The concept of a museum is not Indian and is foreign to most Indians. However, the British colonial rulers initiated the movement and today there are over 500 museums in the country. Those under the central government like the National Museum, New Delhi enjoy special status and funding. Each region has what are called State Government Museums often located in their capital cities and at important historical sites. Inadequate funding to state museums is one of the many reasons for poor maintenance and display, though these museums have very valuable collections.

The Archaeological Survey of India has 33 site museums, some located at World Heritage Sites like Khajuraho, Sanchi, and Agra or near historical buildings and at excavation sites, such as Amaravati and Lothal. The Archaeological Site Museums maintain a standard of cleanliness and display. In addition, the State Archaeological Departments have their museums which again suffer from lack of funds and attention.

There are science museums/centres under the National Council of Science Museums and the National Museum of Natural History, Delhi that have taken up the cause of public education as an important part of their agenda. There are University museums that specialise in a range of disciplines from zoology to the arts.

Other museums like the Air force Museum, Rail Transport museum are run by related government departments. There are museum trusts that also specialise in a single discipline area.

The private museums form the last category and a few of them have set high standards of quality like the Calico Museum of Textiles, Ahmedabad. Today, private art galleries have mushroomed in large metropolitan cities as the demand for art objects has become fashionable.

Most museums in India receive government grants and do not generate an income through their own programmes. This has led to poor motivation levels of museum personnel and inadequate training, few museums in India have catalogues of their collections, guides or any other publications. The government has to fully realise the educational potential of museums and make them an important aspect of public life in India.

Museums in India house some of the most precious, irreplaceable national treasures. The government needs therefore, to urgently address the needs of museums: their security, documentation of objects, publications, educational programmes, scientific conservation, design and display of these priceless collections.

The major cities and historical sites — those that visitors would most likely want to see — have been selected, and the important museums in these places are described in the third section of the book. The four cities of New Delhi, Bombay (now called Mumbai), Calcutta and Madras (or Chennai) are dealt with first, as these are the usual entry points into India for the foreign visitor. Then, in alphabetical order, other Indian cities with important or interesting museums are introduced.

Most museums in India have an incredibly large collection of objects, ranging from paintings, sculptures, manuscripts and textiles to metalware, glass, armoury and jewellery. Apart from the variety in forms, the objects are each representative of a distinct phase or historical period, from among an accumulation of over 5,000 years of Indian history. For this reason, one or two aspects or galleries of a particular museum have been singled out

(overleaf) Vishnu and consorts, late Chola period; Government State Museum, Chennai

for description in greater detail. For instance, for the Indian Museum at Calcutta, a fuller account has been given of early Buddhist sculpture, with only a brief mention of the treasures of medieval Hindu sculpture that one can also see there. This is because the museum has a particularly rare collection of early Buddhist art, and comparable works can be found in very few other places.

For each gallery or section of a museum, mention has been made of only one or two especially interesting objects because this book is not intended as a catalogue but merely as an introduction or orientation to Indian museums generally. It is also possible that the objects that *are* mentioned in the text, or are illustrated in the book, may not be found in the museum during your visit. This may be because some objects have been sent for exhibition elsewhere, or have been lent to other museums in exchange for exhibits from their vast reserve collections. Therefore, the descriptive part of the guide has been kept at a general level. It was also felt that readers would not want to be burdened with an excess of indigestible detail.

Some museums — like the Utensils Museum or the Calico Museum, both in Ahmedabad — have been mentioned for their unique collections and specialised focus of interest. In other cases, a museum has been selected for the historical value of its site, and particular attention has been given to describing the period and place concerned, because these evoke the history of the times in a dramatic way. This is the case with the Fort St George Museum in Chennai and the Tipu Sultan Museum in Srirangapatnam, Karnataka, for instance. In general, different aspects of the various museums have been described both to avoid monotony and to give you a taste of as many facets of India's cultural history as possible.

The Reference Section

The iconography and glossary section briefly defines special terms and describes some of the many Indian gods and goddesses you may encounter on your museum visit. If you become interested in an object not mentioned in the museum description and want to know a little more, the history section and iconographic details may provide the information you are looking for.

The labelling used in Indian museums is usually very brief. For instance, you might read, 'Devi, ninth century, bronze, Tanjore, Tamil Nadu'. Devi, the Hindu goddess, is described in alphabetical order in the iconographical section. In the light of contemporary developments in the field of art history, some of the museum labels are now inadequate. However, for purposes of identification, the museum labels have been quoted in the text and are accompanied by descriptive passages.

Should you develop a special interest in the art of a particular period of history, then you may like to refer to the tabular section of this book, headed 'Chronology, Historical Sites and Related Museums', to find where the best exhibits are to be seen for that particular period.

A short selection of books recommended for further reading has also been appended, in the hope that this will be helpful for those wanting to know more about India and her artistic treasures.

A Brief History of Indian Museums

At the turn of the 19th century, the British in India set up a number of institutions such as the Geological Survey of India and the Botanical Survey. These organisations were entrusted with the task of 'assessing' India's potential as a supplier of raw materials and, in general, as a colony that could be exploited. On the other hand, the Archaeological Survey and the Asiatic Society were established as interest in Indian art and culture grew under the patronage of enlightened, academically inclined officers of the army and administration, and of scholars who were increasingly captivated by India and the mystery of her ancient past. It was an age of exploration in the West and dedicated researchers, braving illness and fatigue, went to distant lands to study the people and their customs. Through their work, the world came to know that Sanskrit was as old and rich a language as Latin, that Indian art was both awe-inspiring and unique. For persons driven by the spirit of Victorian exploration and curiosity hunting, India was a treasure trove of antiquities. Initially, in the first flush of enthusiasm, the 'finds' were transported back to Britain, and even today fine collections of Indian art are to be seen in the British Museum, the Victoria and Albert Museum and the India Office Library. As the collections grew, it became more sensible to house them in India. Credit here must go to the British administrators who salvaged and conserved so much of Indian art for posterity and set up the first museums in India.

BRITISH ORIGINS OF INDIAN MUSEUMS

The first important museum to be established was the Indian Museum in Calcutta, which was ready for occupation in 1875. The earliest Indian

(overleaf) Amaravati Gallery; State Government Museum, Chennai

museums are now over a 100 years old and have separate sections for art and archaeology, as well as galleries for geology, zoology, anthropology, etc. In parallel with these museums, medical, university and industrial museums sprang up, to encompass the wide range of interests and needs of the times.

Lord Curzon (the Viceroy) and Sir John Marshall, head of the Archaeological Survey, together made an invaluable contribution by setting up what are called site museums, located at important places of historical interest. These museums are specialised in content and carry collections of archaeological finds from a particular region.

Museum architecture during the British period followed the imperial style prevalent in each city. The Prince of Wales Museum in Mumbai and the Government State Museum in Chennai are excellent examples of colonial architecture. Though most of the original British museums are housed in interesting buildings, by modern standards they are inappropriate as museums. They lack the basic facilities and requirements for adequate display and maintenance. The exhibits are poorly lit, and the rooms are huge, with very high ceilings that collect dust and cobwebs. The old-fashioned cabinets designed to fill the rooms are more like storage cupboards, with objects crowded together in apparent disarray.

With the awakening of nationalist sentiment in India, a keen interest developed amongst the educated Indian upper classes in the culture of their own country. Private individuals began to assemble collections from material already at hand, and today we can see the evidence of the pioneering work done by such individuals. The Ashutosh Museum of Indian Art in Calcutta, the Tata Collection in the Prince of Wales Museum, Mumbai, the Calico Museum in Ahmedabad and the Raja Kelkar Museum in Pune, each described in this volume, are examples of this kind of museum.

When India became independent, declaring itself a democratic republic, the fabled maharajas of the country lost their estates. Their family collections of art treasures, archives and memorabilia are in some cases housed in part of former palace, or, later set up as a public museum. In northern India, 'palace museums' are concentrated in the area of Rajasthan, and in this book, those at Jaipur and Alwar are described, together with the Baroda (or Vadodara) and Hyderabad museums in western and southern India.

The royal collections of the 19th century are varied and rich, reflecting an eclectic taste, and an indulgence in luxury goods of minimal practical use and in Western art and kitsch. A dining table with a silver toy train carrying dishes was once considered the great attraction of a royal

Relief of the foundation of the Prince of Wales Museum, 1905;
Prince of Wales Museum, Mumbai

collection. However, royalty also preserved its family heirlooms — paintings, textiles and armoury — which are of immense value in the study of the development of Indian art and craftsmanship through the ages.

Towards an Appreciation of Indian Art

India has developed her own principles of aesthetics; quite different from those of Europe, the Middle East or China. Those visitors oriented towards their own cultural heritage may look (as has been done) for elements of realism, naturalism, Giotto's perfect perspective and Rembrandt's deep, shadowy *chiaroscuro*. These concerns, worthy as they are, were not of prime importance to the Indian artist. The paintings are full of sunlight, with figures executed to 'ideal' measurements; where instead of attempting to copy nature, the artist strove to create a poetic symbol, a philosophical statement, an answer to the riddle of life. All the arts, around the world, strive to reach levels of enlightenment beyond technical excellence, but the approaches adopted and the answers proffered differ. It is after all, questions of ideology, philosophy, a way of life and a vision of the world that make each culture unique and special.

THE FAMILY OF ARTISTS

India's socio-economic, political and religious conditions were and are very different from those in Europe. In the village, the local potter or painter was known to everyone, and he did not need to autograph his wares. Furthermore, even today, some of India's finest artists, musicians and dancers are illiterate, and cannot sign their names. They store an amazing wealth of artistic experience, techniques and information in their memory, and hand this wealth down to the next generation by word of mouth and by example. Both parallel to and within the Indian caste system ran the *gharana* system, in which a particular artistic tradition was maintained by one family of artists. (*Ghar* means house, or family.) A musician would teach his son from a very early age the intricacies of his art and all that his forefathers had handed down to him. Similarly, in the home of a potter or sculptor, a dancer or painter, the tradition was handed down from generation to generation. It was unusual for a potter's son to become a blacksmith, though a sculptor and painter were expected to know enough about literature, music and dance to bring a greater depth of meaning to their work. So it was not merely the artist's individuality that was important; it was the family tradition, going back several generations, that found expression in each artistic creation.

INTEGRATION OF THE ARTS AND LEVELS OF MEANING

In rural India, music and dance associated with every aspect of life. Even today there are work songs, songs for festivals and songs for every important stage of human life — from birth, the naming of the child, puberty and marriage to parenthood and death. Every community had its own festivals, songs and dances that brought all its members together in celebration or in sorrow. The songs were created and sung by the people, and were not separate from their day-to-day life. This love of music and dance is also expressed in paintings, sculptures, textiles and other crafts.

Literature, myths and religious legends were communicated through powerful oral traditions coming down from time immemorial. Wandering theatre groups and puppeteers, storytellers and bards helped to unify India by carrying these narratives across the length and breadth of the country. Much of Indian painting, sculpture and even architecture reflects this deep understanding and love of literature. The art forms in India, unlike those in any other country, are totally inseparable from one another. In the *Vishnudharmottaram* text there is a passage often quoted to emphasise this

Interior of Mehrangarh Fort; Jodhpur

ancient notion of the interrelationship of the visual, performing and literary arts: someone asks how sculptures are made, and he is advised to study painting; and in order to learn painting, he should be qualified in both literature and dance; and for an understanding of dance, a knowledge of music is essential.

Literature in India is most often poetry-based, especially that dating from ancient times when it served both religious and secular needs. Poetry involves exceptional economy with words, and the use of symbols and metaphors replete with meaning and potential feelings. Such poetry has served as the source of inspiration for sculpture, painting, architecture, dance and music. It is from poetry that the artist derives the similes that are translated into other art forms. For instance, a beautiful woman's face is likened to the full moon. Here are two examples of Indian verse (*Poems from the Sanskrit*, translated with an introduction by John Brough, Penguin, 1968), one romantic in mood, the other almost angry, but both contain a poetic humour that is very Indian.

> The moon tries every month in vain
> To paint a picture of your face;
> And, having failed to catch its grace,
> Destroys the work, and starts again.
> *   *   *
> Her face is not the moon, nor are her eyes
> Twin lotuses, nor are her arms pure gold.
> She's flesh and bone. What lies the poets told!
> Ah, but we love her, we believe them.

Unless one is familiar with Indian literature and poetry, the soul of Indian art is somehow lost.

ART AS WORSHIP

There is a custom, still prevalent in India, in which a devotee pledges to honour his gods by offering service and gifts. Such service might be in the form of singing in the temple, for example. Or one might promise to 'offer oil for the lighting of the temple lamps', or 'give a golden vessel for worship, or sing for 20 days of the festival season in praise of God'. These kinds of gifts were sometimes recorded by the priests, but most often they remained unrecorded and anonymous. In medieval Europe similar traditions also existed. In India such customs were practised faithfully, and temples — huge mountains of stonework — were constructed without any record of artist, architect or masons. Guilds, or families of artists, worked together to bring an organic wholeness to architecture. Individual sculptors prepared carved stone pieces to be fitted into a wall of the temple, and their work was supervised by the master-artisan, who gave style and continuity to the entire creation. Craftsmen often had to work for years to build just one temple, and the objects now housed in museums hardly reflect with justice the hardship and sacrifice that went into making these masterpieces. Hindu philosophy stresses this aspect of the insignificance of the individual in the splendour of the universe. Human beings were urged by their faith to dissolve into the ocean of life, like a river when it meets the sea. For, 'Who can separate the waters of the river from the mighty sea, and who can claim to have made the waters that sustain life on earth?'

THE ARTISTS AND THEIR MATERIAL

A traditional woodsculptor from Kerala, narrating how he collected wood for his work, said,

> We go to the forests, and choose an appropriate tree that is not deformed in any way. Then, on the auspicious day and hour, we take offerings of sweets and rice and place them at the foot of the tree. In a prayer, we ask forgiveness from all the creatures, birds and insects who live in the tree. We assure them that though we are depriving them of their home and food, we will use the wood for a good purpose, not wasting even a scrap of shaving.

Such a beautiful description, coloured by sentiment, conveys an important philosophical idea. Indian artists believe that all of nature is interdependent and respect should be shown to everything on earth, living or non-living. The *Shastra* — the sacred Hindu writings, some of which serve as manuals for arts and crafts — prescribe a similar attitude for quarrying stone from Mother Earth. The sculptor-builder was expected to follow the rites due to the Earth, and to respect the materials he used.

MYRIAD LEVELS OF INDIAN SYMBOLISM

It is this attitude of respect for nature, expressed in rituals encouraging a deep and lasting appreciation of the natural world, that has been present in Indian art through the ages. In nature, in animals and trees, the artist found symbols for artistic expression. All art is symbolic, making use of symbols to convey meaning and emotions, ideas and philosophical concepts. Indian literature, dance, sculpture and painting abound in symbols derived from nature.

(overleaf) Musicians, detail from painting of the Ramayana *series; Kullu, 18th century*

The lotus flower is one such symbol. You will see it in almost all museums in India. A goddess stands on a lotus, or she is holding a lotus bud. The flower itself may not even be there, for the artist need only show her fingers clasping a make-believe lotus to convey the idea. The lotus grows in stagnant, murky water in a pond, but each morning, with the rising sun, the lotus flower opens its petals, standing clear of the water below, clean and pure. If, in sculpture, a figure is shown standing on a lotus base, it denotes the purity of the soul of that figure, suggesting divinity, something that has not been contaminated by the dirty waters from which it grew. Similar symbols are drawn from trees. Flowering trees represent the blossom of youth, fertility and goodness; water, the earth and sky represent the whole world.

Another source of inspiration, as mentioned earlier, was literature, myths and legends, for they too provided a fund of symbols. Literary symbols and allusions are a little more difficult to understand, for they are specific to India as a region. To understand nature symbols, your imagination can help you, but literary symbols require certain points of reference. For this reason, some attention has been given here to explain the myths behind certain symbols and works of art, and a summary of these is included in the section on iconography at the end of the book.

Colour symbolism differs from country to country. The Christian bride wears white; in India, widows wear unbleached white while brides wear maroon or red, the colour of blood, life and fertility.

Grey clouds give promise of rain, and in India the monsoons are a cause of celebration, music and dance. Paintings that represent rain, lightning and thunder are joyful in character. In England the rain is cold and miserable; in India it is cool and refreshing. Krishna, called the 'blue god', is not painted in just any old shade of blue. In poetry he is likened to a dark blue-grey cloud ready to burst with rain. Krishna is like the rain — to the dusty human soul he brings hope, growth and joy. Similar symbols in art have been derived from geometry, and the principles of science and mathematics. The circle stands for change; the universe of change; which is why Nataraja stands encircled by a halo of fire, balancing birth and death, the cycle of destruction that leads to creation, and so on. The square denotes the constant universal principles, and when a circle is drawn within the square, the two opposites, like ying and yang, signify life.

THE ARTIST AND THE RASIKA

In Indian aesthetic philosophy, great attention is paid to explaining the attitude of the *rasika*, the one who enjoys the artistic experience. There are numerous *Shastras* (sacred manuals, or books of rules) that govern the arts of dramaturgy, music, dance, architecture and sculpture. These *Shastras* explain in minute detail how a sculpture should be made: the proportions, length, height, and how to create movement or a sense of action in the three-dimensional arts. In each age and each region, the artists interpreted these codes to their own advantage.

The sculptures from Pallava temples in south India are based on sculptural principle similar to those of sculptures from Konarak in Orissa. Yet they differ in style, because of the artists' own contribution and, often, the different qualities of the worked material, the stone, lending yet another flavour to the work. It is necessary that both the artist and the *rasika* appreciate the guidelines laid down in the *Shastras*. If the artist is expected to be familiar with the *Puranas*, the myths and legends of the gods, and with mathematics and science — as is mentioned in the *Manu Smriti* — then so is the *rasika*. Visual representations, therefore, provide a unified, all-embracing view that transcends time and evokes a metaphysical vision, kindling the imagination to comprehend the oneness of the universe. The *rasika* or viewer has to 'be' an artist, with imagination and refined perceptions, in order to appreciate art.

The *rasika* must respond to the symbols used by the artist, and his sense perceptions should be alert. There is a sculpture of Vishnu lying on a huge snake, Sesanaga, on the Ocean of Eternity (see the description in the section on the Prince of Wales Museum, Mumbai). Here, the artist shows a mythological representation of Vishnu, the creator and preserver of life. His reclining figure evokes the nature of water, a sense of expanse stretching towards infinity, and there is also a feeling of restful balance, rhythmic harmony of the movement of waters and of life; a stillness that is full of controlled activity and energy, for water sustains all life. The sculpture is merely a carved piece of stone, but it is up to the viewer to infuse it with life and meaning, and to draw out its philosophical essence.

Woven into Indian symbolism in all the arts is the aesthetic theory which has evolved from the nine *rasas* (essences). *Rasa* translates as an experience somewhere between 'taste' and 'fragrance', and it has to do with the all-pervading senses. There are nine rasas, universal to all human beings. Alice Boner, in her introduction to the *Vastusutra Upanishad* (by Sarma and Boner, Motilal Banarsidas, Delhi, 1982), summarises them:

> The basic emotion of all living beings is LOVE (*Srngara*) [sic]. Love creates MIRTH and LAUGHTER (*hasya*), but

often also leads to SORROW and PAIN (*karuna*). Pain degenerates into ANGER (*raudra*), but anger can be sublimated into HEROISM (*vira*), which leads to fight. Fight motivated by anger creates FEAR (*bhayankara*). One party is defeated and feels DISGUST (*bibhatsa*), and so gives up the fight. Who thus relinquishes everything finally finds PEACE (*shanta*).

It is these nine 'emotions' that are described, explained and portrayed in arts such as painting, sculpture, dance and theatre. It is the artist's endeavour to evoke an emotion through the work and to take the *rasika* (who is thus one who can discern and appreciate *rasas*) on a journey of exploration of feelings, thoughts and ideas.

Sringar, or love, is the most all-pervading *rasa*. It has its moods, and many aspects like jealousy, sorrow and separation, and all the nine *rasas* can be rolled into the one, of love. The definition of love includes the feeling expressed by the mother for her child, that felt by lovers, brothers or any human being, so the *rasa* of love can be expressed in all these different ways.

The ultimate goal of life is the attainment of peace, tranquility and calm that is not entangled with desires and longing. The seated or

Madhubani *painter*

standing figure of the Buddha evokes this *rasa* of *shantum*, or inner harmony, and the artist places all details of eyes, face and body in a state of perfect balance and repose, to communicate the notion of peace.

In the case of *vira rasa*, in the sculptures showing heroism, the gods and goddesses are given several arms, legs, and even heads. Each arm (and they are always in pairs) carries a symbol that conveys the power of the deity, the multiple strengths which, if need be, can all be activated simultaneously. In sculpture, especially stone sculpture, it is not possible to show *actual* movement in time, so this device was adopted to show many heads for the all-seeing one, and many arms for the all-powerful controller of the universe.

Universal Themes and Concepts

Indian art through the ages has striven to represent the universe both in form and content. In Indian thought the universe is divided into five elements, earth, fire, water, sky and ether, which are manifest in all arts and rituals. Therefore, a painting may seem very cluttered and 'busy' to the non-Indian eye, for it strives to represent all (or many of) these elements.

A painting, sculpture or an Indian ritual also evokes the five senses, touch, smell, sound, sight and taste, for the aim is to awaken the total being. For instance a painting might show a woman touching the branch of a tree, flowers that perfume the air, and a bee hovering over a lotus to taste its delectable nectar.

The concept of wholeness is encapsulated in every minute detail. For instance, a painting or sculpture may have a border, illustrating a running stream, or a pond, representing the water principle so important to life. The pond will have lotuses growing on it, and each flower will signify the concept of time past, present or future: the bud, the full bloom or the dying flower or fruit; or, like a flowing river, the past, present and future are contained in every wave.

Such totality of vision is attempted in every work of art, however simple or sophisticated. If one were to qualify this as a conceptual philosophical dictum which is the keystone of Indian art, i.e. the notion of the universe, with all its variety and contrasts as one harmonious whole in which human beings are a part of nature, such a philosophy can be said to have directed Indian science, medicine, food habits and every other aspect of life and thought. Human beings quest for this wholeness all their lives; the Indian artist, through the ages, has proved that it is possible to achieve harmony and live in peace in this universe.

Some Aspects of the Cultural History of India

Summarising the history of a country like India, which has a civilisation that is over 5,000 years old, poses many problems. There are problems of what to exclude and include; of how to unravel the complexity of history without oversimplifying the drama and the challenges; of how to describe the process of change and evolution in society, economics, philosophy and language, and in artistic expression as it weaves in and around human life. However, the present purpose being to make visit to Indian museums meaningful, emphasis in the following account is on events related to and influencing artistic and cultural rather than political development. To facilitate presentation, certain liberties have been taken by the totally arbitrary division of Indian history into brief sections, as these are presented below.

SETTING THE STAGE

India is a country of great geographical diversity. To the north lies the world's highest mountain range, to the north-west the desert, to the east the deltaic wetlands, in the centre the great river plains, and the peninsular plateau of the south, washed on three sides by the sea. This diversity has given India an abundance of minerals, flora and fauna.

During the colonial period, the British undertook extensive surveys and exploration to study the natural wealth of India. Their collections of fossils, petrified wood, minerals and precious stones are still on display at the Prince of Wales Museum in Mumbai, at the Indian Museum in Calcutta, the Government State Museum in Chennai and elsewhere.

The National Museum of Natural History, New Delhi, has a small but well-kept collection of Indian plant and animal life. There are older (and more dusty) collections of animal specimens in the Natural History section of the Prince of Wales Museum, Mumbai, and in the Indian Museum, Calcutta.

The natural beauty of the mountains, rivers, animals and plants has always inspired the artist. To the poet, painter and philosopher, nature provided images and metaphors. The varieties of beautiful stone, from soft marble to hard granite, were used for building and sculpture. Minerals of dazzling and subtle hues were ground to produce colours for paintings. To the Indian craftsmen, nature provided an unending supply of materials from which to fashion household items like bamboo baskets, pottery, textiles, jewellery and much more.

It is in this setting of geographical diversity and abundance that the history of India begins. Major museums in India have collections of Stone Age implements and tools from various parts of India. In Madhya Pradesh, not far from Bhopal, there are some caves with paintings dating back to the Stone Age (prior to 2500 BC): delightful drawings of man-the-hunter amidst graceful animals of the wild. A special National Museum of Man has been set up here, devoted to the earliest periods of human history.

With the development of agriculture, in India as elsewhere, human beings moved from cave dwelling to houses clustered in villages, settling near river banks, where water was plentiful and the land fertile. Excavations of such neolithic sites are in progress in various parts of India.

THE INDUS VALLEY OR HARAPPAN CIVILISATION (2500–1500 BC)

A spectacular chance discovery in the 1920s, made when a railway track was being laid in Sindh (now a province of Pakistan) led to the excavation of the remains of an urban civilisation that was more than 5,000 years old. The important cities to be unearthed, Mohenjodaro, Harappa and Chanhudaro, lay on the banks of the River Indus, and so historians have referred to this as the Indus Valley Civilisation. Later, after Pakistan and India became separate countries, excavations continued and more cities were discovered, with similar urban plans, roads and buildings, all built with clay bricks of a standardised size. The uniform urban culture appears to have spread far beyond the Indus Valley region and is therefore now called the Harappan Civilisation. In India, the major sites are at Kalibangan in Rajasthan and as far south as Lothal in Gujarat. Excavations in other areas are in progress, and new insights into this amazing culture are awaited with great interest.

These large cities derived their wealth from even older, prosperous villages on the banks of the river. Agriculture improved greatly with the discovery and use of bronze, and this period is also referred to as the Bronze or Chalcolithic (stone and bronze) Age. It was the surplus produce of the land that led to trade, and the development of the urban centres.

Each city was built to a well-organised plan, as if under the supervision of a committee of architects and urban developers. These cities had broad roads running parallel and crossing at right angles, elaborate underground drainage systems and houses in blocks. Each house had living rooms, a kitchen, a well, and a bathing area. There were also workshops, storage rooms, and shopping centres.

Although the Harappan culture was contemporary with the Mesopotamian and Egyptian civilisations, it shared none of their opulence and ornateness in style and art. There are no monumental figures of pharaohs and gods. The cities of the Harappan culture are austere. The artifacts found there are metal implements and tools, elegant wheel-turned pottery of great variety in shape and design, stone and metal weights and measures, toy bullock carts and boats, and numerous seals assigned to traders, bearing their trademark and inscriptions in a script that has yet to be deciphered. This culture appears to have produced few weapons and what might be firmly identified as religious objects. Surprisingly, hundreds of very tiny figurines of animals, birds and toys for children have been found in these cities.

Many Indian museums have collections of artifacts from the Harappan culture, the best among them being at the National Museum, New Delhi, that has excellent specimens of painted pottery, jewellery of gold and semi-precious stones, of seals, and the tiny animal figurines in clay, stone and metal, which display a sensitivity to nature, a humour and style that is the hallmark of the Harappan Civilisation.

THE IRON AGE AND THE EVOLUTION OF VEDIC LITERATURE (1500–1000 BC)

The cities of the Harappan Civilisation were gradually abandoned and left to fall into ruin as the people moved towards the greater plains of north India. The reasons for the disappearance of the Harappan Civilisation are still being sought by historians; perhaps it was a decline of resources or some natural calamity.

During this period nomadic tribes from Central Asia, in search of pastures for their flocks, moved in groups towards Europe; others turned south to Iraq, Iran and India. These tribes are described by historians as sharing a common linguistic heritage. Across the continents, the movement of the tribes and where they settled can be traced by a study of the roots of the languages and common words.

The tribes that entered India moved eastward and built villages in northern India, the Punjab and further east on the plains of the River Ganga. Excavations at sites in these areas have unearthed some 'grey ware' pottery and iron implements. Iron changed the life of the people, enabling them to produce more, to cut tropical forests and convert them into villages and agricultural farms.

Bronze Cart c. 2500 BC; Prince of Wales Museum, Mumbai

Seal from Mohenjodaro; National Museum, New Delhi

From archaeological and literary evidence it appears that economic life centred around the rearing of cattle and agriculture. The change from a nomadic way of life to village settlements led to the development of a more complex society. Though tribal norms may have governed law and order, more occupational groups came into play as the community grew. These were landowners, cattle owners, priests and craftspeople, and the concepts of monarchy, patriarchal families, and of private property began to appear in the loose tribal-federation structure of these societies.

It was during this period that the sacred texts of the *Vedas* evolved, describing the nature gods, Agni (fire), Indra (rain), Vayu (wind) and many others. These texts, along with legends and epic poems like the *Ramayana* and the *Mahabharata*, were for many centuries not committed to written form; they were passed from one generation to the next by word of mouth, an oral tradition that is still prevalent in India today.

Many archaeologists have attempted to excavate sites that may provide more historical evidence on the dating and times of the inception of the *Ramayana* and the *Mahabharata*. It however appears that these epics evolved over centuries, with each generation adding descriptions and stories of their own and do not denote one event or place.

HINDUISM AND THE BIRTH OF BUDDHISM AND JAINISM (1000–500 BC)

The religious literature assigned to this period provides ample information on rituals and ceremonies, and the evolution of the philosophy now known as Hinduism. This philosophy synthesises many diverse ideas from belief in God to atheism. The literature, such as the *Vedas*, also describes the growing wealth derived from agriculture and trade, the growth of towns and small kingdoms, and a society well divided into occupational groups. From literary and archaeological evidence it is possible to piece together an amazing story of growth and development.

Towns and craft centres famous for their trade and outstanding artisans came into being, which attracted further trade and visitors. Travel from these cities to far off places was possible by road or boat, and this generated vast amounts of wealth concentrated in the hands of a few. The banks of the River Ganga, which was a lifeline for trade and agricultural prosperity, were dotted with important cities that linked commercial activity.

In literature the 'ideal' concept of society is one divided into *varna*, the caste divisions consisting of the *brahmins* (priests and teachers), the *kshatriyas* (the princely, ruling and warrior caste), the *vaishyas* (farmers and traders) and the *sudras* (manual labourers on farms or in trades and crafts). However, with the passage of time, the caste system became much more complex with the addition of sub-caste and *jatis* which varied from region to region. The *jati* system specified by birth the occupation, the lifestyle and the marital relationships permissible for each individual. Nevertheless, Indian history records several instances of caste distinctions being overcome, of how a *vaishya* became the king and of protests against the caste system as occurred in the case of the founding of the Buddhist religion. The worst affected by the caste system were of course the *vaishyas* and the *sudras*, and it was to them that Buddhism offered salvation and liberation.

The founder of Buddhism, Gautama Buddha, was born as a prince of a royal *kshatriya* family, in a kingdom in what is now Nepal. The young prince Siddhartha, moved by the sight of human suffering, renounced his royal heritage and family ties for a life of contemplation. After years of meditation, he attained *nirvana*, or enlightenment (literally, 'extinction') — the wisdom to understand life. The title of 'Buddha', the 'Enlightened One', was then conferred on him.

The place of the Buddha's attainment of *nirvana*, at Bodhgaya in Bihar, is a celebrated centre of pilgrimage. Buddha's first sermon was delivered at Sarnath, now in the state of Uttar Pradesh. (The museum at this site is mentioned in this book.) In his teachings, the Buddha explained that all human suffering is caused by greed and desire, and he urged people to follow the 'Middle Path', that is, to shun excess and embrace simplicity in all aspects of life.

Buddhist sculpture and literature abound in descriptions of nature, animals, birds and even snakes, because the Buddha believed and taught that each living creature had its role to play, and wanton destruction of life would eventually harm human life. This compassionate respect for life and the whole philosophy of non-violence is known as *ahimsa*, a concept used 2,000 years later by Mahatma Gandhi to guide political protest and action during the struggle for independence against the British.

From India, Buddhism spread to Sri Lanka, Burma, Thailand, Korea, China and finally to Japan. In subsequent centuries, trade and religious contact led to the exchange of ideas and artistic traditions in this region of Asia.

Mahavira, during the same period, became a prominent saint of the religion that came to be known as Jainism. Similar in style to those of the Hindus, Jain temples have sculpted images of saints, rather austere and

rigid, reflecting the philosophy of non-violence and renunciation professed by this faith. Although dating from a much later period of the tenth to the 11th centuries, those at Mount Abu in Rajasthan deserve special mention for their wealth of decorative marble sculpture.

These two religions attracted a large number of people, especially people of the lower castes like the merchant and trade community, who, during this period, were achieving financial prosperity from trade with the Far East but were being denied social mobility under the Hindu caste system. Jain merchant communities from Gujarat, Rajasthan, Orissa and a few other places still play a very significant role in India's commerce and industry.

THE SPREAD OF BUDDHISM (500 BC–AD 1)

During this period, more land was brought under cultivation, and there was an increase in trade and agricultural development. Literary evidence points to the rising power of a number of states, tribal federations and kingdoms. In the struggle for power, a number of dynasties emerged, ruling for a few generations, with kingdoms being inherited by some of the family until they were superseded by others. For purposes of law and administration, the rulers evolved systems of tax collection and division of the state into administrative units such as the village, or groups of villages. Such fiscal and administrative control was necessary for the government of a kingdom, maintenance of the army and upkeep of a growing number of rulers, their families and courtiers. Trade increased, through the development of transport and the building of roads, and with the general advances in technology. It was the ruling class, the trading communities, who, having amassed wealth, lent their patronage to the religious orders of Buddhism.

From contemporary edicts and dedication stones, it appears that merchants' and artists' guilds gave money, land and their expertise to the construction of religious architecture for the support of the religious orders.

Over a period of one thousand years, some of the world's greatest Buddhist monuments were built. To begin with, stone funerary mounds called stupas were created to contain the relics of the Buddha. The early stupas look like a huge stone bubble emerging from the earth. Stupas built later tend to be elongated and pointed, like those in Burma and Thailand,

Indra riding on his celestial elephant; Assam State Museum, Guwahati

and in Japan they are transformed into pagodas — shrines with many levels and sloping roofs.

In India, the stupas are solid stone and rubble constructions and have no entrance. They are surrounded by high stone railings with gateways, often nine metres (30 feet) high, carved with reliefs. Buddhist sculptures are beautiful both for their skill and composition. The sculptures of the early period are full of a humour and vitality that many people do not usually associate with the religion. The reliefs depict incidents in the life of the Buddha and stories of the Buddha's previous incarnations as recorded in the *Jataka* literature. Parables and stories of birds, animals and people are depicted on the stone railings, for the education of the pilgrims.

The most famous stupas and Buddhist pilgrimage centres in India were founded during the reign of the Mauryans, Sungas, Satavahanas and Kushanas in northern and central India (see pages 289-90). Amongst the best known are in Bharhut, Sarnath and Mathura in Uttar Pradesh, Sanchi in Madhya Pradesh (not far from Bhopal), and Amaravati and Nagarjunakonda in Andhra Pradesh.

Some of the remains of these stupas have been removed from their sites and are preserved in museums. The Indian Museum, Calcutta, has some fragments of early stone railings with sculptures from Bharhut. The sculptures from the Amaravati stupa are now in the Government State Museum, Chennai, the British Museum, London, and the National Museum, New Delhi; those from Uttar Pradesh and northern India are in the State Museum in Mathura.

Buddhism, as a way of life, stresses simplicity, meditation and saintliness. Yet the sculptures from early Buddhist stupas are a celebration of life, carefree and without restraint. The stone railings are adorned with sensuous figures of women, wood nymphs, elephants and monkeys, flowering trees and snakes. The sculptures are full of a joy and exuberance so unlike the huge, awesome images of the Buddha that were to come centuries later in Burma, Thailand and Japan.

On the basis of contemporary literature from Persia, India and Greece, this period appears to have been one of great activity. The Achaemenid emperor of Persia was said to have crossed the mountain barriers to India. This contact with Persia lead to a considerable exchange of ideas and knowledge in the northwest region of India and Pakistan. During this

Temple at Bodhgaya, Bihar, that marks the place where Buddha attained enlightenment

Terracotta sculptures; Patna Museum

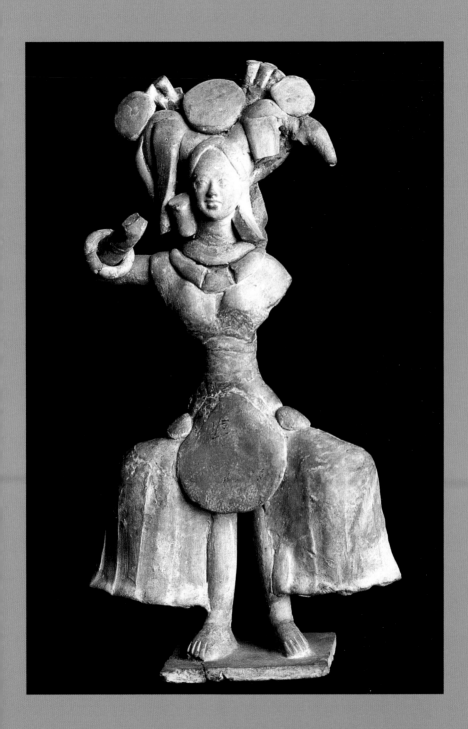

period, Alexander the Great, from Macedonia in Greece, defeated the Persian emperor and sought to expand the limits of his empire. This brought Alexander and his army into northern India but, unable to persuade his rather homesick army to go any further, he was forced to return to Greece. However, Alexander left some of his generals to govern the provinces of what is now northern India, Pakistan and Afghanistan, and so the Greeks, and the Roman traders who succeeded them, left their mark on Indian culture. Great trading cities emerged, some of which were also centres of learning, like Taxila (now in Pakistan), which attracted scholars and craftsmen from all over Asia.

The Greeks and Roman traders may well have brought some of their own craftsmen with them to India, but they must also have engaged local artisans and artists. The result was a happy blend of Indian, Greek and Roman styles that goes by the name of Gandharan art. The museums with the best collections of Gandharan sculpture are in Lahore and Taxila (Pakistan), New Delhi (National Museum) and Calcutta (Indian Museum). Examples of Gandharan art are also to be seen in some major museums in Britain, France and North America.

Apart from sculpture, all these museums display coins, including some gold ones, dating from this period, many bearing Roman inscriptions. As far down as Arikamedu near Pondicherry in south India, coins and pottery of Roman origin, some 2,000 years old, have been found. There is substantial evidence of Roman trade with India, for spices, precious gems and textiles. Pliny is recorded as having remarked that all the gold of Rome was being drained to purchase the marvels of the East.

The southern part of India also grew prosperous through trade and agriculture. Its wealth and splendour are described in the early Sangam literature of the period. Alongside trade that linked India and Europe, there were trade contacts with the Far East. The development of agriculture and trade under various rulers of small states naturally resulted in a struggle for power and greater wealth.

The stage was now set for the building of empires in India. The *Arthashastra*, a treatise on government assigned to this period, described in great detail how the land should be administered. The state was to be divided into regions, the smallest unit being the village. The tax system is spelt out with care, under various categories — agriculture, trade and even

(previous pages) Terracotta sculptures; Patna Museum

the taxation of prostitutes are mentioned in this text. Tax was to be collected by officials, after inspection; law and order was to be maintained at all cost, for the benefit of the ruler. The area along the Ganga River, where cities had mushroomed along the banks, and where mineral and agricultural wealth was abundant, was the target for conquest and control.

From among the small kingdoms emerged the Mauryan empire, with its capital at Pataliputra (in the vicinity of the modern city of Patna, in Bihar). The greatest of the Mauryan emperors was Ashoka — a name one often hears or reads about in contemporary India. He is remembered because he was the first to unite a large portion of what is today called India. His empire stretched from Assam, Bengal and Orissa in the east to the Punjab and the pre-partition North-West Frontier Province, and as far south as present-day Karnataka. The size of Ashoka's empire and the extent of his influence are indicated by the widespread distribution of the edicts he had had engraved on rocks and stone pillars. The script used in most of these edicts is called Brahmi. These royal declarations were inspired by the Buddhist faith to which Emperor Ashoka had became a convert.

It was through many battles that Ashoka had won his vast empire, but finally, dismayed by war and bloodshed, he turned to the philosophy of non-violence, of peace — the way of the Buddha. Some historians have seen political and economic compulsions rather than a genuine change of heart behind this sudden conversion. Ashoka's huge army was a drain on the economy, and the empire had grown too large for effective administration. However that might be, Ashoka has become a model of a great benevolent king.

When India won its independence from British rule, it was from Ashoka and Buddhism that the emblems of sovereignty were drawn for the seal of the Republic of India and the Indian national flag.

The latter is a horizontal tricolour of saffron, white and green. Saffron is the colour worn by monks and saints, the colour of sacrifice and honour; white stands for purity and unity; green for prosperity. On the central white band is a dark blue-black *chakra*, the Buddhist wheel of *dharma* — *dharma* being a word with many meanings: duty, life, action, law, but also social order; the ideal order of the world. The wheel is symbolic of perpetual change and movement, spiritual progress and 'right action'.

The emblem of the Indian Republic, seen on all Indian currency and official notepaper and publications, is derived from the capital of a stone

Bodhisattva, *Gandhara, second century* AD;
Government Museum and Art Gallery, Chandigarh, Punjab

column erected by Ashoka at Sarnath. This capital still exists. It has four
lions, back to back, facing the cardinal directions, carrying the *dharma
chakra* (now broken), and is preserved in the Archaeological Museum at
Sarnath, mentioned in this volume.

The sculpted lion capital is characteristic of Ashokan art: the beautiful
yellowish stone, with its bold carving, has been so well polished that the
sheen is still visible. Another sculpture with the same lustre is that of a
large female figure carrying a fly-whisk, the celebrated Didarganj Yakshi of
the State Museum in Patna. This Yakshi has travelled to exhibitions in
many countries overseas, and is still magnificent despite the fact that
she is 2,000 years old. The Patna Museum also has a great collection
of terracotta figures, excavated from nearby sites, belonging to the
Mauryan Period.

THE RISE OF EMPIRES (AD 1–500)

The first few centuries of the Christian era were extremely interesting in
India. Trade with the Middle East brought Jewish and early Christian

travellers and merchants to India, especially to the west coast of Kerala. However, it was only many centuries later, in the 18th and 19th centuries under the patronage of the colonial powers, that large-scale conversions to Christianity occurred, and church construction was undertaken. In the north-western region, Graeco-Roman influence persisted. Famous and very powerful rulers, such as Kanishka, the Kushana dynasty ruler of the Gandhara region, promoted economic growth, development and the spread of Buddhism.

It was during this period that the image of the Buddha came into vogue. In the previous period (500 BC–AD 1), sculptures on stupas and their railings carried only symbols of the Buddha, important among which were the tree under which he attained enlightenment, an empty throne and the Buddha's footprints. For philosophical and religious reasons, the Buddha was not represented in human form. This was the attitude of what is called the Hinayana School of Buddhism. It was the later Mahayana School that adorned its temples with images of the Buddha in various postures: standing, meditating, preaching and even lying on his deathbed.

The early Buddha images of the Gandhara School show marked Graeco-Roman influence. The sharp nose, wavy hair and toga-like robes are quite easy to identify with Roman art.

The Government Museum in Mathura and the National Museum in New Delhi have good collections of early Buddha figures. In these, the artists' struggle to achieve an expression on the face that would convey inner peace, meditation and tranquility is evident. The seated or standing figures are delicate and small in comparison with the giant Buddha images that are seen in Nepal, Sri Lanka, Thailand and Japan, and which date from later centuries.

Buddhist rock-hewn architecture is to be seen in Maharashtra and Orissa. At Ajanta, along a peaceful, isolated hillside, the rock face has been carved out to fashion *viharas* (cells for Buddhist monks) and *chaityas* or prayer halls for congregational worship. These halls, excavated and sculpted in the solid rock of the hillsides, were designed in imitation of constructions in wood, with pillars and ribbed roofing. The stone walls of the *viharas* and *chaityas* of Ajanta are adorned with famous wall paintings in beautiful, muted mineral colours. Ceilings and pillars of the rock-hewn halls are also similarly decorated with paintings depicting the life of the Buddha, *Jataka* tales (stories of the Buddha's previous incarnations), and decorative panels.

Apart from producing great works of Buddhist art, the early centuries of the Christian era saw enormous developments in a number of other fields. The universities of Taxila (in the Gandhara region) and of Nalanda in Bihar attracted scholars from all over the country, and from the Asian continent as a whole. Scholarly works in the fields of philosophy, linguistics, literature, astronomy, mathematics, science, medicine, art and dramaturgy were written, and have had great influence on the development of Indian culture.

During the reign of the Guptas (third-fifth centuries), a large part of present-day India was united once again into a single empire. The wealth of knowledge, accumulated over centuries, spread through all regions of the country, creating the underlying cultural unity that is so visible today in religious customs, architecture, sculpture, music and dance.

Over the centuries powerful guilds of craftsmen led the way towards great artistic achievements. There are references in literature and epigraphic evidence of merchants and artists contributing to the development of art through their patronage of the major religions of Hinduism, Buddhism and Jainism.

In the religious art of the Hindus, two new trends emerged during the Gupta period: (1) the building of stone temples; and (2) the rise in popularity of the three male gods: Brahma, Shiva and Vishnu. Sculptures often monumental in scale were produced in larger numbers than ever before.

The earliest Hindu temples were presumably built of wood and brick. It was during the Gupta period that Hindu temples were built of stone decorated with sculptures. The standard floor plan was simply of one large covered room, the *garbha griha*, or sanctum, where the image of the deity was placed.

To understand how this temple form evolved, one has to return to the idea and meaning of a Hindu temple. It symbolises the universe. It is built to face the four cardinal directions; the rising sun, and the alignment and position of the zodiacal signs and planets. The temple is then a replica or reflection of the cosmos and the order of the world. The vertical tower of the temple pierces the sky, and fixes the position of the heavens in relation to the earth. The upper regions of the temple walls are inhabited by sculptures in movement, musicians and dancers, and celestial beings offering flower garlands to the temple walls are inhabited by sculptures in

Medieval temple, Osian, Rajasthan, showing position of sculptures on temple wall

movement, musicians and dancers, and celestial beings offering flower garlands to the gods. Air, which is the breath of life, is represented by sculpted figures in movement, never static or at rest. All the elements of nature; air, water, earth and fire are represented, to appease the forces of nature. Images of lovers and beautiful women are also included, as it is believed that these protect the temple from lightning and other destructive forces.

A temple is also a likeness of the universal being. The body of the temple is thought of as a human form; an idea in Indian philosophy used as an analogue and metaphor, similar to the Western (medieval) concept of a church. The central, most holy part of the temple is the small room (the *garbha griha*) housing the idol — the very heart and soul of the building. The room is dark, calm and silent, like the centre of the universe. Within is the object of worship where only the initiated are allowed to enter. The whole *garbha griha* is sheathed in walls of stone, like the flesh and limbs of the human body. The stone clothing reflects the other manifestation of the body of the temple, and sculptures therefore cling to the surface walls. The outward-facing walls have representations of the gods in their appropriate postures and facing the cardinal points, for the temple is also the all-expanding universe. Sculptures protect the temple and guide the devotee towards the stable, quiet centre within the temple and within the mind.

Under the Guptas, both Hindu and Buddhist art appear to have flourished without too much friction between them. Hindu temples and Buddhist religious buildings continued to be built in close proximity, each to some extent influencing the art of the other.

Hindu sculptures in terracotta and stone are sometimes narrative in nature, with more than one figure, depicting in sculptural shorthand the main events of a story from mythology. There are also purely decorative panels depicting musicians and dancers, court scenes, etc. Still other sculptures are of Hindu deities, identifiable by the symbols they carry.

The story of the *Ramayana*, which today appears in many versions and languages, has, in the original Sanskrit of the legendary sage Valmiki, over 100,000 lines. It is, in essence, the story of the exile of a young prince, Rama, his wife Sita and brother Lakshmana, arising out of the jealousy of other members of the family. While in exile, Sita is kidnapped by Ravana, king of Lanka. Rama and his brother, after a fierce battle, rescue Sita and return in triumph to their kingdom. The return of the heroes and their victory over evil are celebrated in the popular festival of lights, Diwali, each

Shiva with attendants

year. The saga is embroidered with many sub-plots and episodes, and is replete with lyrical passages on love, loyalty, jealousy, greed and pride, such human values, which imbue the *Ramayana* with lasting relevance. Even today, episodes from this epic provide a major source of themes for Indian dance, theatre, puppetry and literature.

The *Mahabharata* is the longer of the two major Indian epics. It describes the conflict among members of a royal family over property and land. The Pandavas (five brothers) and their common wife Draupadi are defeated in a game of dice, and lose their kingdom to their cousins, the hundred Kaurava brothers. They are forced into exile, where many events take place. There are stories within stories; a sort of compendium of folklore and folktales. The Pandavas return to fight a great battle against their kinsmen. It is as a prelude to this cataclysmic clash that Lord Krishna delivers his celebrated sermon, the *Bhagavad Gita*, the 'Song Celestial', in which he discourses on the meaning of life, conflict, war, death and duty. This part of the *Mahabharata*, the *Gita* as it is usually called, lies at the core of Hindu doctrines and religious practice, and has deeply influenced the life and thought of Indians over the ages.

Gupta art, architecture and sculpture, the Hindu myths and legends, music and dance — all travelled with sailors and merchants to the East, to Thailand, Cambodia and Java, influencing the construction of the great temples of Angkor Wat and the monumental Buddhist temple of Borobudur. The dance and puppetry of this region continue to draw on themes from the *Ramayana* and *Mahabharata* to this day.

THE AGE OF EXPERIMENTATION (AD 500–1000)

The Gupta empire had evolved a system of administration and taxation with an elaborate network of officials and governors. Land was granted both for the upkeep of these officials and for religious purposes. Since it was not possible for direct control to be exercised by the 'emperor' himself over every corner of the empire, power fell into the hands of lesser administrators. In art too, we see a growing tendency towards the assimilation of diverse elements, rather than centralised control. Animal totems and the religious beliefs of certain communities were amalgamated into the already large pantheon of Hinduism, as were their rituals and forms of artistic expression.

India, after the Guptas, disintegrated into smaller kingdoms, each riding on the ebb and flow of prosperity in agriculture and trade, both internal and foreign.

In south India, a number of powerful empires emerged during this period, each offering a distinctive contribution to the mosaic of Indian culture. The Pallava dynasty's capital was Kanchipuram, a city of temples. At Mahabalipuram, the ancient seaport on the east coast not far from the present city of Chennai, huge granite boulders and parts of the hillside along the beach were hewn and carved into temples, with rooms, pillars and sculpted walls. Despite the enormous technical difficulties involved, the architect-artist chose to experiment with the design of the roof of the temple. From this experiment came the pyramidal temple tower or *Shikhara*, now typical of south Indian temples, with distinct horizontal levels made up of miniature temple-roof designs.

Pallava sculpture is characterised by the pale granite used, and by the soft, elongated lines of the sculpted figures of deities and donors, and the decorative panels depicting attendants and animals. The Government Museum at Chennai has a good collection of sculpture in stone and a few exquisite bronzes of the Pallava period. Nevertheless, it is worth visiting Mahabalipuram and Kanchipuram to see the art of the Pallavas in its full splendour.

Kanchipuram is still a thriving cultural centre today. It has over 100 temples, each with its own elaborate celebrations and processions attracting hundreds of pilgrims. Temples were built by the king, or by donation from the villagers. The village water tank was also built with the contributions of the people, and every south Indian village is proud of its tank, the centre of daily life, even today. Around the temples, shops and market-places developed, where neighbouring villagers bring their wares for sale. Still found alongside the temple complex are the homes and workshops of local artisans — potters, weavers and goldsmiths. Kanchipuram also has a very ancient university, or *gurukula*, where teacher (*guru*) and student live, work and study together. This model of temple town or city is characteristic of south India, with the temple as the centre of all cultural life — music, dance, crafts, education and philosophy. The later temples of Madurai and Chidambaram evolved over the centuries on almost the same lines.

The inspiration and example of the temples of Kanchipuram travelled to the north. Here activity was continuing in the region of Ajanta, in the present-day Aurangabad district of Maharashtra, where Buddhist caves of an earlier period are located. It was during the reign of the powerful Rashtrakutas, the power rivalling the Chalukyas and the Pallavas, that work continued in this region. Not very far from Ajanta, at a site named Ellora, rock-hewn architecture was constructed by Buddhists, Jains and Hindus. The Hindu rock-cut halls have larger-than-life sculpted deities in dramatic and impressive compositions. The most amazing is the Kailash Temple — an entire temple with rooms, halls, porticos and windows, sculptures of figurines and motifs all carved out of the hillside. The temple stands free from the rock, as though it were built from the foundations upwards, whereas in fact it was carved from the top down. This rock temple is modelled on the Kailashnath Temple of Kanchipuram.

There were other kingdoms of importance in this period: for instance, the western Chalukyas with their magnificent temple experiments at Aihole, Badami and Pattadakal in present-day Karnataka. In the Chalukyan cities of Aihole and Pattadakal the prototype of Indian temples was developed. Styles that later influenced the architecture of Orissa and central India, are all to be found here.

At the same time other kingdoms flourished, such as the Pala and Sena dynasties of West Bengal and the eastern region of Bihar. Some good

(overleaf) Camel fight, Mughal School, Jahangiri period, 17th century; Prince of Wales Museum, Mumbai

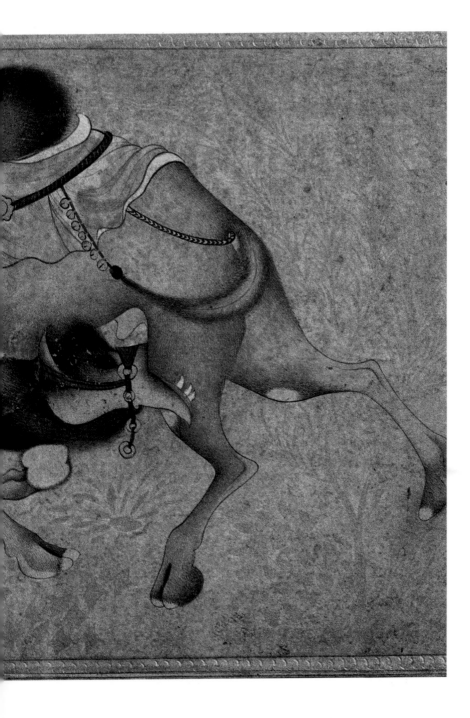

examples of Pala and Sena sculpture are housed in the Indian and Ashutosh Museums, Calcutta, and the National Museum, New Delhi. The influence of Pala and Sena art spread to Nepal, Tibet and Thailand in subsequent centuries. It is during this period (AD 500–1000) that one can see a cultural web beginning to emerge, through the spread of Indian art — both Hindu and Buddhist — that linked distant places together, not only within India but beyond its present boundaries.

The Maturation of Hindu Art and the Introduction of Islam (AD 1000–1500)

During this period, the country was fragmented into several smaller kingdoms, each vying for power and control. In a system akin to feudalism, kings granted the government of land to others in return for loyalty and the supply of armies and men in times of trouble. Such power in the hands of governors of states enabled feudatories to rise to power, claiming in turn their own kinghood and the right to govern the land under their jurisdiction. Time and again small rulers ascended to power, overthrowing neighbouring rivals and eventually their own king himself. This political and economic system may have been the cause of the social insecurity, continuous strife and the constant intrigue which prevailed during this period. However, in the world of art it led to the development of a number of unique schools of regional art, using forms of expression that were both individual and energetic in style.

The kingdoms of importance were the Cholas, the Cheras, the Pandyas and the Hoysalas in the south; the Rastrakutas, Chalukyas and Chandellas in the centre; the Pratiharas, Rajputs and Chauhans in the west; and the Palas, Senas and the Eastern Gangas in the east, with kingdoms of importance also in Assam, Nepal, Tibet and Kashmir. Architectural achievements were matched by those in the fields of sculpture, painting, literature, dance and music. Each region began to develop its own regional language derived from the roots of Sanskrit, Tamil and other spoken dialects.

It was this period that saw the maturation of Hindu artistic expression, after centuries of experimentation. In south India, the Cholas had emerged as a powerful dynasty, with trade contacts with the Far East and marriage alliances with Sri Lanka and also other kingdoms within India. Their capital was in the region of present-day Thanjavur district, which is today the rice bowl of Tamil Nadu. The Cholas, who were great patrons of art, built beautiful temples and encouraged poets and scholars. The city of

Tanjore has the great Brihadeswara Temple, and the Tanjore Art Gallery has some of the finest bronze and stone sculptures of the Chola and Pallava schools. The collection of the Government State Museum, Chennai, is also outstanding in quality of workmanship. In Tanjore today, there are still craftsmen who fashion bronze figures.

In the Hoysala kingdom in the region of present-day Karnataka (Mysore, Hassan district area), magnificent, ornate temples profusely decorated with sculptures were constructed. The design of the Hindu temple, common to all parts of India, evolved into a unique form with a star-shaped plan and bands of sculpture in which each figure was laden with carved details of jewellery and stylistic ornamentation. This was neither a period of 'the dark ages' nor a period of decadence, but one of maturation and flowering of a number of styles, each coloured by its region of origin.

On the east coast, the region of the present-day state of Orissa came under the rule of the Eastern Gangas. The relative peace and tranquility enjoyed by this region, thanks to its matrimonial and military alliances with the Cholas, created conditions favourable for the building of beautiful temples. Those at Bhubaneswar, Puri and Konarak represent the Orissan style of architecture at its best. A regional variation in the pattern of architecture and sculpture was the conical shape of the *shikharas*, embellished with sculptures of deities, dancers and other secular themes, which today provide interesting information on the life of the people at the time the temples were constructed. Orissa developed its own form of classical dance, linked with temple worship, now called Odissi and much of the style reflects the sensuousness of Orissan temple sculptures.

Some of the Orissa temples are open to all visitors, while others like the Lingaraja Temple at Bhubaneswar and the Jagannath Temple of Puri, are important pilgrimage places open only to Hindus. The temple at Puri celebrates a chariot festival every year when the presiding deity, feeling the heat of June–July, is moved to his summer abode in a huge wooden chariot that is drawn by his devotees. The temple cart or chariot, decorated with flowers and banners, and the surging throng of pilgrims that surround it as it is drawn through the streets of Puri, is a spectacle unmatched by chariot festivals elsewhere in the country.

The idea of the *rath* or chariot was used in a remarkable way in the building of the Sun Temple at Konarak, Orissa. The entire temple is fashioned to resemble a magnificent carriage, complete with stone wheels and horses, representing the chariot of the Sun God.

Sculptures removed from these temples are on display at some major museums. The Orissa State Museum in Bhubaneswar has some excellent examples, along with a magnificent collection of early illustrated palm-leaf manuscripts.

Khajuraho is a town in present-day Madhya Pradesh, in central India. Here, in the 11th century, the Chandella rulers built a complex of elegant Hindu and Jain temples raised on high platforms, so as to give the impression, in profile, of a range of ascending mountains. The Khajuraho temples will always remain famous for their sculptures, and infamous for the erotic themes of some of them. Good collections of Chandella sculptures from these temples can be seen at the Khajuraho Site Museum, the Indian Museum in Calcutta and at the National Museum, New Delhi. The delicacy and subtlety of the sculptures — of amorous couples, women dressing and undressing, playing and writing love letters — echo the richness of Indian love poetry, music and dance.

The tradition of Indian love poetry dates back 3,000 years or more, but in the period we are now discussing, a new wave of poetry and music emerged in what is called the *Bhakti* movement. *Bhakti* means faith/devotion, which was the cornerstone of the Hindu revivalist movement to which it lends its name. The Bhaktis stressed that single-minded devotion to God brought man closer to Him. They expressed this devotion in poetry and song, which they repeated tirelessly. This devotional poetry caught the people's imagination and spread everywhere. The metaphor used by these poets was that of human yearning for one's beloved, signifying human adoration of the divine. The embrace, the passion, the yearning of the lover could have a literal significance in human relationships and yet evoke an almost erotic symbolism on a metaphysical plane.

The eighth–ninth century also heralded the arrival in India of the followers of Islam. Arab traders had for centuries been passing through India, along caravan routes that linked China and Europe, providing horses and other items of trade to ports on the west coast of India. They brought to India and took from it many ideas, inventions, jewels, spices and other commodities. Paper, invented in China, was carried by the Arabs to India and Europe; they did the same for silk.

Apart from traders, there were others who were attracted by the wealth of India — the gold and precious stones amassed in its temples and palaces — and predatory raids from the north-west occurred in the tenth and 11th centuries. Taking into account a natural tendency to exaggerate, the evidence suggests that India was unbelievably wealthy, and the temples

Seductive pose

and palaces sufficiently well endowed to attract the interest of these invaders. Was it years of accumulated wealth, or the prosperity of the era, that glimmered like a lighthouse? Whatever the answer, the arts were thriving, as were the crafts and India looked a greener pasture to many. Soon the Islamic raiders were tempted to make India their home. The Delhi area, traditionally ruled by Hindu kings, was taken over by a succession of Muslim sultans. The first Muslim dynasty built a new city, in which Qutb-ud-din Aibak constructed Delhi's first mosque and the towering Qutb Minar. It is obvious that Hindu craftsmen and masons worked on the mosque along with Muslims, to build the arched corridors and carve the intricate calligraphy in stone of the Qutb complex. The Khaljis and the Tughlaqs were followed by others who built their imperial cities in the Delhi area.

As the power of the Delhi sultanate declined, a number of small, new kingdoms, some with Hindu and some with Muslim rulers, emerged in Gujarat, Rajasthan, Kashmir, Bengal and in the south. Contemporary literature speaks of the wealth and grandeur of the Vijayanagar empire and today extensive excavations are in progress at Hampi in modern-day Karnataka. In kingdoms under Islamic rule, beautiful mosques and secular buildings were constructed, each carrying a touch of the distinctive flavour of the regional culture, grafted on to the basic features of Islamic architecture.

With the rise of regional kingdoms in India over the last thousand years, there has been a remarkable development of distinct regional styles in architecture, sculpture and painting, and in the literature of languages like Hindi in north India, Gujarati in western India, Bengali in the east, Marathi in the Deccan, and Malayalam, Kannada and Tamil in the south. The court language of the Lodi Sultanate at Delhi was Persian, replacing Sanskrit in many regions of north India.

The administrative needs of the Islamic rulers of north India, with their Turkish and Persian heritage, led to the development of a new and very lyrical language, or rather an assimilation of a substantial number of Persian words into the vocabulary and grammatical structure of Hindi, to form, the language that is now called Urdu and which is extensively spoken in north India. Urdu literature is noted for its lyricism and elegance of expression, both in prose and poetry.

THE LAST FIVE HUNDRED YEARS (AD 1500–2000)

The Mughal Empire

Babur, the founder of the Mughal dynasty, conquered a large part of northern India. With him, Babur brought new technologies, systems of administration and warfare, and new armaments. He laid the first formal garden in India. A formal garden is seen in Islamic Thought as man's attempt to create a near paradise on earth, similar to that in heaven, with trees, flowers, birds, butterflies, and, running through it, canals and fountains (for water is the symbol of life) — all arranged in perfect harmony and order. Many Mughal monuments and palaces were surrounded by beautiful gardens and orchards.

Babur's son, Humayun, reigned for a short period and was then defeated by his rival, Sher Shah Sur, the Afghan ruler of Bihar, and driven out of Delhi. He took refuge in the Persian court, where he was assisted in his plans to reconquer his Indian territory. The supremacy of Persia and its culture naturally affected Humayun, who, on his victorious return to India, brought with him Persian artists, scholars and poets who created great works of art and music in India. Humayun's capital was once again established in Delhi and, when he died, his wife had a beautiful mausoleum built for him, in which the Persian engineering principle of the double-dome and some other concepts were incorporated in the already current Indo–Islamic architecture that had evolved in the previous period.

Humayun's son, Akbar, extended the Mughal empire to Bengal in the east, Gujarat in the west and the Deccan in the south. This huge territory brought him great wealth but required a highly organised administrative, transportation and communication system to ensure effective control of even the remotest regions in his extensive domains. Despite Akbar's years of exile with his father Humayun, his inability to read, and his accession to the throne at a very young age, he became a great patron of the arts. Artists and craftsmen produced illustrated manuscripts, such as the *Baburnama*, of the extraordinary sights recorded in Babur's diary. The *Baburnama* has illustrations, almost scientific in their representational detail, of animals such as the rhinoceros and elephant, and of birds and plants which Babur had never seen before.

Akbar had many Hindu wives, a policy of political matrimony that enabled him to have allies in many Hindu courts. His eclectic tastes extended to many subjects, including the fields of philosophy and religion, and he even attempted to synthesise a new, universal religion. During his

Royal procession, Vijayanagar period; Government Museum, Bangalore

region, which art historians readily label as the 'reign of red sandstone', he built the Red Fort in Agra. Not far from Agra, on a hilly outcrop, Akbar created Fatehpur Sikri, a beautiful royal city, built entirely of local red sandstone. The palace buildings are roomy and airy, and the pinkish red of the stone glows in any light. It was here that Akbar gave his patronage to the synthetic architectural style now called Indo-Islamic, which borrowed and adapted features from both Hindu and Islamic buildings. The royal city, sadly, had to be abandoned and Akbar returned to Agra.

Just before his death, Akbar began the construction of his tomb, as was the practice in those days. It is a truly remarkable structure, bearing many Hindu elements and very unlike the tomb of his father, Humayun. It was constructed with open, pillared halls placed one above the other. The engineering principles of pillar and beam were traditionally used in Hindu architecture, while Islamic buildings were characterised by the use of arches and domes. In Akbar's tomb, as in his palaces, there is a combination of Hindu-style flat roofs, pillared halls, with wide spanning Islamic or Persian arched openings.

The influence of Persian art and ideas during Akbar's reign is quite evident. Yet it was in his reign that the synthesis of Indian and Islamic aesthetics found the widest scope for experimentation and creation. Under Akbar's rule, many illustrated manuscripts on court life and his achievements were compiled as the *Akbarnama*, examples of which can be found in the Victoria and Albert Museum in London, and in other museums. There are also manuscripts that Akbar had ordered to be translated from Hindu classics and epics like the *Ramayana* and *Mahabharata.*

Akbar tried in all aspects of his life to blend the two cultures he represented. To his royal courts came artists from all parts of India; craftsmen who prepared the finest armour, utensils of metal, gold jewellery and textiles. Artifacts belonging to the reign of Akbar, his son Jahangir, and of Shah Jahan (his grandson) have been preserved in the National Museum in New Delhi, the Salar Jung Museum in Hyderabad, and the Victoria and Albert Museum in London, and also elsewhere. These are very rare objects, of great beauty, prepared by the best artists of the land.

Jahangir, Akbar's son, in a comparatively uneventful reign, continued the tradition of excellent architecture and production of exquisite paintings.

Illustration from Baburnama *painted by Banwari, Mughal School, late 16th century; National Museum, New Delhi*

His father had ensured that Jahangir's childhood was more privileged than his own, and Jahangir gained the reputation of being less interested in politics than in the joys of luxurious living.

Shah Jahan, Akbar's grandson, inherited a vast and very powerful empire. He therefore had ample resources to indulge in extravagant architectural projects. He is, of course, best remembered for the construction of the Taj Mahal, the tomb of his beloved wife, Mumtaz Mahal. It was begun in 1632, and several hundred people were involved in designing and planning it, and in supervising its construction. Precious stones and other materials were brought to Agra from all parts of India and elsewhere to prepare the intricate inlay work on the marble tomb. In style, the building itself resembles the tomb of Humayun in Delhi. Shah Jahan's architecture can be distinguished, however, because he preferred (or could afford) buildings faced with marble. The stately gateway of the Taj Mahal in Agra, its location by the River Yamuna (Jamuna), the clear skyline without distractions and the well-laid out garden with its fountains and channels — all form a perfect setting for the tomb.

While the Taj Mahal was being built, Shah Jahan moved his capital from Agra to (Old) Delhi (then known as Shahjahanabad), and began the construction of yet another fortified royal palace, now famous as the Red Fort of Delhi. Within the fort are excellent examples of Shah Jahan's taste in architecture — regal rooms and halls, gardens and pavilions. Later, for his Friday prayers, he had the Jama Masjid built, a mosque magnificent both in scale and design.

Thousands of visitors go each year to see the Taj Mahal and the Red Fort. These buildings are now bare, stripped of much of their original ornamentation and of the accessory items that must have formed a vital part of their ambience. To reconstruct the magnificence of the Mughal court, one has to turn to museums, to examine Mughal paintings, textiles, arms, objects of jade, jewellery and, of course, contemporary literature.

Mughal paintings have been preserved in almost all the major museums in India. The National Museum (Delhi), the Bharat Kala Bhavan Museum (Banaras), the City Palace Museum (Jaipur), the Prince of Wales Museum (Mumbai), and in England the Victoria and Albert Museum have very good collections. From these delicately coloured compositions, one can derive a lot of information on the costumes, jewellery, customs, festivals, celebrations, armaments, sports and domestic life of the times.

Mughal illustrations cover many subjects: hunting scenes, court celebrations, exquisite paintings of birds and animals, and a few portraits.

The tombs of Mumtaz Mahal and Mughal emperor Shah Jahan at the
Taj Mahal; 17th century, Agra

The use of the term 'miniature' for Mughal illustrations is somewhat loose. In India, dried palm leaves three to five centimetres (an inch or two) wide and 25 to 30 centimetres (10 to 12 inches) long were used to form books before paper was introduced. The leaves were illustrated with paintings which accompanied the text. Paper was introduced from China and through Islam (the 'Religion of the Book'), and later Hindu rulers used it to prepare illustrated manuscripts. The palm-leaf and paper illustrated books were both small in size and required minute handling of details. They were miniatures in comparison with mural and ceiling (fresco) paintings, or the oil canvas paintings to which Europeans were accustomed. Hence the English term 'miniature paintings' is a relative term, coined during British rule.

Some excellent examples of textiles, arms and royal household objects can be seen in the Salar Jung Museum (Hyderabad), the City Palace Museum (Jaipur) and in the Bharat Kala Bhavan (Banaras). They include jade dagger handles, bowls and books stands studded with rubies and gold. Jade is not found in India, but the Mughals had the stone brought from China and fabricated into objects in their workshops.

Shah Jahan's descendants were unable to hold the empire together for long, and it soon broke up into smaller states and kingdoms. These continued to patronise the arts, often emulating the Mughal style of music, painting, architecture, costume and customs.

Colonial Rule

During the disintegration of the Mughal empire, many of the court artists are said to have migrated to other areas, in search of patronage. During the 17th, 18th and 19th centuries the court paintings of the Rajasthani, Pahari, Deccani and other schools or style came into their own. The architecture promoted by the rulers of the various states was usually an amalgam of the imperial Mughal style and their own, often resulting in incongruous mixtures.

The centuries of interaction between Hindu and Islamic ideas, arts and language led to the creation of a new religion, Sikhism, which is India's youngest. The Sikh saints drew inspiration from contemporary philosophies and established a fine tradition of literature and, later, architecture of their own.

India had had trade links with countries in the east and west for over 2,000 years. However, Arab trade was displaced by that of the Portuguese, French, Dutch and British, who established their respective East India companies in 17th–18th centuries. They developed trading centres and 'factories' in India, and built large storage houses and offices. Indian industry responded to this new trade alliance, producing fabricated goods for the West. The Calico Museum of Textiles (Ahmedabad) has some excellent examples of Indian fabrics, designed and created for Western consumers.

Later, as the trade brought enormous prosperity to the home countries, they saw the need to gain administrative control over Indian territory. In the colonial period, the greater part of India was under British rule, only present-day Goa and Pondicherry, with a couple of other minor enclaves in each case, being under the Portuguese and the French respectively.

Colonial architecture began with imposing administrative buildings, churches and offices, followed by residential quarters, parks, hospitals and schools. Interestingly, there are differences in the styles adopted in various regions, reflecting the dominant art of the colonial ruler superimposed *on an Indian essence.* It was, after all, Indian artisans and masons who constructed the buildings under the direction of European architects. Apart from offices, residential houses were built in the cities of Calcutta, Bombay, Madras, Bangalore, Goa, Pondicherry and, eventually, Delhi, when it was made the capital of the British Indian empire in 1912. An Indo-European

Farewell to Napolean Bonaparte, France; Salar Jung Museum, Hyderabad

architecture emerged, complete with gardens of both tropical and European flowers and plants.

Apart from buildings, objects relating to colonial India such as documents, coins, weapons, prints, illustrations and household items are to be found in the Victoria Memorial Museum (Calcutta) and in Fort St George Museum (Chennai).

The British developed India's railway and postal network, and established a copy of the British administrative and educational system in India. Enlightened and dedicated European scholars undertook studies of India's heritage, flora and fauna, which led to the preparation of beautiful books on Indian art, botany and zoology.

The influence of the West on costumes, customs and lifestyle began to be felt, beginning, of course, from the top. Indian princes, under British rule, adopted many new affectations. Their former palaces, some of which have been converted into museums in places like Gwalior and Baroda (or Vadodara), are full of curios and kitsch from Europe — cuckoo clocks, marble garden-sculpture, cut-glass, and four-poster beds coexisted in uneasy juxtaposition with Indian artifacts. The Salar Jung collection in Hyderabad has such mixed material along with genuine work of art.

The Independence Movement

During the Independence movement, when the Indian people united to end colonial rule, a number of cultural events took place. Mahatma Gandhi, inspired by ideas of self-rule and self-reliance, called for the boycott of foreign goods, and by his personal example made Indian cottage industries and homespun cloth the very symbols of liberation.

There was a conscious attempt by artists and poets like Rabindranath Tagore to encourage indigenous forms of artistic expression in theatre, poetry, painting and crafts. The struggle against foreign rule inspired some of finest of Indian poetry and literature in all the regional languages — Bengali, Tamil, Gujarati, Marathi, Malayalam, Hindi, Urdu and others. Museums directly concerned with documenting the freedom movement are the Gandhi and the Nehru memorial museums in Delhi and Gandhi Ashram Museum in Ahmedabad, Gujarat.

The National Gallery of Modern Art (Delhi), Rabindra Bharati Museum (Calcutta) and Santiniketan University in West Bengal have representative collections of paintings and sculptures of leading artists associated with the freedom movement.

Contemporary Times

The post-Independence period, from 1947 to the present day, has witnessed a dramatic change in the cultural life of the Indian people, especially the urban population. An expanding middle class, with its colonial hangover, turned its eyes to western Europe and America for cultural inspiration. However, small groups of urban intellectuals, government agencies and universities continued the British tradition and opened a few more museums in India for the study and preservation of India's rich cultural heritage.

The National Gallery of Modern Art (New Delhi) has a very comprehensive collection of Indian art (mainly painting and sculpture) dating from the post–1857 period. City art galleries and exhibition halls, and dance, music and theatre performances give some idea of present-day urban Indian art trends.

Running parallel to the urban cultural stream are the rural and tribal streams, which involve 80 percent of the entire population. The wealth of traditional Indian crafts in clay, metal and other natural materials like wood and bamboo, is still in evidence. Government sponsorship and pioneering work by dedicated individuals have brought crafts that were nearing extinction back to life. The major cities of India have cottage industries and emporia that sell a variety of craft products.

The Crafts Museum (New Delhi), the Raja Kelkar Museum (Pune) and the Ashutosh Museum (Calcutta) are examples of a type of museum that seems to be mushrooming all over the country. These specialise in Indian everyday arts.

Many of the problems that India faced on attaining Independence still await resolution, but much has been accomplished, including the setting up of a framework for the preservation of its cultural and historical heritage. A substantial responsibility for this falls on over 500 museums distributed in all parts of India.

Museums

New Delhi

The National Museum

The National Museum is one of India's finest. It has a vast and almost completely comprehensive selection of Indian art, ranging from the prehistoric to the late medieval periods. With its modern extension and display areas, it provides a representative introduction to the development of India's artistic traditions and also includes small collections from Central Asia and of the pre-Columbian art of the Americas.

The origin of the museum goes back to the days prior to Independence when it was established and housed in Rashtrapati Bhavan. The nucleus of the collection consisted of items that had been sent to London in 1947 for an exhibition at the Royal Academy. Instead of returning these objects to their respective museums, it was decided to keep them in Delhi for what was to become the National Museum and the foundation stone was laid by India's first prime minister, Jawaharlal Nehru, on 12 May 1955. The museum was moved into its present building in 1960. The building encircles a small inner courtyard, and has three floors of galleries to house the museum's huge collection of over 150,000 works of art. Art purchases each year add to the wealth and splendour of this museum.

The galleries of the museum are organised to follow a general historical and chronological sequence, and this pattern will be followed in this short survey of the museum's collections.

The Indus Valley Civilisation Gallery

Until the 1920s, when the remains of this urban culture were discovered, it was believed that Indian history stretched back only as far as the third century BC and the reign of the Mauryan dynasty. The dramatic and accidental finding of more ancient cities placed Indian civilisation on par with that of Egypt and Mesopotamia, both in antiquity and artistic merit.

The earliest of such cities to be discovered were those now called Mohenjodaro ('Mound of the Dead'), Harappa (from which the term

Dancing Girl, bronze, Indus Valley Civilisation, circa 2500 BC;
National Museum, New Delhi

'Harappan culture' is derived), and Chanhu-daro. These were excavated by teams led by R D Banerji, Rai Bahadur Daya Ram Sahni, then serving with the Archaeological Survey of India under Sir John Marshall. Inadequate scientific methodology and the use of inaccurate carbon dating hindered the work of these early excavators, but they nevertheless unearthed thousands of artifacts that tell the story of this ancient culture. With the partition of the subcontinent into two separate countries, India and Pakistan, at the time of Independence the finds from the excavations were also divided. So, whilst Pakistan gained the excavated cities of Mohenjodaro and Harappa, India was able to keep a substantial number of the artifacts discovered, many of which are displayed at the National Museum. Excavations are still in progress, and today India has uncovered a number of cities and sites that belong to the Indus Valley Civilisation.

This culture, that spread its influence along and around the River Indus and beyond, is dated to the period between 2500 and 1500 BC. The Indus Valley Civilisation appears to have flourished for over these thousand-odd years, during which time over 400 well planned cities were built. What has amazed historians is the suggestion of a uniform culture, with standardised, common city plans, building designs and even a uniform size of bricks used in construction. This is despite the fact that the sites lie as far apart as Rupar in the Punjab and Lothal in Kathiawar district in Gujarat, and running right along the Indus River in Pakistan.

In the gallery is a display of the elegant **pottery** of this culture, representative of the popular (and similar) taste that was prevalent in all the major cities. This pottery was produced mainly on the wheel, and was usually baked with a red slip, and black, painted decorations. From the shape of the pottery, one can assume the functional use of each piece: for cooking, storage of water or grains, and smaller vessels for precious oils and perfumes. There are plates, dishes with lids, gracious stands and lamps. The painted pottery is especially beautiful. The designs range from natural motifs for water, rain and the earth in wavy, dotted or speckled lines, to those of animals, birds and fish. A large, brick-red, painted pot depicts a rural scene with a farmer tilling the land, using two buffaloes. The animals and the loneliness and hard labour of the farmer are touchingly portrayed.

Another pot, perhaps used as a funerary urn for burial purposes, has a panel of rather joyful-looking peacocks (from Cemetery H). The artist has placed a figure of a human being inside the stomach of one of the peacocks, possibly in reference to a myth or legend, a ritual or belief. There is great variety in the clay ware displayed, some of the most contemporary-looking designs coming from the Nal site. These are specimens of painted pottery with geometric designs in pale yellow, blues and greens, against a white background. The shapes of the round, squat pots with diameters greater than their height, and those of the square lamps with fluted rims are very beautiful.

From the abundant clay available from the river banks, the artist of the Harappan culture fashioned not only pottery but also **toys** and **figurines** — the most charming and endearing feature of this riverine culture. The **sculptures of a bull, ant-eater, pig and monkey** are miniature masterpieces. There are also modelled images of a **flying bird** and a little **monkey** climbing a pole, with its tail looped up on its back. One **toy bull** has a movable, nodding head, which the artist has devised using a hinge and thread.

Among the human **figures**, there are many that reflect something of the life of the people who inhabited the ancient cities: a woman lying on a bed, breast-feeding her child; a woman kneading dough; a person carrying a bird, perhaps a pet duck, securely under the arm. These figures are tiny, often not more than eight centimetres (three inches) high, but they carry the mark of playful and observant artists, whose humorous and gentle touch has the joy of a child as its purpose.

From the metal and clay **toy carts**, we gather something of the mode of transport that must have existed within the cities, between the village and cities, and perhaps between cities too. There are six different types of carts, in various shapes and proportions, with large, solid wheels. We also learn of the domestication of animals such as the **bull** from these toys, and there is even one specimen of a **toy bird-cage**.

There is a variety of items made out of stone, from **jewellery** to **toys**. The semi-precious stone **necklaces** have been reconstructed from the rounded beads found at the excavation sites. There are bone and shell **buckles** and carved **pendants** and **bangles**, a lovely little group of **squirrels** eating nuts, and stoneware **bowls**.

The steatite **seals** of the Indus Valley Civilisation have puzzled many historians. On display in glass-topped cabinet tables is a sample of the many small seals found — some three to four centimetres (an inch or two) in size, and square or rectangular in shape. Each seal carries a representational or a geometric design in *intaglio* relief, with the curious

Harappan script inscribed on top, or along the side. The relief has been so executed as to render an inverted impression when it is pressed on to soft clay. The fine workmanship of the seals is especially noteworthy.

Amongst the collection is one seal which is especially interesting; it portrays a seated man, wearing a huge bull-horn crown or mask identified by some scholars as the oldest representation of an anthropomorphic guru or god, or the origin of the God Shiva. Beside and beneath the figure are animals, such as the rhinoceros, bull elephant, tiger, stag, etc. What has set the historians thinking is that today the area around Mohenjodaro, where the seal was found, is virtually a desert — dry and uninhabited by the rhino. Moreover, the rhinoceros and elephant are now found only in north-eastern India, more than a thousand miles away. It may be, as Zimmer suggests in *The Art of Indian Asia*, that the

> domestic animals of Mohenjo-daro indicate that at the time, the climate of the Indus Valley must have been damper, the vegetation denser and the water supply more abundant than now.

Other scholars feel this was not so. Still others suggest that the Harappan people denuded their rich forests to build cities and for fires to bake thousand of bricks for buildings, thus changing the environment and climate so drastically that they had eventually to forsake their houses and abandon the cities. Surely such environmental destruction is the sole prerogative of 20th-century cultures!

The Indus Valley Civilisation period is also referred to as the **Chalcolithic Period** in Indian history, in view of its use of metal in addition to stone and clay. **Copper and bronze implements and sculptures** have been found at various sites. **Silver** and, more rarely, **gold** was used for the preparation of items of **jewellery**. (See Harrappan Civilisation jewels in Jewellery Gallery of this museum). Famous amongst the bronze objects is the so-called **Dancing Girl**. She stands naked, 10.5 centimetres (a little over four inches) high, wearing bangles right up one arm and a simple necklace. Her hair is swept into a long roll behind her head. One arm is placed on her hip, and one leg bent slightly; her head is raised proudly as she looks down on the world as it passes by.

Head of a woman, 11th century, Rajorgarh, Rajasthan;
National Museum, New Delhi

The talent of the Harappan metalworkers is also to be seen in two almost contemporary-looking pieces: an **elephant on wheels**, and a **cattle cart** from Daimabad, Maharashtra. These two unbelievably elegant sculptures are significant examples of the sophistication of the Harappan artists. Even in the tiny objects such as the **Buffalo from Mohenjo-daro** (c. 2500 BC), the artist has achieved a life-like rendering of the animal with its swishing tail, and head slightly uplifted, as though it were about to moo.

Mauryan, Sunga and Satavahana Art

A most dramatic period in India's cultural history in terms of sculptural remains begins in the third century BC, along after the end of the Indus Valley Civilisation.

The museum has some excellent examples of **Mauryan sculpture** and **Sunga art**. Lent by the British Museum are a few sculptures from the Buddhist site at Amaravati. These sculpted panels of marble have a soft, delicate style. To be noted in these panels is the depiction of the beauty of the female form in a number of postures and stances. The best collection of Amaravati sculptures is, however, at the State Museum in Chennai. The collection at the National Museum has one panel of the **stupa from Amaravati**, the venerated funerary mound built by Buddhists to enshrine holy remains. Though the original Amaravati stupa in Andhra Pradesh was destroyed by vandals, this panel gives some idea of how the stupa may have looked, with its hemispherical mound, surrounded by a tall sculpted railing. From the proportions of the figures depicted in front of the railing, it would seem that the stupa was very tall, which explains the size of panels displayed here which formed part of the stone fencing and decorations of the stupa.

The Art of Gandhara and Mathura

The north-west of the sub-continent, now forming parts of present-day Pakistan and Afghanistan, has yielded a wealth of sculpture which is attributed to the **era of Graeco-Roman influence**, following the invasion by Alexander the Great of Macedonia in the third century BC. Greek and Roman trade with this region continued for centuries, during which period Buddhism was patronised by the rulers. The result was a style of art referred to as **Gandharan** (Gandhara being the name of the region). A famous university also functioned in this region, at Taxila, attracting scholars from the whole Buddhist world in Asia for pilgrimage, study and research.

Laughing Child, stucco, Gandhara, third–fourth century;
National Museum, New Delhi

The **figures of the Buddha**, in shiny, black-grey schist, are rendered in the classic Gandharan style. The robes hang like a Roman toga in deep, heavy folds, while the face of the Buddha appears tranquil and meditative. The hair is fashioned in thick waves, drawn up into a top-knot. There are also panels of sculptures from the stupas of the region of Gandhara, depicting various scenes from Buddhist literature. Among the sculptured busts and damaged heads of figures, one sees the artists' attempts to imitate Greek and Roman ideals of figurative art. The expressive faces of a **young child** and an **old man** are given a touch of realism, to copy nature, as it were. Generally, realism rarely occurs in Indian art, rather artists strove to render abstract concepts and ideas through figurative symbols.

The **sculptures from Mathura** in Uttar Pradesh, of the first few centuries of the Christian era, are easy to identify as they have been worked in a delightful red sandstone, mottled with white. The excavations at Mathura yielded a number of sculptured panels that formed part of the **railings of stupas**. The Government Museum in Mathura (see page 215-21) has the best collection of both **Kushana and Mathura masterpieces** in sculpture. The railing panels or balustrades are also easy to identify, for they consist of upright sculpted columns (the balusters) which used to be linked by horizontal beams (the coping) decorated with lotus motifs. Some of the vertical columns are just a metre (three feet) high with figurative sculptures of women devotees and tree nymphs or **salabhanjikas**.

There is a panel with a woman holding a branch of a tree (**Ashokadhana**) — a reference to fertility myths in which the Ashoka tree (*Jonesia ashoka*) is said to be so sensitive that it bursts into bloom at the touch of an embrace from a woman. It was in a grove of Ashoka trees in Lumbini, now Nepal, where the Buddha was born, and hence this tree holds a special significance to Buddhists. Its long tapering green leaves and slim branches are often represented in Buddhist sculpture.

There is another sculpture, in the same sequence, with a woman bathing under a waterfall (**Snana Sundari**, Mathura, second century), a mother and child playing with a rattle and a woman gazing into a mirror. Another well-known panel is of a swooning woman, named **Vasantsena** (Kushana, second century). A small male figure carrying a cup supports the collapsing form of the woman, while another strives to pull her up by the arm.

In all these Buddhist railing panels, the women are depicted barebreasted. Stitched blouses are a much later fashion. Even today, in Hindu rituals, unstitched cloth is considered pure and uncontaminated. Women wear a thick belt which holds a finely draped cloth around the lower portion of the body. Jewellery of great variety and sophistication appears in the form of long, heavy earrings, necklaces, belts, armlets and anklets. Often, bangles are worn in dozens, to dress the entire arm.

The Art of the Gupta Period
During the Gupta period (third to sixth century), a large swathe of India came under centralised rule, which served to influence many later regional styles of art. It was during this period that the first stone Hindu temples were built, supplanting clay, brick and wooden structures. The sculptural decoration of these temples paved the way for experiments in the art of adorning the religious buildings of the Hindus. The Guptas, however, extended their patronage to Buddhist communities as well, and here too a

Surpanakha being punished by Lakshmana, episode from the Ramayana, Gupta *period, fifth century, Deogarh, Uttar Pradesh; National Museum, New Delhi*

fine synthesis of earlier styles from Mathura and Gandhara is perceptible in the sculptures.

The **figure of the Buddha** (Sarnath, fifth century, Gupta) is a classical example of the acquired confidence of the Indian artist. The Buddha stands with one hand raised in the gesture of protection, *abhaya*. Seen faintly behind the robes, one knee is gracefully bent in a relaxed standing position. The robe no longer needs to be depicted in busy folds, as the Gandharan artist had shown it, but has been simplified or abstracted into just a covering. So beautifully has the drapery been shown, that the youthful body of the Buddha is apparent, full of warmth and pulsating with life. The face of the Buddha is oval, elongated by a broad forehead, and the facial details are in perfect repose, symmetrical as if to reflect the equilibrium of the Buddha's peaceful mind. His half-closed eyes symbolise his contemplative mood.

In a similar mood, the artist has attained the same inward power in the **sculpture of Vishnu** (Mathura, fifth century, Gupta). The torso is intact, but the arms and legs are broken. The body of the figure has been superbly handled, particularly the sensitive portrayal of the gentle swell of the stomach above the garment. The region of the chest has been made expansive, and shows off the jewellery to its full advantage. The necklace, of many rows of pearls, hangs in a very elegant way. The variety of textures depicted by the artist in this sculpture is quite incredible: the hard, metallic quality of the jewellery, the weight of the string of pearls, the patterned textiles and the soft, sensuous body. The Indian artist had by this time acquired complete control over his medium; what he chose to highlight, what was eliminated or selectively ignored was a matter of aesthetics and iconography, far beyond the realm of realism.

There are other Gupta sculptures in this gallery that are narrative in composition. Unlike the early Buddhist story-telling panels, the Gupta artist summarised the myth or legend in one major episode with the assumption that the viewer was familiar with the entire story — what came before and what happened after. A typical example is the panel of **Surpanakha being punished by Lakshmana** (Deogarh, fifth century, Gupta). In this story from the *Ramayana* — the epic poem, Rama, his wife Sita and brother Lakshmana are exiled to the forest as a result of court politics. Rama, an incarnation of Vishnu, is portrayed as the ideal hero-king in this poem. In the forest, Surpanakha, the sister of Ravana, the king of Lanka, falls desperately in love with Rama, who ignores her. She then tries to seduce Lakshmana. In this panel, she is being punished for her lustful advances by Lakshmana, who has been ordered to cut off her nose and ears. Sita demurely watches the whole drama. The forest scene has been symbolised by just one tree, above. What follows in this story, is that the injured Surpanakha hastens back to Lanka to complain to her brother. Ravana, hearing of Sita's beauty, kidnaps her and a great search and battle between Ravana and Rama ensues, with the good side gaining victory over evil.

Besides stone sculptures, the Gupta temples and buildings still made out of brick were adorned with **terracotta panels**. The National Museum has a fine collection of terracottas dating back to the fifth century. The **figures of Ganga and Yamuna** (Ahichchhatra, fifth century, Gupta) are examples of the personified goddesses of the holy rivers of the Hindus. Carrying a waterpot, Ganga rides on the back of a *makara* or crocodile, while Yamuna rides on a tortoise. Such figures of the two river goddesses later adorned the two door jambs of the shrines of temples, to signify purity and absolution from evil on entering the temple. Other terracotta panels are of animals and people, and one depicts the might battle of the *Mahabharata*, with the warriors riding in chariots, with bows raised high, ready for action.

Medieval Sculpture Galleries

These rooms, containing examples of medieval sculpture from the seventh to the 17th century, from different parts of India, are extremely difficult to describe, as they are very varied both in style and emphasis. By way of introduction, it may be said that after the dissolution of the Gupta empire, up to the rule of the Mughals, the Indian sub-continent was politically fragmented and governed by a host of dynasties and rulers. In each territory and under each dynasty, a regional style of art flourished, with an individual approach to architecture, sculpture, painting and the performing arts. This is not to say that traces of a unified past, of common ideals, are not perceptible in these artworks. Most of the artistic work was oriented towards Hinduism. Buddhist art only flourished in pockets in Bihar, Bengal and some other areas, after the 13th century.

In these galleries of medieval sculpture there are some superb examples of the cultural achievements of various schools and regional forms of art. From south India, there are the magnificent granite **sculptures of the Pallava period**, such as the **Shiva Bikshatan murti** (seventh century, Pallavan, Kanchipuram). Pallava sculpture, like all temple sculpture, must be appreciated in the context of the building to which it belongs.

Mahabalipuram and Kanchipuram, not far from Chennai in Tamil Nadu, have some of the most well-preserved temples of this era. The temples, like the sculptures seen here, have a powerful, solid presence, full of quiet dignity, with little ornamentation and very subdued features. The sculptures are elegant, tall, slim figures of various gods and goddesses.

In Karnataka, there are several temples and rock-hewn shrines of the **Chalukya period**. A very influential school of art developed in this region at Badami, Aihole and Pattadakal. The sculptures of this school displayed in the museum carry some of the dramatic quality of this highly innovative and creative Chalukyan style. The **Flying Gandharvas** (seventh century, Chalukyan, Aihole, Karnataka) depicts a pair of sky-nymphs floating with graceful ease across the skies, their fine drapery billowing and flowing with the breeze.

The **Tripurnataka** (eighth century, Chalukyan, Aihole, Karnataka) is a brilliant sculpture with drama and movement. Shiva, on an aerial chariot drawn by the gods, stands astride to aim his mighty arrow at the three fortresses and kingdoms of the powerful Asuras. These Asuras had received a boon from Brahma to build three fortresses, one of copper on earth, one of silver in the sky and a third of gold in the world beyond. When they began to assume that they were indestructible, Shiva destroyed all three regions with a single arrow.

Artists throughout the world have been challenged by the task of representing movement and suspense in the visual arts like sculpture. In Chalukyan art, especially the sculptures still to be seen at Badami and Aihole, the sculptor has mastered the technique of creating in stone a moment of great drama, filled with the thrill of suspended action.

From western India, there are a few specimens such as the **Chamunda** (12th century, Parmara, Madhya Pradesh) and the marble figure of **Saraswati**, the goddess of learning (12th century, Chauhan, Bikaner, Rajasthan) which are equally beautiful but executed in a slightly different style and, of course, different stone. Several of these masterpieces are displayed at the entrance of the introduction gallery of the museum.

From eastern India come the famous **sculptures from Konarak** in Orissa, easy to identify as they are in a shiny, almost black, chlorite stone. The mighty King Narasimha of the Eastern Ganga dynasty built the fabled Sun Temple or *Surya Mandir* in Konarak in the 13th century. We have here a few very lively portraits of this ruler, in various panels and scenes. **King Narasimha as Archer**, **King Narasimha on a Swing**, with details of the brass swing chain so realistically depicted, and **King Narasimha discoursing**, where he is shown seated on a low stool, holding a palm-leaf manuscript in one hand. Another panel is of **King Narasimha Worshipping**, in which he stands before two small shrines, one containing Jagannath, the Lord of Puri, and the other the goddess ahishasuramardini. The details of the cloth with its woven designs, the hairstyles, the depiction of the temples and houses, swings and household objects, are both minute and informative. The fund of detail in these panels gives them a theatrical quality, with all the objects as part of a 'set', as it were.

There are several sculptures of **Pala** and **Sena periods** of the region of Bihar and Bengal: **Vishnu and his Consorts, Chamunda**, and others of the 12th century. Distinctive and very moving is a sculpture entitled **Mahishasuramardini** (Pala, tenth century). There is a legend that there was a mighty demon called Mahisha, who had grown too powerful and was disturbing the equilibrium of the gods. He had received a boon that he would not be destroyed by any man or god. So together, the gods created a 'super-goddess'. With Shiva's energy, her face was formed; through Vishnu, her arms; her toes by the Sun, her eyes by Agni (fire), and so on. Zimmer, in *The Art of Indian Asia*, poetically describes the scene of the battle between the mighty goddess and the bull-demon Mahisha:

> He beheld the goddess, pervading the cosmos with her light, causing the earth to bow at the touch of her feet . . . shaking the underworld with the playful twang of her bowstring, and filling the sky with her numerous hands.

During the battle, she cuts off the head of the bull-demon, and he escapes from this body and appears as a man, till finally the goddess kills him, thereby gaining the title of the 'one who conquered the Asura Mahisha', or Mahishasuramardini. In this sculpture, the gorgeous goddess, filling the sky with her numerous arms, has just decapitated the bull; the tiny human-demon figure is shown emerging from the prostrate body of the bull and, unfortunately for him, walking straight into the mouth of a tiger, the mount or companion animal of Durga. Wherever you see a sculpture of this goddess, Mahishasuramardini, it is worth having a closer look to see how the artist has portrayed this wonderful tale of female power that left all the male gods speechless.

Late medieval sculpture tends to be elaborate, even fussy, with profuse ornamentation, as in the examples of the **Hoysala period**, from Karnataka, of **Kaliya Krishna**, the cowherd god trampling and dancing on the head of the serpent Kaliya, and of **Musicians, Mohini,** and **Lakshmi and Narayana** (Lakshmi and her husband Vishnu) flying on the wings of Garuda.

The Indian Bronze Gallery
The art of bronze sculpture in India is an ancient one, dating back to the Indus Valley Civilisation. The bronze **Dancing Girl** described earlier is over 5,000 years old, and even today, in cities like Tanjore in Tamil Nadu, artisans produce works of great beauty. The National Museum has a representative collection of bronzes from different historical periods and places in India. They range from small, almost miniature bronzes from Kashmir and Kerala to larger ones from Tamil Nadu in the south. There are Buddhist sculptures and Hindu ones, all produced by the *cire perdue* or 'lost wax' process.

A wax model is first made and covered in a clay mould. The mould on the enclosed model is then the base. The empty clay mould is then filled with a special mixture of molten metals. In the end, the liquid, wax-like delicacy of the modelling is reproduced in the hardness of the metal. This is what makes these bronzes so special.

Since the stone temple sculptures were immovable, it was the bronze ones that were used in the home and in processions outside the temple, when they were taken into the city streets where thousands gathered for a sight (*darshan*) of the deity. The stone sculptures in the temple may have been plastered and painted, but today we must appreciate them in their shorn, stoney splendour; so too with the bronzes. In the temples, these magnificent statues were dressed in clothes, jewellery and flower garlands, and one wonders why the artist strove to include such delicate detail in moulding these bronze sculptures, when few would see their real, naked beauty. Such perhaps is the power of faith, and the unseen greatness of the anonymous Indian artist through the ages.

The late Dr C Shivaramamurti, one of India's greatest scholars and an outstanding art historian, served as the Director of this National Museum for several years. His favourite bronzes in the museum were undoubtedly the **Kaliya Mardan Krishna** (Pallava-Chola, ninth century), and the **Nataraja** or **Natesa in** *chatura* pose (Early Chola, tenth century, Tiruvarangulam, south India). He wrote numerous articles and books, and never failed to mention these two pieces: 'The collection of bronzes has lately been greatly enriched with the acquisition of a Nataraja in chatura — *tandava* pose — a unique bronze' (1959); and The 'National Museum can

Nataraja: Shiva the cosmic dancer, Chola bronze, 11th century, Tamil Nadu; National Museum, New Delhi

well be proud of a unique bronze, aesthetically also of the highest order, Nataraja in *chatura* pose' (1980).

The **Nataraja figure of Shiva**, as the cosmic dancer and creator, also appears in stone sculpture, and is today also choreographed in dance. In one hand, Shiva holds a drum, symbolising the source of all creation — sound, rhythm and life-giving energy. In another hand, he holds a flame, symbol of destruction. The third arm is raised in the gesture of protection, while the fourth draws attention to the position of Shiva's feet — trampling a dwarf figure, a personification of Ignorance. Shiva danced to the thunder of the drums and the elements, awakening the heavens. His figure is lithe and youthful, with slim legs, and arms in full movement, the tinkling of his ankle bells filling the universe. Modestly bejewelled, often with his hair flying in the wind, Shiva's face is always calm, showing no trace of exertion. Snakes, blessed to all agricultural communities in India, form part of the ornamentation of Shiva, for he is also the Lord of the Earth, the Underworld and the Sky, and all the secrets of the hidden world are known to snakes as well as to him. In this one dance, the *Nataraja* symbolises all — creation, protection, destruction, removal of ignorance and the attainment of bliss.

The Kaliya Mardan Krishna depicts yet another story. Krishna, as the cowherd, is an incarnation of Vishnu. Once, it happened that he noticed that many cattle were being poisoned when they drank water from the river where he and his friends took the animals for watering every day. Krishna found the culprit, the giant serpent Kaliya, and in this sculpture, Krishna is seen dancing on the five-headed hood of the serpent. Realising his mistake, he raises his hand in worship of the young boy Krishna, who holds up Kaliya's long tail in triumph.

The Gallery of Manuscripts and Paintings
This first floor gallery has a splendid display of the art of **calligraphy**, **illustrations** of texts and **paintings**. In India, the use of **palm leaf** for the preparation of early **manuscripts** governed the unique aesthetic quality of composition within this art form. The long, tapering shape of the palm leaf required subtle handling of the stylus in writing, and the composition of each page. Bound together by string and wooden covers, palm leaf manuscript bundles were usually wrapped in a protective cloth. At times, a page was divided vertically, to form narrower columns to facilitate reading, with margins, framing lines and small oblong areas of illustrations. The use of mineral colours gave rise to the dominance of pure, unmixed primary colours — red, blue and yellow — with black, white and gold in the paintings. The *Mahaparaniravana of Buddha* (Bengal, Pala, AD 1000), the *Mandu Kalpasutra* (1439, Mandu, central India) and the *Astasahasrika Prajnaparamita* (1350, Nepal) are good examples of this style of page design and early manuscript art. A noteworthy collection of palm leaf manuscripts is also on display in the Government State Museum in Bhubaneswar, Orissa.

The influence of Islam on the art of book illustration and calligraphy in the medieval period was quite significant. The museum has a specimen of the *Quran* **in Arabic** (ninth century, Kufic) which is a superb example of the elegant art of calligraphy.

The *Jahangirnama* (Mughal, 17th century, Persian Nastaliq) is a more ornate example of the art of writing and page composition. The use of paper which could be cut to different sizes led to a different compositional form. The edges of the paper were often strengthened with painted borders, and the art of calligraphy flourished because of the initial Islamic hesitation to draw human figures.

When the two streams of tradition met — Persian and Indian — a new synthesis emerged. In the early Islamic works on display, such as the *Baburnama* [labelled 'Babar Nama'] (Mughal, 1598) and illustrations from the *Tutinama* (Mughal, 1580), or the *Bustan* (Sultanate, 1500-2), the written text is placed very prominently on the page, with the illustrations around it serving merely as an adjunct to the written word. Gradually the text and illustrations were given into a variety of shades and hues, and Indian and Islamic abstractions melted into one another.

The Mughal emperors maintained huge ateliers or workshops where artists from many parts of the country worked. Painters were commissioned, as were jewellers and textile workers. Under royal patronage, an influential and artistic style of painting emerged. There are nature-study paintings, for example, conceived by Babur to record the new and curious creatures of the land of the Indus. Dating from the reign of Jahangir is the animal painting *Camel Flight* (Mughal, c. 1615-20), in which the camels look decidedly young and playful. Another painting *The Falcon* (Mughal, c. 1630, by Mansur) is a fine example of an artist's keen observation of nature. With what care each feather has been depicted!

Another important phase in this Mughal School's development was that which flourished under Emperor Akbar. Among the National Museum's prize possessions are the folios of the *Baburnama*, the illustrated diary of Emperor Babur, the founder of the Mughal Empire. *Babur Supervising the Construction of a Reservoir on the Spring of Khwaja Sih-yaran near Kabul* (*Baburnama*, Mughal, 1598) is a rare and interesting portrayal of the emperor. He is standing in a garden, in which a canal and pond are being constructed. His courtiers stand around observing the activities with some concern. At the bottom of the painting, some gaily coloured tents have been pitched for the emperor's sojourn. Babur will always be remembered in India as the great garden builder. It is to him that we owe the introduction of the concept of formal gardens as an integral part of Mughal architecture. The painting is crowded with people, animals and birds; in the far distance lies a rugged landscape, where animals roam wild and free. The artist's name, Prem Gujarati, suggests that in the Mughal ateliers Indian as well as some Persian artists worked together, each assimilating the style of the other to produce what we now call the **Mughal School of painting**. In the painting *Akbar Hunting* (Mughal, 1595), we catch a glimpse of the cruel, little-known side of the emperor. The golden

(overleaf) Krishna Steals the Gopies' Clothes, an illustration from the Bhagavad Purana, *Kangra School, late 18th century; National Museum, New Delhi*

landscape and the fleeing animals with a look of terror in their eyes have been captured by the artist with tremendous skill and patience.

In a different mood, *The Meeting of Sufis* (Mughal, c. 1640, Shah Jahan's period) creates a sense of tranquility and peace by depicting a quiet landscape undisturbed by the soft whispers of learned sages in discussion. In style, the painting is meticulous in its concern for detail, every leaf of a tree, every hair of a beard, each fold of a gown is painstakingly painted. Often the artist used a single-haired brush to capture minute features.

A new and favoured art form was the painting of portraits of rulers. The National Museum has the best-known one of *Emperor Jahangir Holding a Picture of the Madonna* (Mughal, Jahangir period, c. 1620). It is a tiny portrait affixed to a larger page which is decorated with flower borders and inscriptions, and gold has been used to enrich the subtle decorations of the paper. Jahangir proudly holds in his hand a painting of the Madonna, perhaps a gift from one of the European ambassadors such as Sir Thomas Roe who visited his empire. Dressed in a brocade tunic and adorned with a necklace of pearls, his turbaned head glows under the light of a halo. The artist is flattering the emperor perhaps, in his portrayal of him as an art-loving, wise king.

Other paintings of the Mughal period are equally noteworthy, and the range of the artists is admirable. *The Marriage of Dara Shikoh* (Mughal, Oudh, c. 1750) is full of pomp and splendour. The well-dressed horses, surrounded by nobles and members of the royal family attired in the fashions of the day, walk in procession to the music of drums and the flickering light of the fireworks display.

The art of portraiture continued in other region within the Mughal empire and beyond, as we see here in *Raja Medini Pal of Basohli* (Pahari, Basohli, c. 1735) and *Raja Sansar Chand of Kangra* (Pahari, Kangra, c. 1780). This last painting from Kangra is extremely rich in colours, full of oranges, browns and creams. The room in which Raja Sansar Chand sits is decorated with flowers, paper lanterns and smoky, flickering lamps, while he witnesses the celebration of Janmashtami (the birth of Krishna) with music and dance.

Paintings from the region of Basohli are especially noteworthy. *Krishna Making Love to Gopies* (an illustration to the *Gita Govinda*, a Sanskrit poetic work by Jayadeva, Pahari, Basohli, 1730) is an undisputed favourite. The riot of Indian colours proclaims the essential joy of the theme of the painting. A row of trees, like a colourful pattern, fills the top part of the painting. Below, a band of orange-red earth sets the stage for Lord Krishna with his lady friends, and a river runs by the lower border of the painting. All the elements of nature are present and rejoice in Krishna's love: the earth, water, sky, the air and all living things. A close look at the highlights of the jewellery reveals the artist's use of tiny pieces of a luminous beetle's scales and wings that glimmer in the light. From a distance, one can appreciate the artist's innovative use of colours, where seemingly contrasting shades have been juxtaposed to form an internally harmonious composition, something that became 'acceptable' in the West only in the 20th century.

All the paintings from Kangra and Basohli, of the Pahari School, displayed here are of first-rate quality. The painting, **Radha and Krishna Sheltering from the Rain** (Kangra, Pahari, c. 1790) is a tender scene. Krishna extends his arm to Radha in protection, and in the same mood of love the cow calls to her calf. Among other stories of Krishna's prankish childhood, the one of how **Krishna Steals the Gopis' Clothes** (Kangra, 18th century, an illustration to the *Bhagavad Purana*) is an old favourite. The women have left their homes in the village, depicted at the top end of the picture, and are wandering down to the river to collect water in their pots, and to bathe. Divesting themselves of all their clothes, the young women plunge into the flowing waters, frolicking in the rippling stream and playing with each other in gay abandon. Krishna, who happens to pass by, spies on them and mischievously collects the garments lying on the river bank, and with them climbs up a tree that overlooks the bathing women in the river. From the safety of the tree, he calls out to the women. They are unable to get out of the water because their clothes have all been taken away. Krishna then teases them, asking each one to emerge, naked, and request him to return her clothes, with hands raised in prayer, not covering herself. The unfortunate young ladies have to comply. The whole painting covers various parts of the story, with sequences that occurred both 'earlier' and 'later', all placed together in the picture. The story is naughty and playful, but the painting is charming in the elegant handling of the nude figures in the water, the gestures of female distress and the self-assured arrogance of young Krishna. How often must this story repeat itself in the villages of India, where bathing in rivers is so common and where there is no dearth of naughty boys and pretty girls! It is impossible not to respond to the native charm of this story that so endears Krishna to the Indian people.

Another exquisite painting is of **Krishna Installing the Parijata Celestial Tree in His Palace in Dwaraka** (from the *Parijataharna* of the

Harivamsa Purana, Pahari, Kangra, c. 1810). The composition of the large painting is very bold, with substantial use of architectural detail. There is a central courtyard where Krishna has planted the celestial tree obtained by him from the realm of Lord Indra. His wife, Satyabhama, places a garland around Krishna and the tree. There are men and women looking on at the scene from windows and doors. There are female musicians in the courtyard; a number of other people peer out of windows with cloth curtains rolled up; and doorways with designed panels give us some idea of the décor of the times. The colours of white, orange, red and black are balanced in a pleasing symmetry.

Also from the Pahari School comes another painting of *Mahishasuramardini* (Pahari, Nurpur, c. 1770-1800). The story of this painting has been described in the section on medieval sculptures in this museum. Here, the same theme has been rendered in paint, with the artist using the same iconographic details. Yet in this composition, the artist's individual perception and style add a unique flavour to the portrayal of a youthful, almost girl-like goddess astride her tiger mount, slaying the demon Mahisha. The gods above, hiding amid the clouds, can only look on in amazement at the power of this wondrous goddess.

If the *Mahishasuramardini* extols the strength of the goddess, there are paintings of the gentler aspects of the Hindu deities that are like family portraits. Shiva, Parvati and their children: Ganesh (represented with an elephant head) and Karttikeya (with many heads), with their mounts, the bull, tiger, rat and peacock respectively, are depicted in paintings from the Pahari region. *Shiva's Family and Banasura* (Kangra, Pahari, c. 1760) is one such scene where the holy family is having a picnic, playing together, sewing a patchwork quilt, walking on their annual descent from the Himalayan mountains. From a non-religious point of view, this family of gods is much like any human family. However, the religious iconographic details are not eliminated altogether, but are included almost casually in the painting. The baby Ganesh hangs around the neck of Shiva, or wanders off to play with his brother. Creatures that are never seen together in nature are composed in these pictures into a happy unit of the animal mounts of the gods. The bull sits next to the tiger, the rat near the peacock. When the gods are at rest, what does one have to fear? All the world is suffused with harmony.

Birth of Mahavira, illustration from Jain Manuscript, Mandu Kalpasutra, western Indian Style, 15th century; National Museum, New Delhi

Apart from the theme of love, and the exploits of gods and man, there are paintings that are essentially mood pieces, reflecting nature and human life, transient moment, emotions and feelings. The *Raga Megha* (Narsinhgarh, Malwa, c. 1680) and the *Raga Megha Malhar* (Kotah, Rajasthan, c. 1750) are two paintings inspired by the replenishing glory of rain. Krishna, who appears in both the paintings, is seen dancing to the accompaniment of music, the beat of drums and the melody of stringed instruments. In the *Raga Megha* from Malwa, the sky is a dark band, with the rain falling like a curtain of white flowers. In the *Raga Megha Malhar* from Kotah, the sky is swirling with dark bluish-purple clouds, heavy with rain. Lightning snakes through the sky to create a visual metaphor for a literary phrase. And in this rain, humankind is happy, joyful, for the earth, like the human soul, is thirsty, and rain brings with it a promise of growth and a soothing calm after days of heat and toil.

The term *raga* refers to music; there are legends of great musicians who, on singing *Raga Megha Malhar* compositions, brought dark clouds and rain. In Indian dance, too, rain is described through movements: through fast footwork and hand gestures, the dancer can portray the rolling clouds, thunder and lightning, and the joyful mood that accompanies the monsoon season.

There are two other paintings that individually are of great artistic merit, but for purposes of comparison they will be discussed together to illustrate an Indian sentiment towards nature. The painting entitled **Radha Offering Flowers to Yogi Krishna** (Kishangarh, Rajasthan, c. 1760) is in the **Kishangarh style**, characterised by slim, elegant figures, with faces in sharp profile, and very elongated eyes. Here Radha meets her lover Krishna (dressed as an ascetic). They are surrounded by birds and animals who are in pairs, both male and female, rejoicing in the union of the gods. In the painting, **Majnu in the Company of Wild Animals** (Mughal, c. 1614), the mood is very different. Here the lover sits pining, alone; the animals empathise: they too come alone, without their mates, or in pairs, looking sad and mournful. The emotion in each of the two paintings is one that is quite familiar to all of us. When one is happy, the world seems happy too, and in sadness one finds many images that echo the same sentiment.

Central Asian Antiquities
The ancient 'silk routes' that linked China with Europe brought trading caravans through China, Russia, Iran, Iraq and India. There is evidence of

settlements and trading posts along the routes dating back to the early centuries of the Christian era. On these hard, difficult and often dangerous journeys, the traders sought refuge from nature and human marauders in the oases of civilisation and religion along the way. The settlements developed over the centuries, with their own synthesised culture born from the cross-fertilisation of many strains, from different lands and people.

The National Museum has a unique and unusually large collection from Central Asia of objects discovered and found along the silk routes that were explored by Sir Aurel Stein between 1900 and 1916. On display are some **silk banners** from Dunhuang that had been donated by traders praying for their safety along these arduous routes. Remnants of **wall paintings** have also been carefully preserved. *Buddha and Six Disciples from Miran* (third to fourth century) shows influences from India and Gandharan art. Stein, in his excavations, found some graves furnished with utensils, furniture, pots, figurines and silk palls or hangings. On display are a few long, **hand-painted silk banners** (Astana, seventh to eighth century), some decorated with the serpentine, entwined figures of Emperor Fuxi and his wife Nuhua, the 'sky gods' of Chinese mythology. Emperor Fuxi is said to have invented the characters of Chinese writing. There are fragments of silk paintings, also from Astana (seventh and eighth century). In *Ladies in the Garden*, the delicate brushwork of the Chinese artist is clearly noticeable.

Among the figurative sculptures are grave horses and riders. The *Damaged Stucco Horse* (Sorchuk, sixth to seventh century) is a sprightly piece that exemplifies the wealth of Chinese art and culture.

Other Important Galleries
The National Museum has a representative selection of **Indian textiles**. The variety of Indian weaving techniques displayed includes brocades from Banaras, some dating back to the Mughal period; ikat tie-dye weaving from Andhra Pradesh and Gujarat; and woven gold and silk work. There are embroidered items from different parts of India, including some exquisite shawls from Kashmir. Gold and silver embroidered cloth and canopies are examples of the richly ornamented fabrics for which India has been famous throughout history. There are delicate embroideries from Himachal Pradesh and Kashmir called *rumal*, that was used for covering gifts and items of religious value. Cloths printed with handmade blocks, a separate one for each of the several colours, carry intricate designs of flowers, birds and animals.

Another section of the museum is devoted to the **decorative arts**, with displays of **ivory work** of great delicacy and superb craftsmanship. Metalware, in the form of ornate pots, bases, hukkah (hookah) stands, money boxes and pen stands have been decorated in a variety of ways. There are **Bidri work** samples, bell-metal objects in a dark grey colour inlaid with silver or brass paterns. Repoussé, enamel and gem-studded work adorns other metal objects used by royalty in days gone by. Tall, regal oil lamps carrying images of birds and deities vie with smaller household items to attract the attention of the visitor.

The National Museum also has a large collection of **tribal art** which is worth seeing if only to appreciate the continuity and creativity of India's artistic traditions. Figures in wood from the Bastar region in Madhya Pradesh are elegantly proportioned, the *Mother and Child* (20th century) being an exquisitely beautiful piece. There are also **metal images**, abstract and symbolic, which are appealing to the contemporary eye. It must be remembered that the rich tribal tradition formed a parallel stream in India's ancient cultural history, and was often one of the many sources of inspiration for rural and courtly art.

The specially designed **Jewellery Gallery** contains 27 showcases projecting the development of jewellery art during the last five thousand years. The first showcase represents the ornaments from the Indus Valley sites, which are made of gold, silver and faience. Besides, precious and semi-precious stones were also used for beads and pendants.

To create an awareness of the rich maritime history of India, a **Maritime Heritage Gallery** has been added to the National Museum. This Gallery has a modest collection of artifacts displaying glimpses from India's glorious maritime heritage extending over four thousand years.

Museum Services

The National Museum has a sales counter, in the same area as the reception and ticket counter. The museum has produced a number of well-researched monographs, based on exhibitions, and an expensive museum catalogue. There are prints, slides and postcards on sale. Plaster-cast models of sculptures belonging to the museum collections are popular as souvenirs. There are models of Indus Valley Civilisation toys and animals, a Buddha's head from Sarnath and early medieval sculpture.

Ekamukhalinga, fifth century, Uttar Pradesh;
National Museum, New Delhi

The National Museum,
Janpath,
NEW DELHI.

Hours: 10 am–5 pm everyday except Monday and major government holidays.

Admission: 50 paise; nominal charge for a camera. A camera with a tripod requires special permission.

Suggested viewing time: 2–3 hours; perhaps spread over more than one day.

The National Gallery of Modern Art

Most tourists, both domestic and foreign, tend to miss a very important and significant aspect of present-day Indian life — **contemporary art**. This may be because India has so much to offer by way of ancient and medieval masterpieces, that there is no time for any more. The National Gallery of Modern Art is one of India's best maintained museums, and is devoted exclusively to Indian painting and sculpture of the post-1857 era. Some galleries have permanent displays; in others, special exhibitions are mounted periodically, with an emphasis on what may loosely be called contemporary art.

Jaipur House, where the gallery is housed, is situated at one end of the parade ground and lawns of Raj Path that lead up to the former Viceregal Lodge, now the Rashtrapati Bhavan where the President of India resides. To echo the imperial mood, the palaces of the old states of Baroda, Hyderabad and Jaipur, built by the same architect, follow the same plan with spacious gardens. **Jaipur House** has a dome similar to that of the Rashtrapati Bhavan, with a butterfly-shaped building plan. The gardens around the Jaipur Palace buildings are manicured and well tended. It is a joy to walk in this **garden** on a winter's morning, when all the roses are in full bloom. Over the years, the garden has won several prizes at the annual Delhi Flower Show. Today, an open-air sculpture garden has been arranged on the back and side lawns of the building.

As you enter the gate, in front of the museum building is a huge bronze sculpture by D P Roy Chaudhury, called *Triumph of Labour*. The artist, who was trained in Tagore's Santiniketan in Bengal, served as Principal in the Madras Government School of Art for several years, and is considered one of India's most renowned sculptors of the 1940s and 1950s. The sculpture depicts a pathetic sight, often seen in India, of poor labourers hauling a huge boulder for some construction work. During the Independence struggle, this sculpture acquired a metaphorical significance, symbolising team work and the struggle of life, the labour of love and freedom. Several casts of this sculpture are to be found in different cities, including Chennai (on the Beach Road).

The National Gallery extends over two floors. The first floor is reached by a staircase near the entrance doorway.

The period 1770–1850 saw the gradual decay of traditional Indian schools of painting, sculpture, architecture and handicrafts. In their place, under the patronage of the British East India Company officials and the weakened sections of Indian royalty, grew what is commonly called the **Company School**. Paintings and sculpture (even architecture) were influenced by ideas from Europe during this period. Portraits of British governors, Indian royalty, records of daily life and Indian landscapes were commissioned by the new patrons. The composition, technique and subject matter were new to India, and carried the stamp of 19th-century taste brought from the West to India. There are a number of examples of royal portraits of the **post-Mughal Style**, such as the one of *Ghulam Ali Khan*, in this gallery. The most amusing portrait belongs to the **Punjab School:** *Queen Alexandra and King Edward VII* (tempera on paper). Here the British king and queen sit like an Indian couple — on the floor, bedecked with jewellery, executed in a style that is unmistakably Indian.

Among the paintings and prints, **works by Hodges and Daniell** (uncle and nephew) are of great importance. A good collection of their work is on display in the Victoria Memorial Museum in Calcutta and at the museum at Fort St George in Chennai (see pages 151-4 and 166-7). There are water-colours by Thomas Daniell: *Part of the Fort at Vellore* (Tamil Nadu) and the *Observatory at Benares*. The famous and most familiar one, *The View of the Fort at Trichinopoly*, and another, *View of Mathura on the River Yamuna*; both these aquatints show characteristically delicate drawing and subtle shading of colour.

It was in the British-run schools or colleges of art in Madras, Calcutta, Bombay and other cities that the next phase of Indian artistic expression was born. It was through colleges, often run by British principals, that the European style and techniques of painting, unfamiliar and foreign to the Indian artist, received emphasis and gained popularity. This gallery has the

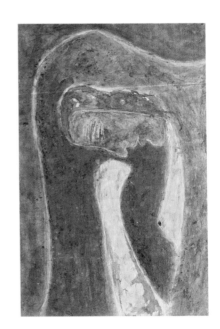

works of some artists of this period. **Ravi Varma** (1848–1906) is representative of this style of Indian Victorians. *A Woman Holding a Fruit, A Woman in Moonlight*, etc are all oil paintings on canvas. The Indian subject has been reframed, as it were, to a Western style. Dark backgrounds, a romantic atmosphere and the warm glow of light on jewellery characterise this school of painting. Similar in style is the **work of M F Pithawala**, such as *A Girl Praying Near Fire* (1911).

The turn of the century, the 1900s, saw the development of a very influential movement in Indian art history, referred to as the **Bengal School**. Though the origins of this school are rooted in Bengal, at Calcutta and Santiniketan to be specific, there is often no common denominator in the works of the outstanding artists of this group. Each evolved an individual style and technique that are almost impossible to link with the work of others. However, the Bengal School, often abused for its revivalist tendencies of attempting to be Indian and yet not so, formed a bridge between the Company School and what was to follow in the 1950s.

Senior-most among the Bengal School group was **Abanindranath Tagore**, a student of E B Havell who taught in the Government School of Art at Calcutta. E B Havell had written a number of books on Indian art and architecture. His interest in the Indian cultural tradition brought new inspiration to the lives of his students.

Abanindranath Tagore's works in wash and tempera show marked Western, Japanese and Mughal influences. The gallery has a good collection of work by this pioneer. *Advent of the Rainy Season* is a delicate wash and tempera rendition of a peacock (the bird associated in India with the coming of the monsoon) and a flowering plant, drenched in rain. Other noteworthy works on display are *Twilight*, and a pastel, *Landscape*.

One of Abanindranath Tagore's students was the outstanding artist **Nandlal Bose** (1883–1966), whose life and paintings inspired generations of artists. There are framed composite collections of drawings of people and animals. The paintings of the *Head of Shiva* and *Pratiksha* are examples of the range of experimentation that the artist undertook during this period.

Ramkinkar's (1910–80) is known more as a sculptor. However, *Seascape* (1951) and *Goat and Coolie from Shillong* are examples that confirm his amazing talent for painting. Other artists associated with the

Drawings by Rabindranath Tagore, India's poet laureate for literature; National Gallery of Modern Art, New Delhi

Bengal School are **Asit Kumar Halder** who worked in Lucknow, **Venkatappa** of Mysore, **Sailendranath De** who lived in Jaipur, and **Kshitindranath Majumdar**. In the gallery there are some examples of Majumdar's work which convey that very lyrical quality that is associated with his individual style.

The 'giant' and best-known member of the Bengal School was **Rabindranath Tagore**, India's poet laureate. He was born in 1861 in Calcutta, to an aristocratic family, and throughout his life played an important role in India's freedom movement and cultural development. In 1901 he established a school, later to become a university, called Santiniketan ('Haven of Peace'), similar in spirit to the traditional *gurukul* of India, where the guru or teacher lived and worked with his students in idyllic rural surroundings. This school was a brave departure from those established in accordance with the British school system, so alien to the Indian ethos. Santiniketan produced scores of brilliant artists, painters, dancers, sculptors, and the like, who worked in different parts of India spreading a new wave of inspiration everywhere.

Doodling on his manuscripts, correcting verse, and deleting lines, Tagore discovered his innate talent for drawing and painting. His doodles came alive as strange creatures of the subconscious that reflected the dark mood of the period of history through which Tagore lived. Between 1928 and 1941, when Tagore died at the age of 81, he painted about 2,000 pictures. A collection is on display at Santiniketan and the Rabindra Bharati University Museum in Calcutta. The National Gallery of Modern Art has a small but representative collection of his work, the best-known being *Veiled Lady* (ink on paper) and the *Head Study* (ink on silk). There is a strange, sombre quality in the paintings, touched with flashes of humour and mystery.

Returning to the other members of the group, mention must be made of the work of **Binodi Behari Mukherjee**, who studied and taught in Santiniketan, and **A R Chugtai** who worked in Lahore (now in Pakistan). In the gallery there are a number of Chugtai's paintings which today seem like book illustrations of another era. The examples, *Laila* and *Omar Khayam*, have an eastern fairy-tale quality.

Gaganendranath Tagore (1867-1938) was the elder brother of Abanindranath Tagore. Unlike his brother, Gaganendranath had no formal education in the arts. His paintings on display here are delightful both in technique and in their mystical quality, enhanced by the experiments in cubist composition. The paintings, *Temple Door, Meeting at the Staircase* (which has spaces created with just the use of blacks, greys and white), and the famous one, *Magician*, have a distinct Japanese flavour, a characteristic of Gaganendranath Tagore's work.

An undisputed favourite and much loved artist is **Amrita Shergil**. Her father was from the Punjab and her mother was a Hungarian pianist. Amrita Shergil was trained in painting in Paris, and returned to India in 1934-5. Unfortunately, she died suddenly of an illness in 1941, at the age of 29. In her short life as a painter, she produced some exquisite paintings that are greatly treasured, and have earned her a prominent place in the history of Indian art. The Gallery of Modern Art has one of the best collections of her work, though, sadly, most of them are locked away in a storeroom. It is hoped that when this museum completes its new building, an entire gallery will be dedicated to the work of the artist. Among her portraits of women, there are *Sumair* (1936), an Indian woman attired in urban finery, and *Self Portrait* which gives us some inkling of her vibrant and vivacious personality. Her paintings in India derived their inspiration from scenes from everyday rural life. *The Brahmacharis, Two Musicians* and *The Bathers* are well-known examples of Shergil's work, strongly influenced by Gauguin, and bathed in light and flamboyant colours. Executed in an elegant style — slim, with limbs elongated and serene expressions — her figures are often huddled together to create a sensation of warmth and humane gentleness.

Another very charming painter is **Jamini Roy** (1887-1972). He too studied art in Calcutta at the Government School of Art. Born and bred in Bengal, Roy looked for his muse not in the Western tradition in which he had been trained but in the artistic heritage of Bengal. On display is his painting of **Krishna and Balarama**. The essence of this work is derived from the *pata* of Orissa, traditional rural paintings. He adopted indigenous colours — Indian browns, ochres, black, white, greens and blues — and some of the *pata* compositional details, such as the bold flat background, often sprinkled with flowers falling from the sky. Another source for his ideas was the Kalighat paintings of Calcutta, as seen in *Yasodha and Krishna* in this gallery. It is in paintings like *Kirtan*, of a group of musicians playing devotional music, that the lively spirit of Roy's art can be best enjoyed. There is a sense of rhythm in the repetitive, pattern-like drawing of the musicians, their elongated eyes, the dark thick outlines, and the use of a minimum of figurative detail. The figures are almost squashed into the tight frame or composition of the painting. Was this a conscious effort to revive older Indian painting traditions, or to find a truly Indian language of painting that could serve modern times? Whatever the artist's purpose may have been, the style he evolved stood in sharp contrast to the Western painting ideals in which he was trained, and which were patronised during his time.

There have been many more, important artists since Independence. Unfortunately, because of lack of space in the present gallery, a sizeable selection of any one individual artist's work is not available for study and appreciation. Major artists of contemporary India have but one or two samples of their work on display, which makes the task of describing and viewing them difficult.

M F Hussain is today one of India's most prolific painters. His style is abstract, with a bold use of colour, line and texture. Coming from a working-class family, he supported himself by painting cinema hoardings at the start of his career, and he is always comfortable on large, often huge canvases, for scale has never inhibited his style. After India's Independence in 1947, he became part of an important association, the **Bombay Progressive Artists Group**. His painting *Zamin* (1955) in this gallery is a long, almost narrative, scroll-like work, illustrative of his mature style. Today, Hussain — slim, with a long flowing white beard and hair, and always barefooted — is India's most sought-after and highly priced artist.

Also on display are some works of **Souza**, **Raza**, **Hebbar**, **Bendre** and **Chavda**, along with **Swaminathan's** characteristic rocks, birds and bright skies, as in his painting entitled *Journey I*.

Of the eminent Baroda Group of artists, who actually do live in the city of Baroda, Gujarat, there are the works of **Vivan Sundaram, Bhupen Khakar** and **Gulam Mohammed Sheik**, each with an individual and powerful style. Sheik's *Man II* (1970) is a large canvas with striking use of contrasting colours and moving subject and content. Bhupen Khakar's paintings are represented by one of his works, entitled *Man with a Bunch of Plastic Flowers* (1975). Khakar's strength lies in his satire, his humorous vision of contemporary Indian life, which he expresses with the additional use of narrative details. These draw one's attention to some mundane, seemingly insignificant fragment of life.

Among other paintings are those of **Tyeb Mehta**, *The Gesture No. 2* (1977), **Ram Kumar's** abstract painting entitled *Flight*, and **Anjoli Ela Menon's** *Mataji* (1983).

Mask for Chhau *Dance, eastern India*

Romancing Couple, Rajasthan

Toy Horse, central India

Museum Services

The Museum has a publication counter which has on sale prints, posters, slides, postcards and monographs on contemporary Indian art from its collection.

Look in the newspapers for the advertisement of special exhibitions.

The National Gallery of Modern Art,
Jaipur House,
NEW DELHI.

Hours: 10 am-5 pm every day except Monday and
                                     government holidays.

Suggested viewing time: an hour, at least.

The Crafts Museum

This is perhaps one of the most important museums in the country for here you will see what makes Indian culture so special and unique. Not many other countries of the world can boast an artistic tradition that is 5,000 years old and is alive and thriving today. The Crafts Museum honours the craftspersons and artists who have kept alive this ancient artistic tradition in all its wondrous diversity and originality.

This museum was established in 1956 by the All India Handicrafts Board and occupies over eight acres within New Delhi's main exhibition grounds (Pragati Maidan), next to the impressive fortress of **Purana Qila**. Following an exhibition on Rural India in 1972, the museum took over the running of the Village Complex that had been built to display exhibits. This complex has miniature or small-scale **replicas of village houses** from different parts of India, including Arunachal Pradesh, Orissa, Tamil Nadu, Gujarat, Bengal and Rajasthan. All the houses have been built with authentic materials, by artisans from the respective regions. Within the houses are some items of daily use, commonly found in their states of origin. The **Kullu hut** of Himachal Pradesh has been made of wood and stone, slate tiles on the roof, and carved balconies. The houses of Gujarat and Rajasthan are in mud brick, decorated with wall paintings.

Wall paintings in Indian villages differ from place to place. Often, powdered white lime (which also serves as a disinfectant) was sprayed and painted over the freshly laid mud wall so that the painting was fixed to the drying walls of the house. In some regions colours were also used for painting. These were obtained from minerals. The paintings changed every season, every time the mud walls were re-done, and for the celebration of

festivals and marriages, or to announce the birth of a child. As in
Madhubani (mural paintings named after the district of Madhuban in the
state of Bihar where the women paint the outer walls of the village houses),
each painting carried a personal style and expressed the artist's concerns.
Apart from paintings, the mud/clay walls were often modelled into reliefs,
and objects like shells (even bottle caps and glass pieces) were attached, to
enhance the beauty of the walls. For the busy tourist unable to visit rural
India, the Village Complex of the Crafts Museum provides a unique
glimpse into the more beautiful side of 'Real India'. It is a lovely walk
through the houses and courtyards on a winter's morning.

Another interesting section of the museum is the **crafts demonstration
area**. Here, in a small courtyard which has been formed by a quadrangle of
mud huts, is the work area for demonstrations. The Crafts Museum often
organises special, theme-based demonstrations by artists from different parts
of India. Embroideries of India, clay work, metal crafts, pottery and toy-
making are some of the themes of such activities. Artists, both men and
women, work in this area and are also permitted to sell their wares. Of
greatest interest is to actually sit and watch the artists working, to
understand the process, and to even talk with them. It is through
demonstrations such as these that one comes to understand the diversity
and richness of the Indian crafts tradition. In a commonly used medium
such as clay, artists from different states in India have their own
technique and procedure, almost unique to their region. There is also a
great variety in the things they make out of clay, from religious objects to
playthings for children, household objects, pots and plates and even
storage cabinets.

The museum collection of 20,000 items comprises of Indian crafts
from all regions of India, in a variety of media. The myriad forms of clay
from pots to huge storage cases, toys to images of gods. Wooden furniture
to entire wooden façades of houses, ornamental carriages to the rare
wooden Bhuta deities of southern Karnataka. There is a superb textile
collection that explores the many weaving skills for which India is
renowned. Basket work in cane and bamboo and stone and metal from
small votive figurines to gigantic pots and vessels are all part of the
wonders of this museum.

Exhibitions in this museum are announced throughout the year in the
Delhi newspapers. The museum also holds exhibitions of craft objects and
has a significant collection that is housed in its new buildings.

Potter at work; Crafts Museum, New Delhi

Museum Services

The museum has a few publications and organises tours, workshops for children, and audio-visual programmes and lectures. Look out for announcements in the newspapers. This museum is a must.

The crafts museum shop is a must for all visitors. Good quality crafts from all parts of India are available on sale here.

The National Handicrafts and Handlooms Museum,
Pragati Maidan, Mathura Road,
NEW DELHI.

Hours:	Display Galleries daily, 10 am–5 pm, except on Mondays and government holidays.
Crafts Demonstration Programme:	Oct–June open all day, 9.30 am–6 pm.
Admission:	free.
Suggested viewing time:	two hours at least.

The Archaeological Museum at the Red Fort

The Red Fort was built by Emperor Shah Jahan around 1649, when he transferred his capital from Agra to Delhi. Within the huge red sandstone fortress are the royal palaces, some in marble, beautifully inlaid and painted to perfection to match the superior aesthetic standards of the emperor. Along the riverfront are six palaces, including the **Diwan-i-Khas**, the **Khas Mahal**, **Rang Mahal** and further to the south, the **Mumtaz Mahal** where the Archaeological Survey has set up a site museum. The Mumtaz Mahal was built of rubble, the lower half of the walls and pillars being faced with marble. It consists of six chambers divided by arched piers, with stucco and painted plaster work.

The museum displays a collection of objects belonging to the **Mughal period** and is interesting to visit in the context of the Red Fort. The present-day emptiness of the palaces of the Red Fort can be filled in one's imagination from the evidence derived from paintings, fabrics and other items in the museum.

There are documents — *farman* or royal decrees carrying the stamp and signature of the emperors; and there are **maps**, **engravings** and **paintings** of great historical value.

Old **arms** — finely decorated swords and daggers — have been displayed. In the **textile section**, there are samples of embroidered canopies and cushions that must once have adorned the palace rooms. Costumes of the Mughal royal princes, made of fine brocade with exquisite workmanship, speak of days gone by. Today they lie a little dusty, waiting for the imagination of visitors to infuse them with the glory that was once theirs.

The Archaeological Museum,
The Red Fort (Lal Qila),
NEW DELHI.

Hours:	every day of the year, 9 am–5 pm.
Admission:	free.
Suggested viewing time:	20 minutes.

(overleaf) Diwan-i-Am, Red Fort, 17th century; Delhi

The Gandhi Memorial Museum at Raj Ghat
The Gandhi Smriti Museum on Tees January Marg

There is a chain of museums referred to as the Gandhi Smarak Sangrahalaya, dedicated to the memory of Mahatma Gandhi, the freedom fighter and philosopher, the Father of the Indian Nation, who fought for India's independence from British colonial rule and strove to build a united, modern India. Apart from those in New Delhi, the other major museums of the chain are at Sevagram in Maharashtra and at Sabarmati in Gujarat, where Gandhiji (as he is respectfully called in India) first set up his *ashram* — an experimental village refuge, where caste, colour and class had no part, where people from different places and professions could live and work together. Similar museums are to be found in Madurai in Tamil Nadu, Lucknow in Uttar Pradesh, Mumbai, Mangalore in Karnataka and Patna in Bihar.

There are two museums and a monument at Raj Ghat, where Gandhi was cremated in Delhi, which relate the story of his life. The Gandhi Memorial Museum at Raj Ghat has a photo documentation section on the life of Gandhi, along with records, relics, documents and a few of his personal belongings like letters, paintings and books.

The Gandhi Smriti Museum, in Birla House on Tees January Marg in New Delhi, is the place where Gandhi was assassinated on 30 January 1948. This site has become a memorial. The room where he stayed has some of his things in it — a simple bed, a mat on the floor, his spinning wheel, books and his spectacles. There are pictures of his wounded body riddled with bullet wounds, and of the huge procession, miles long, that accompanied his body to the cremation grounds at Raj Ghat, where a simple monumental platform marks the place where the last rites were conducted and his body consumed by fire.

For those interested in Gandhi's life and philosophy, these museums provide a very moving documentation of his work and his untiring efforts to serve the poor, to uplift the suffering and bring about a harmonious society without divisions.

Mohandas Karamchand Gandhi was born on 2 October 1869 in Porbandar, a small town in Gujarat. He came from a conservative section of society and was brought up as a Hindu both in religion and lifestyle. Gandhi went to England where he trained in law, and was then offered a job in South Africa. It was there that he first experienced racial discrimination and abuse when he was thrown out of a railway carriage for trying to travel first class, refused entry to a barber's shop and to a hotel reserved for Whites. It was in South Africa that he combated racial discrimination by resorting to his strategy of 'self reliance', a philosophical/ political plan of action that he brought to India on his return.

Gandhi soon became the leader of the struggle against racism in South Africa. He returned to India in 1915 at the age of 46. Over the years, till 1947 when India won her Independence, he became the undisputed leader of the freedom struggle. His philosophy of life can be summed up in one short quotation:

> The only virtue I want to claim is truth and non-violence.
> I lay no claim to superhuman powers: I want none.

By 'non-violence', Gandhiji meant to show a path of peaceful resistance to wrongdoing. He had no hatred for the British law makers in India as individuals; it was the system that oppressed and exploited people that he deplored. His appeal, and sudden popularity when he rose to become the leader of the movement, lay in his identification with the 'Real India' — the people in villages, the poor and the exploited. Where other leaders had failed, with their European approach, their foreign education and ideas, Gandhi struck a chord with his ideas and the simplicity of his clothes and personal lifestyle, which won him the active support of Indians. They followed him, listened to him and were ready to die for him.

He practised his political philosophy of self-reliance in everything he did. The spinning wheel became a symbol of the self-sufficient India that he dreamt of. India as a colony was exporting large quantities of cotton and other raw materials to Britian and importing finished goods like textiles, at very high cost. Gandhi believed that if every Indian spun and wove his own cloth, this aspect of exploitation and dependency would end and dignity would be restored to all Indians. Every day, even when in jail or when he was ill, Gandhi sat and spun yarn and exemplified his ideal of self-reliance. Thus, unbleached khadi, handspun and handwoven cloth, became the symbol of resistance, self-reliance and freedom. Today khadi has been refined and has become fashionable; the old meaning and symbol are remembered only by a few after 50 years of Independence.

Museum Services

These museums in memory of Gandhiji have produced a wide selection of publications of his writings, biographies and the history of the Indian freedom movement.

The Gandhi Memorial Museum,
Raj Ghat,
NEW DELHI.

The Gandhi Smriti Museum,
Birla House,
Tees January Marg,
NEW DELHI.

Hours:	9 am–5.30 pm. Closed on Mondays and national holidays.
Admission:	free.
Suggested viewing time:	half an hour at any one of the museums.

The Nehru Memorial Museum and Library

Teen Murti House, where the Nehru Memorial Museum is located, was built in 1929–30 as the residence of the British commander-in-chief of India. The Teen Murti or Three Statues refers to the war memorial built at the roundabout on the road in front of the main building, which is dedicated to the Imperial Service Cavalry Brigade. After Independence in 1947, the house became the official residence of India's first prime minister, Jawaharlal Nehru. He lived with his family — his daughter Indira Gandhi, who was to become India's third prime minister, and her two sons. His grandson, Rajiv Gandhi, grew up here, and became prime minister of India after the assassination of his mother in 1984.

After Jawaharlal Nehru's death in 1964, the Teen Murti building was converted into a museum, and to the right of the entrance gate is the **Nehru Planetarium** with a noticeboard outside to indicate the timings of the shows. Towards the left of the main building stands the Nehru Memorial Library and auditorium, and the administrative building. Here research on the life and times of Nehru, and the history of the Nehru era, is undertaken.

Within the memorial museum are rooms that have been maintained as they were when Nehru lived there. One can catch a fading glimpse of Nehru's lifestyle and tastes in these rooms. The bedrooms, drawing room and study have collections of art objects, gifts from abroad, paintings and personal belongings. The staff of the museum are careful to see that the

Nehru Memorial Museum, Teen Murti House; New Delhi

flowers remain fresh in the vases, and the spectacles are placed correctly on the table where they should be. How different is the lifestyle displayed here from that chosen by Mahatma Gandhi!

On the first and ground floors, some of the rooms have been converted into photographic documentation galleries that record the main events of the freedom movement. There are photographs and portraits of leaders of the movement and of various episodes and events. The display is well labelled in English and Hindi, and serves as a graphic account of India's long struggle for independence.

The sprawling lawns at the back of the building, still very well maintained, were once the playground of three Indian prime ministers.

In the garden near the building, there is a small, inconspicuous eternal lamp burning in memory of Nehru. There is also a granite rock on the front lawn on which is inscribed Jawaharlal Nehru's famous speech, delivered on the night of 14-15 August 1947 on the declaration of India's Independence. It is a very moving speech that echoes the thrill of that historic hour, after years of struggle, sacrifice and hardship:

At the stroke of midnight hour, when the world sleeps, India will awake to life and freedom. A moment comes, which comes but rarely in history, when we step out from the old to the new, when an age ends, and when the soul of a nation long suppressed, finds utterance.

Museum Services
The Nehru Memorial Museum has a publication section where biographies of Nehru are available on sale, along with prints and pictures.

The Nehru Memorial Museum,
Teen Murti House,
Teen Murti Marg,
NEW DELHI.

Hours: 10 am–5 pm. Closed on Mondays.

Admission charge: nominal.

Suggested viewing time: one hour.

Mural of Mahatma Gandhi, Hall of the Nation Building; Delhi

Mumbai

The Prince of Wales Museum

Amid the hustle and bustle of Mumbai stand some stately buildings, remnants of the British Raj. Among them is that of the Prince of Wales Museum, named after Prince George (later George V) who visited India in 1905 and laid the foundation stone of the building. Not far from the museum, its architect George Wittet also built the famous **Gateway of India** on the seafront, near the Taj Mahal hotel. Through the arch the Prince made his royal entrance to India as King George V for the Delhi Darbar in 1911.

The Prince of Wales Museum can be broadly described as a British interpretation of Mughal architecture, the so-called Indo–Saracenic style. The structure forms a long rectangle of three storeys, raised in the centre to accommodate the entrance porch. Above the central arched entrance rises a huge dome, tiled in white and blue flecks, supported on a lotus-petal base. Around the dome is an array of pinnacles, each topped by a miniature dome. Indian motifs such as brackets and protruding eaves are combined with so-called Islamic arches and tiny domes. The whole museum complex is situated in a garden of palm trees and formal flowers beds.

The plan of the museum is simple, with a central hall from which the staircase leads to the two upper floors with galleries branching out on the right and left. An extension on the right-hand side of the main building (as you stand facing its front entrance) houses the natural history section. The second floor houses the Indian miniature painting gallery, the pride of the museum, and next to it are the galleries of decorative art and, to the left of the central well of the staircase, the gallery of Tibetan and Nepali art. Above, on the second floor are the European painting, armoury and textile galleries.

The central hall on the ground floor has been converted into the **key gallery** with specimens of art from all the galleries of the museum. To walk around the key gallery is like experiencing 5,000 years of Indian art in a capsule. There are **terracottas** of the Indus Valley Civilisation: animal sculptures and figurines including a mother with a child suckling at her breast. Some sample terracottas of the pre-Mauryan to Gupta periods in the pinched and handmoulded style are also on display.

The art of the Mughal period is represented by a few exquisite paintings, including the *Portrait of Daniyal* with the characteristic Mughal

turban. The latter is actually a sketch for a painting and gives an idea of how the artist worked. There is also the well-known painting, *Black Buck and Doe*, a typical example of animal representation of the 17th century. The buck, with his head held high even in captivity, struts along, while his mate, the dainty doe, looks suspiciously around her at those who have tied the bell chain round her neck and harnessed her pretty head. The aquamarine background, produced by the use of mineral colours, is also characteristic of the period.

There are also some classic examples of jade and armoury on display in the key gallery. **Jade**, not found in India, was imported from the Far East and was treasured by the Mughal rulers. The pale, waxy pieces of jade in hues of green, white and pink were carved into variety of objects: boxes, wine bowls, buckles and handles for daggers. Not content with simply carving delicate designs on the surface, the artist often encrusted jade objects with inlay patterns in gold embedded with precious stones. The jade bowls are well displayed to show off the mastery of the craftsmen in carving them so fine that they are almost translucent, with light appearing to be trapped within the jade.

The **sculpture gallery** on the first floor has some excellent exhibits from historical sites in different parts of India. Along one of the longer walls of the hall are examples of **Gandharan art**, with steel-grey stone figures of the *Bodhisattva* (the 'Spiritual Guide'). The Graeco-Roman influence can clearly be seen in these sculptures in the way of draping the 'toga', the thick wavy treatment of the locks and the rather fashionable moustaches. A beautiful example is that of a **Maitreya** (third century), in the key gallery. His head, surrounded by a halo, is slightly inclined. The gentle, sensuous curves of the torso are draped in garments and jewelled chains to suggest texture and movement.

Displayed in the main section of this gallery are three huge **ceiling slabs from temples in Karnataka** dating from the eighth century. This group of temples at Badami, Pattadakal and Aihole was built by the **Chalukyan** rulers who undertook a very significant experiment in temple architecture which was to influence many generations after them. In their temples, the ceiling of the main hall and side chambers was fitted with carved stone slabs of enormous proportions. What you see in this gallery are sculptured stone panels propped upright, though they would actually

Prince of Wales Museum, Mumbai

have been viewed originally from below, as they ran across the ceiling.

The three panels on display here depict Uma Mahesvara, Vishnu on Sesha and Brahma. The **Uma Mahesvara panel** depicts Shiva, Lord of the Universe, seated beside his equally powerful companion-wife, Parvati. The *Nandi* or bull, the vehicle of Shiva, is seated behind him as if to provide a backrest; little Ganesh, the elephant-headed god and their son, is prancing around at the left-hand corner. Shiva, holding a snake in his hand, is portrayed with immense grace and elegance. The iconographic symbols necessary to identify Shiva are included in the panel relief in an almost casual manner, as can be seen in the positioning of the trident and the *linga* (the phallic symbol of Shiva), at the back. In Shiva's long, matted hair is a skull ornament at one side which exemplifies one of his attributes: as the Conqueror of Time. He is shown wearing a tigerskin and fine jewellery, for he is both the ascetic and the divine lover.

The sculptured **panel of Brahma** from Aihole, from the same temple as the other two sculptured panels, is a rare representation of this deity of the Hindu trinity. Hindu mythology has it that Brahma lusted after his own daughter, and for this Shiva cursed him, decreeing that no temple would be built in his honour. Some historians suggest that this story explains why, while two powerful sects — the Shaivites and Vaishnavites — developed, which worshipped Shiva and Vishnu respectively, no such sect developed around Brahma worship. Whatever the rationalisation may be, Brahma's name is widely evoked in prayer even though sculpture and temples dedicated to him are not common. He is shown here seated on a lotus throne, being worshipped by sages, saints and heavenly beings. Beside him is his vehicle, the animal reflection of his essential being, the *hansa* or swan of Brahma. This mythological creature is said to be a truth-finder, able to separate water from milk.

The sculpture of **Vishnu on the Sesha** shows the Lord of Creation resting in the ocean of eternity on a huge serpent, Sesha. For many hundreds of light years Vishnu rests undisturbed, only to stir when the time for creation comes again. He is completely relaxed in this sculpture; he has cast aside his emblems, the conch and the disc, and they just float on the waves of the ocean. On one arm he rests his head, two others are relaxed, and the fourth is held in the gesture of blessing over the creatures

Lamentation, illustration of the love story of Laur Chanda, Sultanate period, circa 1550; Prince of Wales Museum, Mumbai

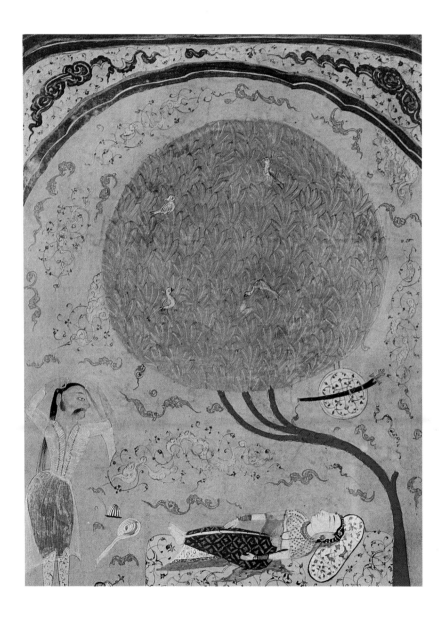

of the sea. His legs are crossed in a rather strange way, but the sculpture was meant to be viewed from below, in its position on the temple ceiling, and perhaps looked all right in its original context.

The landing between the ground and first floor has a gallery devoted to **pre- and photo-history**. It is well labelled and displayed, offering information on various aspects of life in cities of the Indus Valley Civilisation over 5,000 years ago. Reconstructed models of the townships of those times, based on excavations at sites in India and Pakistan, are on display. The layouts of the towns are so well designed as to appear almost modern. Huge storage pots and vessels were used in the homes and shops to store water and grain. Evidence of the inhabitants' eating habits comes from remains of charred grain and wheat husks. Also displayed are **seals**, small **clay and stone tablets** carrying inscriptions and what might be the **personal emblems of traders** — something which will only be established when the script has been deciphered. **Jewellery** found at the sites — ornamented with semi-precious stones, cut *en cabochon*, or rolled and polished — is strikingly simple and elegant, the hallmark of the art of the Indus Valley urban culture.

On the first floor central balcony of the museum are displayed objects of **decorative art in ivory, silver and wood of the late 18th and the 19th centuries**. Some paintings have also been displayed in this area, which leads the visitor into the **picture gallery**. The latter is divided by partitions to create enclosed cubical spaces. The paintings, donated by various patrons, form one of India's best public collections of work, representative of many styles and schools.

At the entrance of the gallery, to the left, in the first cubicle, is an illustrated manuscript of the *Kalpasutra* and the *Kalikacharyakatha* of western India, dated to the end of the 15th century. Paper, introduced into India after the tenth century, began to replace the older palm leaf, used traditionally in India for manuscripts. In these examples we see how the artist-scholar created the superb composition of the page, part written text, part illustrated in the primary colours of red and blue, with gold and black, in techniques that were derived from the ancient palm-leaf traditions.

As painting evolved and the demand for illustrated manuscripts grew, many streams or schools of art mingled in varying proportions, as it were, in different regions of India. The **illustrations of the *Gita Govinda***, poems on the love of Krishna and Radha, show one stage in the evolution of painting, in which there is a continued use of primary colours and a profusion of details of birds, animals, trees and flowers, and nature in general. A kind of 'essence-of-a-mood' style of illustration is used in these paintings, in which the sky is just a band of colour, a forest is depicted by just two or three trees, the leaves of the tree are 'summarised' to create an illusion of the whole tree, and when lovers are united, the artist shows nature rejoicing and even the birds fly around in pairs.

In the illustrations from the *Anwar-i-Suhailli* of the Mughal period (1575), another style of page composition — of distribution of text and illustration — is clearly discernible. From the heritage of Persian painting, one now sees the introduction of many Persian details in landscape, figure and animal drawing. Even the colours are now not only primary ones but mixtures, used to produce a great variety of subtle shades of orange, brown, grey and green. The blending of such individual styles — the Persian and the palm-leaf manuscript tradition of India — gave rise to numerous other schools, each with its own characteristic features.

Of the Mughal School, there are some brilliant examples of paintings of birds and animals in this gallery. The *Baburnama*, the diary of the founder of the Mughal empire, was illustrated during Akbar's period with paintings of animals and birds that he had encountered for the first time in this strange land of the Indus. These drawings are almost scientific in their accuracy as visual descriptions. The tradition and technique of nature drawings was developed by subsequent Mughal rulers, and in this museum there are the **Portrait of a Black Buck**, the **Lapwing** and the **Wood-cock** — all of the 17th century, from the Mughal period. The paintings have ornate borders — a series of narrow, decorated frames round the main composition. The artists have concentrated on the central animal or bird, and there is often little or no other detail in the background. It was here for the first time that animal life was painted in its own right, and not simply as part of nature, to reflect an appreciation for nature's diverse creations, their forms and colours. The artistic portrayal of animals reaches a new level of sophistication in these paintings, which are charming in conception and brilliant in their display of technical skill.

Whether the animals are painted by themselves, as part of nature, or alone with a human — such as a horse or elephant with its rider, or a hawk seated patiently on the arm of a nobleman — the depiction of the animal is always careful, accurate and executed with a delicate touch. In the portraits, the artists lost none of their careful style, and every detail of hair, jewellery and costume is recorded with subtle brush strokes. The pride of the museum are the portraits of *Jahangir with His Attendants in a*

Garden, and of *Dara Shikoh*, favourite son and heir apparent of Shah Jahan, who was brutally murdered by his brother Aurangzeb, who usurped the throne of the Mughal empire. Dara Shikoh will be remembered in history as the great aesthete who loved and patronised the arts. The faces of Jahangir, his son Shah Jahan, and grandson Dara Shikoh in these paintings are recognisable because the artist has portrayed them with slightly larger heads than the others in the pictures, with neatly trimmed beards and dressed in the lavish fashion of the Mughal court.

The court-patronised art of painting and of illustrating manuscripts did not disappear with the gradual decline of the Mughal empire. In deed, both during and after Mughal rule, neighbouring princely states continued the tradition. Though the scale was smaller, these scholar-painters were equally fastidious in their study of detail and the delicacy of their brushwork.

The 19th-century **Pahari School** provides a wealth of evidence of a thriving tradition in the hill states of Punjab and Himachal Pradesh. This school, concentrating on Hindu themes, depicted the divine Shiva and Parvati, Radha and Krishna as though they were contemporary kings and queens. The expressions of these divine Shiva and Parvati, Radha and Krishna as though they were contemporary kings and queens. The expressions of these divine characters are suggested simply by a slight inclination of the head, or by an embrace, which makes the gods almost human in the most perfect sort of way.

Some superb examples of this school of painting in this gallery are **Shiva and Parvati** (Kangra), **Uma Worshipping Shiva** and a second **Shiva and Parvati** (Guler, 18th century), in which Parvati is offering Shiva a garland of skulls as if it were as beautiful as one made of flowers. **Krishna with the Cow Herds** (Garhwal, 18th century) and the work drawing of the **Holi Festival** (Kangra, 19th century) shows Krishna and his friends throwing colour on Radha and her companions to celebrate the spring festival of Holi. Even today in north India, on the occasion of the spring festival at the beginning of summer, dry or wet colours are scattered over the earth; friends and families shower one another with the hues of springtime, for this is a time of renewal, growth and love.

Other paintings of importance on display include **Aurangzeb Reading the Quran** (Pahari, Jammu). Bent and with whitened beard, after years of difficult rule, the emperor of the crumbling Mughal empire is depicted deep in prayer and contemplation. In the painting of **Raja Balwant Deva with his Barber** (Jammu, 18th century), you can almost read the barber's

Uma-Mahesvara, sixth century, panel from Aihole, Karnataka;
Prince of Wales Museum, Mumbai

thoughts: 'Be still', he appears to be telling the ruler, as he fashions the ruler's beard. The artist has captured the mood of the moment in the stance of the figures, the details of the garments and the headgear, which are the significant features of this important school of painting. *Lady with an Attendant and a Peacock* (Pahari, Kangra, 1775) is a remarkably beautiful and lyrical work. This painting is evidence of the fact that as early as the end of the 18th century in India an artist would dare to use three apparently uncomplimentary colours, mauve, pale green and orange, together in the same picture. The lady lover is standing in front of a tree which is in full bloom, and there is no mistaking the symbolism of the flowering tree juxtaposed with the young lady, or the use of the same colours for both the flowers and the woman's clothes.

Similarly, to the south, the **Deccani School** of painting also gained inspiration from the Mughal School and evolved its own unique and very characteristic style. There are some typical examples of Deccani paintings in this gallery that have pale green, mineral-coloured backgrounds with figures placed squarely in the foreground. It is in the treatment of flower vases and the floral borders, however, that the identifying features of the

Deccani School can be seen. The flowers are very stylised; around them are insects and butterflies. The arrangement of the petals of each flower is more like a design than an attempt at naturalism. The combination of colours with extensive use of gold paint is a technique often used in this school of Indian painting.

In the region of Bundi in Rajasthan, another style of painting developed. In size and format it is very similar to certain other Indian schools of miniature painting, but we shall leave it to the experts to identify styles and quarrel about dates. The collection of **paintings from Bundi**, of the 18th century, in this gallery deals with the theme of love.

In painting, theatre and dance in India, the emotion of love is a universal *rasa*, the very essence of human life. Love is believed to be a permanent and everlasting emotion, though it is often overshadowed by transient feelings. The joy of meeting the lover, pining in the absence of the loved one and love-making itself are themes of the fleeting moods of love depicted in paintings and well illustrated in the Bundi collection. In *Lady Looking in a Mirror* (Bundi, 18th century), the artist has created a courtyard with a lush garden in the background and a pond of lotuses in the foreground that blossom in reflection of the glory of the young girl, or lover. She is shown in a mood of great excitement and, like all lovers, she is struggling to find the appropriate clothes to wear to meet her beloved. He is shown peeping from a window upstairs where he catches a glimpse of her in the mirror. Details of the house and costumes are also interesting.

A *Nayika in Agony* (Bundi, late 17th century) is a painting in another mood. The young lady lover is in agony, suffering the torment of separation from her lover. Nothing seems to console her, she is being offered food and drink by her companions, but these are poor substitutes for the beloved. In love poetry the mood of separation is described evocatively: it is said that even the moonlight is too hot, and delicate moonbeams appear to scorch the fevered body of the lover. In this painting the lady is being offered fans and sandalwood paste to cool her brow, though these appear quite inadequate to sooth her pain. For those who have been in love, this, and many other such moods illustrated in these paintings, will be quite familiar! But all is not lost in the game of love and this is depicted in another painting, the *Dalliance of Krishna* (Bundi, 18th century), and in *Krishna Sitting with His Beloved* (Bundi, late 18th century) in which the lovers are united and nature celebrates with humankind by bringing life-giving rain. Once again, all is well with the world.

Next to the painting gallery is the **hall of decorative arts**, with samples of Indian jewellery and objects in silver, enamelled jars and hookah stands. The samples on display are superb, contrasting starkly with much of the work of today, which shows the sharp decline in standards of craftsmanship since the 19th century.

Bidri work, associated with the region of Hyderabad, in particular the small town of Bidar, is made in bell-metal. Carved on the object, the designs are then filled out with silver and brass. The surface is then burnished and smoothened until the inlaid silver and the metal blackened with charcoal paste become inseparable.

Some **jade objects** are also on display: a spoon with a curved handle, bowls with fine relief work in which the artist has enhanced the beauty of the stone and set its colours and hues aglow.

The **Nepal and Tibet Gallery** faces the painting gallery on the first floor. The collection was donated by the Tata family, a large industrial house with interests in the sciences and the arts. For those who might travel to these neighbouring countries, the artifacts are particularly interesting because they may help visitors distinguish between genuinely valuable art and the tourist 'junk' that is now being sold.

There are *thankas*: cloth hangings either painted or embroidered with geometrical mandala compositions of tiny figures and symbols of Buddhist origin. The lotus-shaped, square and circular mandala designs are alive with patterns of seated Buddhas, little stupas and other religious motifs. The **Buddhist and Hindu images in metal** are gilded, and studded with gems. Statuettes of Tara, the Buddhist goddess of compassion, Vajradhara, Lord of the Thunderbolt, and of Lakshmi Narayana are studded with turquoise, ruby and diamond. Most beautiful of all is tiny Avalokitesvara from Nepal, of the 17th century. The little figure is seated on a mountain of blue turquoise. Avalokitesvara is a *Bodhisattva*, or teacher, who is so compassionate that he chooses to stay on Earth to lead people to the path of the Buddha rather than to enjoy the benefits of eternal salvation himself. This tiny figure, lost in meditation on its ingenious turquoise stand, has a very moving quality.

For those interested in **glass, jade** and **porcelain**, the gallery on the second floor presents an extensive collection of art objects donated by Sir

Ratan Tata and Sir Dorab Tata. The collection includes objects carved in rock crystal, metalware and lacquered woodwork. There are samples of elaborate **ivory work** from Japan, like the **Cock on a Tree**, with feathers of ivory. There is a small but exemplary collection of miniature sculpture work for belts and snuff boxes, brilliantly executed in Japan. There is also a wide range of Chinese blue and white **porcelain and cloisonné ware**. In this technique, the pot is designed with tiny metal wire compartments, that are filled with powdered glass, and is heated till it melts to create the enamel designs over the surface of the object. The multicoloured Japanese ceramics are bathed in hues of gold, brown and deep vibrant reds.

On the same floor are the **European painting** galleries. On entering this area it immediately becomes clear that European art historians dubbed Indian paintings 'miniatures' because they were indeed much smaller than the huge oil-painted canvases the Europeans were familiar with. In this collection there are some interesting samples of small landscape paintings by Constable, and many copies and works of less well-known artists. Rather charming are the two portraits of *Lady Ratan Tata* and *Lady Dorabji Tata*, which, if viewed from a distance look exactly like portraits of English ladies, complete with gloves and fans, dressed in the fashion of their British rulers.

A word must be said in honour of those generous donors who, in the early years of the 20th century, donated from their private collections, works that form the nucleus of this museum. Indian and European paintings, the Chinese porcelain and jade, metalware, textiles and armour were given to the museum by Sir Ratan Tata and Sir Dorab Tata. Their original gesture helped to inspire the many other donations that were subsequently made to this museum.

The Natural History Section

Should you plan to visit any of the game sanctuaries or parks in India, it would be worth your while to look at this museum's exhibits on **birds, mammals and fish**, for a foretaste of what you might see in the wild. The Natural History Section was added to the museum from the collection of the Bombay Natural History Society. This organisation, with founder members and notable scholars like the late Salim Ali, has contributed greatly to the study and understanding of India's natural heritage. Today, due to their efforts, a start has been made to create an awareness amongst

The Guessing Game, Malwa School, 1680;
Prince of Wales Museum, Mumbai

the general public of the urgent need to preserve Indian wildlife. The first room houses an impressive collection of birds, classified according to species, and the exhibits are all well labelled. Among them are the beautiful but untidy magpies, the flash of blue of the kingfisher and well-dressed partridges and pheasants. Dioramas and display panels attempt to provide a natural setting for the taxidermist's art.

The Prince of Wales Museum,
Mahatma Gandhi Road,
MUMBAI,
Maharashtra.

Hours: 10 am–5.30 pm except on Mondays and three government holidays.

Admission: nominal

Suggested viewing time: two hours at least.

Calcutta

The Indian Museum

This is the oldest museum in India, dating back to the 19th century when the Asiatic Society felt the need to establish a museum in Calcutta. Explorations and surveys conducted to investigate the economic potential of the Indian sub-continent led to the collection of items of mineralogical, botanical and zoological value. Artifacts of archaeological significance were also documented, and in sum, an amazing collection had been assembled that had to be properly catalogued and preserved.

In 1875 the building of the Indian Museum, designed by Walter L B Granville, was ready for occupation. Granville was the architect of several other famous Calcutta buildings such as the University, the Senate House (which sadly has been demolished), the Post Office, and the impressive edifice of the High Court. The Indian Museum, facing Chowringee, is built in two storeys around a central open quadrangle, with corridors and verandahs supported by huge Ionic columns.

The building is a splendid solid construction of the Victorian era in India, but is very inappropriate as a museum. As you enter from the main street, to your left is the **Mineralogy Gallery**. This section, though dusty and poorly layed out, has a very extensive collection of minerals from all parts of India. It provides a fascinating display of the diversity of India's mineral wealth. Further down this gallery is the renovated anthropology section, and up the stairs is a gallery with rather old-fashioned dioramas of various tribes of India. The baskets and other craft products on display are specimens of artistic techniques that are under threat of extinction today.

The Bharhut Room

To the right of the main entrance is the Archaeological Section and its first room contains an invaluable collection of stone railings with sculptures of the second century BC from a Buddhist religious site at Bharhut in Madhya Pradesh.

The story of how they came to the Indian Museum is quite interesting and had been narrated in Randhawa's book, *Indian Sculpture*, 1985.

Yakshi (detail), pillar from the Bharhut stupa, second century BC;
Indian Museum, Calcutta

General Alexander Cunningham, who was responsible for many archaeological finds, discovered the ruins of the Bharhut Stupa in 1873. The solid mound of the Buddhist stupa was surrounded by a huge stone railing and gateways bearing relief panels, which Cunningham found scattered in a ruined state around the site. He decided to transport the remaining sculptured railings to Calcutta and have them installed in the Indian Museum. Professor Childers in England, hearing of this plan, wrote: 'It is impossible to read General Cunningham's most interesting account of these sculptures without a sigh of regret that they should be so far beyond the reach of our inspection.' Childers was keen to have the Bharhut sculptures in the British Museum in London. He continues: 'I hear of a proposal to remove them from Bharhut. The scheme carries with it certain aroma of vandalism (fancy carting away Stonehenge).' Cunningham, however, knew that he was saving the sculptures since much of the ancient stupa had already been taken away by the local villagers for building purposes. Today it is well worth a visit to Calcutta, just to see this gallery of early Buddhist sculpture and to gain an insight into a philosophy of life still relevant despite the great antiquity of its roots.

The sculptures from Bharhut are indeed amazing. The railings stand nearly three metres (nine feet) high. This stone fencing, in imitation of an older wooden construction, has upright posts linked together by horizontal beams, and a massive curved railing stone on top. The railings, consisting of vertical posts and horizontal crossbars, are decorated with almost life-sized female and male figures that stand like guardians of the stupa, and at regular intervals there are panels and circular medallions carved out in low relief. Some of these depict episodes and stories from the *Jataka* tales that describe previous incarnations of the Buddha. In every incarnation, Buddha led an exemplary life of service and kindness, whether he appeared in the form of a deer, of the self-sacrificing monkey or any other form.

Amongst these relief sculptures is a **circular panel of a large stag** resting on the bank of a river, facing a hunter with a bow and arrow. This is a good example of how Buddhist lyrical poetry is depicted in stone. The narrative style in the sculpture is a single frame in which many events that constitute the story are all shown at the same time, in one panel. The *Jataka* tale goes like this:

> Once upon a time, in a previous incarnation, the Buddha came to life as a young stag, which grew to be a beautiful and graceful creature with a coat the colour of gold. The doe, his mate, was also a handsome creature and they lived happily

together. One day a hunter set snares to catch some deer and the beautiful stag got caught in one. The doe, realising the threat to her husband's life, said,

> 'O golden foot
> No effort spare
> To loose thyself
> From the tangled snare.
> What joy is there,
> Bereft of thee,
> To roam amidst the woodland free?'

The doe then fearlessly appealed to the approaching hunter to spare her husband's life. The stag was freed, but the hunter was struck with amazement and remarked: 'Even human beings give not their lives for their King, much less the beasts. What can this mean?'

The stag then explained to the hunter the golden rule of life: 'Friend, henceforth take not the life of any creature; set up a home and give alms to the poor and do good work.'

Another of the many narrative panels tells the story of the **monkey incarnation of the Buddha**, *Mahakapi Jataka*. On a circular relief panel is a forest scene through which there flows a stream. On one bank of the stream, monkeys are shown clambering up a tree, and crossing to the opposite bank on a monkey bridge. The monkey who endangers his own life by creating a bridge for his companions is an incarnation of the Buddha and thus represents his ideals. It was through animal tales and parables like these that devotees were able to understand the teachings and principles of Buddhism. Spiritual inspiration, through compassion for animals and all other living creatures, was the objective of these didactic sculptures.

Following the railing on the right, on the outer side past the gateway, is a depiction in a relief panel of a **group of monkeys trapping an elephant**. On the parallel railing on the left-hand side from the entrance to the gallery is depicted the amusing episode of a **group of monkeys extracting a tooth** of a tall and burly man. The monkeys have tied the troublesome tooth by a long cord to an elephant, while one monkey sits poised to give the tail of the elephant a good hard bite, so that it will charge in pain and the tooth thus be extracted!

There is no representation of the Buddha in human form in the sculptures of Bharhut, as they were executed during Buddhism's Hinayana

Lower Part of a Lady

phase when only **symbolic representations of the Buddha** were depicted on stone sculpture. The symbol most commonly used is that of the *pipal* tree, under which the Buddha attained enlightenment. The tree, the Bodhi tree, is shown in sculpture surrounded by a fence, or platform, and being worshipped with flowers and garlands. There are also several circular lotus medallions, some with faces carved in the centre. These shallow-relief decorations are unique as they are carved in many levels and the varying depths create a subtle illusion of space. The lotus, employed in Buddhist art and later in Hindu sculpture, is a symbol of purity and signifies the miraculous birth of a holy or great person, whose example stands distinct from the rest of humanity.

On the railings there are also several **female figures**, some almost life-size, in various poses: holding a musical instrument, looking in a mirror, holding the branch of a tree. They are dressed in a simple loincloth, and wear exquisitely designed jewellery in their hair and around neck, waist and arms. Such silver jewellery is still worn by women of various communities in India. A sculpture of a young girl holding a branch of a tree has been interpreted as a fertility symbol, and it is easy to see why. The tree behind her, with flowers and buds ready to burst into bloom, reconfirms an ancient tradition that was absorbed into the Buddhist belief of paying homage to trees and the spirits who dwell in them, and acknowledging their close relationship with human beings.

This entire gallery of early Buddhist sculptures is full of life, vitality and humour, attributes not usually associated with religion, particularly Buddhism, by most people. They form a very important link in the chain of development of Indian sculpture. For centuries Buddhist and Hindu religious buildings were adorned with didactic sculptures that taught pilgrims the myths and legends associated with the gods. A touch of humour, some reflection of contemporary life, and the use of natural motifs formed part of this tradition. A big thank you must be whispered to General Cunningham for rescuing the Bharhut sculptures back in 1873.

Gandhara Sculptures

Further down, in the next gallery, are sculptures from Gandhara. This collection is the finest in India, and is only equalled by the one in the Lahore Museum in Pakistan. The north-western region of India, and parts

Sculpture from Indian Museum, Calcutta

of what are now Pakistan and Afghanistan came to be known as Gandhara in the early centuries of the Christian era. This area came under the influence of the Greeks after Alexander's conquest, and later, when trade links with the Roman Empire were strengthened, Roman influence. In Gandhara, princely states and cities were established which flourished with increasing commerce and trade. A famous Buddhist university of the times, Taxila, attracted Buddhist scholars from China and other parts of the Far East, and from Asia generally. Excavations at Taxila and neighbouring sites have revealed a wealth of stupas, sculptural remains, coins and artifacts, each with its distinctive Greek or Roman influence.

Amongst art historians a great controversy developed some years ago on whether it was the Graeco-Roman influence that created the first 'human' images of the Buddha. Research today confirms that sculptures of the Buddha evolved in many parts of India at approximately the same time as the Gandhara images were being made. Figurines in wood, terracotta, stone and even metal had been modelled by Indian artists for centuries, and this was not their first attempt at creating figurative sculptures. What challenged the artist at the outset of the **Mahayana (Buddhism) period** was the task of evolving an image of the Buddha that would reflect the goodness and purity of the Buddha's mind in a meditative mood. The early sculptures show evidence of the artist's experimentation with the facial expression, clothing and stance of the Buddha, often with a smile accidentally appearing on the Buddha's serene face.

Some of the sculptures in this galley were donated by General Cunningham, they belong to the Mahayana period of Buddhism when it was thus found acceptable to present the Buddha in human form. There are small votive stupas which would have been donated to the holy shrine as offerings by devotees. From such votive objects, which were often inscribed, it was possible for historians to piece together information on the nature of the patrons of Buddhism. It was found that among the large mercantile community many had become followers of this new faith, and their wealth supported its growth and dissemination to different parts of Asia. As stupas mushroomed along trade routes, the original Indian hemispherical stupa became taller and more elongated, till it assumed the form of the towering pinnacles still seen in the Far East.

The Numismatic Gallery

The museum has attempted to display its excellent coin collection in chronological sequence, beginning with the **punch-marked coins** of the fifth century BC to AD second century. There are **Greek and Arab coins** that provide historical evidence of trading contact with the Indian sub-continent centuries ago. The **gold Gupta coins** are especially beautiful, with tiny reliefs of kings, horses and lions faithfully depicted with details despite the small workable surfaces of the coins. Years ago the excavation of hordes of gold coins led historians to describe the Gupta period as a 'golden age'. The value of its currency is of course indicative of the relative prosperity of a particular period in history.

The **Mughals**, who ruled north India from the 16th century until the British took over, produced in their early years of glory magnificent coins in gold and silver. On display are coins with zodiac signs and calligraphic designs. The scale of the coin did not reduce the power of its visual appeal, and in these examples it is possible to see the artist's skill in composition of the design, in his selection of the details to be represented and in creating the final effect.

There are very few museums in India where the coin collection is so well presented.

Indian Sculpture of Different Regions

From the Gandhara Gallery there is a door that leads into a large hall that runs along the side of the open courtyard of the museum hall that runs along the side of the open courtyard of the museum building. This gallery has been divided into small niches with samples of sculptures from different regions, periods, styles and schools of Indian art. An attempt has been made to group sculptures of one style together in one niche, beginning with earliest examples. It is however impossible to examine all of them in a single visit. In the Buddhist section there is one group of long white marble panels of sculptures obtained from the now ruined **stupa at Amaravati** in Andhra Pradesh. One of these panels depicts the **Miraculous Birth of the Buddha**. The legend records that the Buddha's mother had a dream in which there appeared a white elephant, this symbol being interpreted as a portent of the birth of a child that would be a 'gift to mankind'. Maya, the Buddha's mother, is shown sleeping in one section of the long panel, her attendants also asleep beside her, while a small baby elephant hovers above her in the top right corner, in what can only be a portrayal of her dream.

A representative collection of Hindu sculptures from various regions is displayed in this gallery, covering every major school of the different historical periods. Amongst them the Bengal style of the **Pala period**,

Woman gazing at herself in the mirror,
Chandella period, 11th century,
Khajuraho, Madhya Pradesh;
Indian Museum, Calcutta

Standing Yakshi with figures in the
balcony, pillar from stupa, second
century, Mathura;
Indian Museum, Calcutta

around the eighth to the 12th centuries, is important and easy to identify; shiny black stone was used and a famous example of this style is a sculpture of a **Mother and Child Lying on a Bed**.

There are some excellent examples of sculptures from the **temples of Khajuraho** in Madhya Pradesh, in this gallery. These once adorned temple walls, often high up, in unreachable places. Here they are available for study at close range. The sculptures of Khajuraho belong to the tenth to 12th centuries. For years art historians have tried to explain why the Khajuraho temples displayed so many sculptures of lovers and the art of love-making. Whatever the theory, love is a universal theme in all Indian art, whether it is sculpture, painting, poetry, music or dance. Though there are only a few sculptures from Khajuraho in this museum, it is a pleasure to study such fine examples of images that are both sensuous and charming.

The *Lady Writing a Love Letter* (Khajuraho, 11th century) has her back to you, with her head turned so that you just see her rather mischievous smile. The lady lover seems uncomfortably hot, and she has let her fine clothing fall from her shoulder (or perhaps the artist has lowered the drapery), so that you can view her exposed armpit where tell-tale nail marks have been left by her lover. Is she writing a lover letter, and recalling the night before?

There are also some **sculptures from Java and Cambodia** in this gallery. Indian art and religion travelled with traders and merchants to neighbouring countries, and it is interesting to see how Indian influences were adapted in other countries.

The Zoological Section

The galleries on the first floor contain specimens of unbelievable size and quantity — of animals, fish and birds collected during British expeditions in the Indian sub-continent. The layout of the display is appalling, though the collection is quite valuable. For the visitor keen on wildlife in India, these galleries can serve as an introduction. Sadly, the vibrant colours of the birds' feathers have faded and the labels fail to tell you where these birds can be found in India. For such information there are some excellent books available (see Recommended Reading).

On the first floor, near the Egyptian room and the elevator landing is a passage that leads to the **Art Gallery**. Here, though again poorly displayed, is a fine collection of Indian textiles — fine reed mats of Bengal, printed fabrics of Rajasthan, shawls with the woven and embroidered designs that made Kashmir so famous, brocades from Banaras and much else besides.

Down the hall is a clutter of decorative art objects in wood and metal, that can be broadly classified as kitsch.

The **Nahar Gallery of Oriental Art** is a small room which has some good examples of Persian miniatures of the 17th century, of the Mughal School of painting, including examples from the Akbar period. It is interesting to see in these paintings the kinds of clothes and jewellery that were worn by those emperors who built their royal capitals in Delhi and Agra, and then to walk back through the textile gallery to get a first-hand impression of the fabrics represented in the paintings of the different periods.

The Indian Museum,
27 Jawaharlal Nehru Road,
CALCUTTA,
West Bengal.

Hours:	10 am–5 pm (March–November); 10 am–4.30 pm (December–Feburary), except on Mondays and government holidays.
Admission:	nominal.
Suggested viewing time:	two hours.

The Ashutosh Museum of Indian Art

This museum, named after a great educationalist, Sir Ashutosh Mukherjee, was set up in 1937. It was originally located behind the university, in the Senate House which was unfortunately demolished in 1961 to be replaced by the monstrous, characterless structure, on two floors of which the museum in now housed.

The museum has sculptures donated by scholars, and collections obtained from archaeological excavations in Bengal. Apart from art objects from the past, the museum also holds an exemplary collection of craft items, some of which are still produced and used in Bengal. However, either through lack of funds or from lack of genuine interest on the part of the university, the museum has a dismal appearance of disuse.

Calcutta University has an outstanding record of producing brilliant scholars in a number of disciplines, beginning from 1873 when it was established. The coffee shop near the museum is a meeting place for Calcutta's intellectuals and students. The example of Sir Ashutosh Mukherjee in the field of art inspired the foundation of other university museums in India, like the Kausambi Museum in Allahabad University, the museum of the Deccan College, Pune, and many others. Established some ten years before India won its independence, the Ashutosh Museum reflects the awakening pride and interest of educated Indians in their culture and its preservation during the colonial period.

The museum has a collection of **sculptures of the Pala and Sena periods**. The territories of the Pala and Sena rulers extended over parts of Bengal, Bihar and Orissa between the eighth and 12th centuries. Through trade and commercial contact the influence of these rulers extended far beyond India's shores to the east — to Java, Sumatra and Tibet.

The Palas patronised the Buddhist faith and during their reign a number of religious buildings with sculptures were erected. The famous

Seated Priest, Kalighat painting, 19th century;
Ashutosh Museum, Calcutta

ancient University of Nalanda (in Bihar) attracted scholars and Buddhist pilgrims from all parts of Asia and excavations here have revealed a wealth of artifacts. The Senas were Hindus, and a predominance of Hindu sculpture marks their era. The reign of the Palas and Senas ended with the invasion by Muslim armies from the north-west in the 13th century. The art of the Palas and Senas is characterised by the use of a hard, grey-black basalt stone which lent itself to intricate carving and which, when burnished, glowed with a surface sheen. It is not difficult to discern the mutual influence of Buddhist and Hindu art and ideas in the sculptural remains of this period.

Pala and Sena sculptures were inspired by their earlier **Gupta** sculptural heritage, though in scale the sculptures are much smaller. The sculptures exhibited here were once part of the walls of religious buildings and are therefore carved in high relief on only one side, usually with a broad base. While sharing iconographic conventions with sculptures from the rest of India, the Pala and Sena figures have a distinct quality associated with the eastern tradition.

The museum has a large collection of **sculptured clay panels** from Bengal's unique group of **temples in the Vishnupur region** situated 200 kilometres, west of Calcutta. Most temples in other parts of India from the late medieval period were built in stone. The Vishnupur temples were built in brick, their structure resembling the typical bamboo and thatch huts of Bengal. The curved bamboo roofs of the huts were recreated in the brick temples though it served no structural function. It did, however, contribute to the creation of a characteristic style of temple building. The Bengal hut inspired Akbar on his campaign, and became a feature of Mughal architecture as well. The pillars and façades of these temples were gaily decorated with clay panels depicting both religious and secular themes. There are interesting portrayals of boats carrying passengers, and narrative sequences that provide some idea of the life of the people during the 17th and 18th centuries, when these temples were constructed.

The Collection of Crafts

A visit to this museum is especially worthwhile, because of the collection of craft products displayed in a gallery on the first floor. There are **ritual objects, toys** and **dolls**, the most popular being the **painted owl**.

Along the walls are **painted scrolls**, *Patachitra*, once used by storytellers. India has a very ancient oral tradition; the storyteller roamed from village to village, entrancing children and elders alike with his narration, music, poetry and his scroll of illustrations. The storyteller would arrive in a village and announce his programme. Then, seated under a tree, in the village square or in the courtyard of a patron's house, he would pull out his scroll of paintings and narrate the story. The scroll, divided like a vertical cartoon strip with each frame depicting an episode of the narrative, would be unrolled for viewing to match the progress of the story. The legends were well known to the villagers, but the art of the storyteller kept the audience entranced into the small hours of the morning.

The museum also has some **illustrated manuscripts**. Special mention must be made of the *Kalpasutra* **manuscript** (Gujarat, 16th century) and the *Ramayana* **manuscript** (18th century) from the Bengal district of Midnapur. Also on display are some **wooden covers** which were used to protect the manuscripts. These are decorated with paintings in splendid colours — brick red, sunflower yellow, black and white.

A small collection of hand-painted circular **playing cards** brings up the question of where this game was invented. Some say that card playing was invented in India and was taken to other parts of the world by gypsies and Arab traders. The cards, some of them hardly five centimetres (two inches) in diameter, have decorative numbers and figures corresponding to their suit and value, each one individually hand painted.

A few **palm-leaf manuscripts** provide examples of the art of writing in India before paper was brought to India from China by the Arabs in the tenth century. The leaf was dried, and the text was etched on the surface with a steel stylus. The illustrations were painted. The inscribed palm leaves were stacked and placed between wooded covers, the borders and covers being held together by a cord running through the full set. Thus the pages were held in their proper order; the 'leaves of the book' could be opened and read at any convenient point, and then closed between the two covers and tied together securely with the string.

On the side walls of the gallery are some samples of **textiles** for which Bengal and present-day Bangladesh are famous. In a book published in 1880, *Industrial Arts of India*, George C M Birdwood mentions that cotton and silk cloth were manufactured in Bihar, Bengal, Orissa and Assam. Dacca (now in Bangladesh) was then a major textile centre and Birdwood's comments are broadly applicable to the region as a whole:

> The once celebrated Dacca muslins are now almost a thing of
> the past. James Taylor, in his *Sketch of the Topography* and

Statistics of Dacca, published in 1840 deplores the ruin which had overtaken its muslin trade: but he records that thirty-six different denominations of cotton cloth were still made at Dacca. Since Dr Taylor wrote, the manufacture has still more greatly fallen off. In the time of Jahangir, Dacca muslin could be manufactured fifteen yards long and one broad, weighing only 900 grains, the price of which was 40 paise. Now the finest of the above size weights 1,600 grains and is worth only 10 paise, and even such pieces are made only to order. The three pieces presented to the Prince of Wales and which were expressly prepared for him, were twenty yards long and one broad, and weighed 1,680 grains (three and a half ounces) each. Tavernier states that the ambassador of Shah Safy (AD 1628-1641), on his return from India, presented his master with a coconut, set with jewels, containing a muslin turban thirty yards in length, so exquisitely fine that it could scarcely be felt by the touch. A rare muslin was formerly produced in Dacca, which when laid wet on the grass became invisible: and because it thus became indistinguishable from the evening dew it was named *subhnam*, i e, 'the dew of evening'. Another kind was called *ab-rawan*, or 'running water', because it became invisible in water. The demand for the old cotton flowered and sprigged muslins of Dacca in Europe has almost entirely fallen off, but there is a brisk and increasing demand for *tussur* embroidered muslins, denominated *kasidas*, throughout India, Persia, Arabia, Egypt, and Turkey.

Among the **saris** specimens on display are Baluchar saris from Murshidabad, which were intricately woven in silk with scenes that must have amused weaver and wearer alike. An Englishman wearing a top hat and a gentleman smoking a hookah were carefully woven into the sari border and the *pallu* (the part that hangs over the shoulder), and became the trademark of this region. The art of weaving the Baluchar sari like many other traditional skills is fast disappearing, and much would need to be done to revive this wonderful craft.

Noteworthy is the **quilting and patchwork** technique of Bengal, called *kantha*, which was a vehicle for both artistic expression and the exercise of ingenuity and skill of village women. Old saris, softened by wear, were stitched together to form a light quilt. The quilting and embroidery became so fine that geometric designs, characters and animals were all created from

Durga; Ashutosh Museum, Calcutta

the tiny stitches. No doubt children were enthralled to have quilts with parades of horses and elephants in pinks and blues. The *kantha* was also made for specific functions in the home, like covering books and valuables. Some interesting specimens are on display.

The Ashutosh Museum of Indian Art,
University of Calcutta,
Centenary Buildings,
CALCUTTA
West Bengal.

Hours: 11 am–5 pm except on Sundays and university holidays.

Admission: free.

Suggested viewing time: half an hour.

The Victoria Memorial Museum

Calcutta is one of India's younger cities. Its growth and development began in the 18th century when it was chosen as the capital of the British possessions in India. For the British living elsewhere in India in the 18th–19th century, Calcutta was the 'Little London' of the East. Over the years it attained the status of the second-largest city of the British empire. It was here that the laws were made, the fashions set and where all the real 'action' took place. Its strategic position on the Hooghly River (the most important of the channels of the River Ganga) gave the city its commercial importance, especially for trade in cotton textiles. The name 'Calcutta' is derived from an ancient and venerated temple dedicated to the goddess Kali, and its environs of Kalikata. Even today, every street and lane of Calcutta carries some memory of those days of glory of the British Raj.

Amidst the traffic and activity of Calcutta stands the Victoria Memorial Building which houses a museum, with a collection almost exclusively related to the British colonial period. This impressive building — with its white marble facing, its domineering dome reaching a height of some 57 metres (184 feet) and its setting in an expanse of garden — stands out prominently in the city landscape. The idea of building a memorial to Queen Victoria, who had died in 1901, is owed to Lord Curzon, the Viceroy. He specified quite clearly that Calcutta, a city of European origin and construction, should have a memorial building that was not 'native' in design, and that 'a structure in some variety of the classical, or Renaissance style was essential'. And so it came to be. The English architect, William Emerson of the Royal Institute of British Architects, designed the building to look something like St Peter's in Rome and St Paul's in London. It was completed in 1921. The white marble was brought from Makrana, the place which had supplied the marble for the Taj Mahal. Towering above the dome, which was the fifth-largest in the world at that time, is a bronze revolving *Angel of Victory*, six metres (19 feet) high and weighing three tonnes. The garden and drive to the entrance of the building are decorated with marble sculptures, including one of Lord Curzon.

In the main, central hall of the museum is Sir Thomas Brock's life-size **sculpture of the Empress** as a young woman. The walls have friezes and panels depicting incidents from Queen Victoria's reign. The Queen's proclamations of 1858 (placing India under direct British rule) and 1877 (when she assumed the title of 'Empress of India') are inscribed on the walls of the central hall, in different languages.

Nearest to the entrance on the right is the **Royal Gallery**, with enormous **oil paintings** depicting various episodes in the life of Queen Victoria — her coronation in Westminster Abbey, her marriage to Prince Albert, etc. A huge oil painting, *The Entry of King Edward VII into Jaipur in 1876*, is by a Russian artist, Verestchagin. A few of the **Queen's personal belongings** on display in the museum include a piano and an inlaid writing desk.

In the adjoining gallery are some interesting **photographs** — including one of the Queen with her faithful Indian attendant, Abdul Karim — together with some letters and other personal items.

The **Portrait Gallery** to the left of the entrance contains paintings of British administrators and scholars, and some manuscripts. Among the **books** displayed in the glass cabinets are some that relate to life in India during the days of the Raj — customs and habits, and the costumes and uniforms of soldiers. In one of the books there is an interesting article describing the luxury and joyful lives of the English 'memsahibs' in India, and the employment of an Indian *ayah*, or nanny. Today, these passages have a certain comic appeal, for their style is quaint, and the attitudes quite patronising. It would be entertaining if we could contrast this with a similar account written by an Indian *ayah*, describing her English memsahib.

The **Sculpture Gallery** is in the south entrance hall, with life-size statues of Lord Clive and other governors–general.

This museum is best known for its large collection of paintings and prints, many of which, as described above, are displayed in various galleries. There are, however, concentrated displays in one particular hall on the ground floor and in many of the rooms on the first floor.

Until 1770, the British public had no visual representations of India by British artists. Subsequently, a number of professional and amateur artists began recording their experiences in India in vivid drawings and paintings. Apart from landscapes of towns, countryside and the life of the people, a need arose — with increasing British administrative and political control — for portraits of leading personalities. Within these broad categories of painting and prints came a slowly evolving change in emphasis and style.

William Hodges (1744–97) is the best known early British professional artist to visit and paint in India. His work in oils, his drawings and engravings cover a variety of subjects from landscapes to ruins of palaces

(overleaf) Krishna and Radha celebrating Holi, Kangra, late 18th century;
Indian Museum, Calcutta

and tombs. He visited Calcutta, Bihar and the northern areas of India, where he painted scenes from Agra and Lucknow. On his return to England he exhibited some of his work, especially the oil paintings, at the Royal Academy. His collection of aquatints was compiled in the volume, *Select Views in India*, published between 1785 and 1788. This museum has a painting by William Hodges of the *Allahabad Fort*.

The museum also has a very good collection of work done by the two professional artists **Thomas Daniell** (1749–1840) and his nephew, **William Daniell** (1769-1837). This uncle and nephew team spent nearly eight years in India, travelling quite extensively around the country. Their **paintings, engravings and drawings** depict scenes of Calcutta, Hardwar, Agra, Delhi, Banaras, and to the south in Madras (Chennai), Tanjore (Thanjavur) and down to Cape Comorin (Kanyakumari), to mention just a few. On their return to England, they too exhibited at the Royal Academy and published an album of views of India.

These Daniell paintings and engravings are excellent in technique and the landscapes have an almost sombre mood accentuated by the use of pale dull browns, whites and greys. Today, with colour photography capturing so vividly the colours and vitality associated with India, these prints appear to be almost deliberate attenuations of the general brightness of the Indian landscape. However, strict realism was not the aim of these artists; their work has a subjective quality, presenting an interpretative vision of a 'new' land that was an object of curiosity for those back home in England.

Among the works by other artists on display in the museum are **Johann Zoffany's** dramatic historical scenes: *Embassy of Haider Beg to Calcutta, Tiger Hunt,* and *Claude Martin with His Friends;* **Tilly Kettle's portraits; water colours by Samuel Davis**; and **Fraser's drawings of the Himalaya**.

From this 'age of curiosity' emerged a period when artists and scholars took a more serious interest in India as a country, its culture and history. The 19th century saw the development of an academic movement promoting study of Indian languages, religions, customs, flora and fauna. In the sculpture gallery of this museum, there are a number of portraits and busts of dedicated scholars who strove untiringly to unravel the mystery of India, and to present information about its culture for the world to study. During this era, serious investigative drawings, plans and surveys of India's monuments were undertaken for the purposes of documentation. Academic journals relating to various disciplines were published, and both

British and trained Indian apprentices worked towards compiling a more accurate account of India, both past and present. These dedicated people and their contributions in the fields of natural history, archaeology, language and literature are still gratefully remembered in India today.

There are only a few museums that specialise in collections of objects of the British colonial period. In India, the one at Fort St George (Chennai) and the Victoria Memorial Museum of Calcutta are the best. The documentation sections in these museums and the India Office Library in London provide assistance to those interested in research on the British Raj in India.

The Victoria Memorial Museum,
Queen's Way,
CALCUTTA,
West Bengal.

Hours: 10 am–4 pm except on Mondays and government holidays.

Admission: nominal.

Suggested viewing time: one hour.

Coins from Indian Museum, Calcutta

Chennai

The Government State Museum and National Art Gallery

The architecture of many of the museums built during the British period is often unique in style, and the Government Museum at Chennai is no exception. This large complex consists of the Museum, a theatre and the National Art Gallery. This last was formerly the Victoria Memorial Hall and Technical Institute, designed and built by Henry Irwin in 1909. It has a very distinct Mughal character, the façade resembling the gateway of the Mughal emperor Akbar's royal city of Fatehpur Sikri, near Agra. Today, new buildings have mushroomed between these older buildings, without any attempt to maintain integrity of form or style for the complex as a whole.

The story of the origin and development of the museum reads like a litany of laments. In 1828 the Madras Literary Society, a branch of the Asiatic Society of London, wanted to set up a museum like the one in Calcutta. By the time approval and money arrived, it was the turn of the century! The present buildings are bursting with objects, in crowded displays in an attempt to accommodate as much as possible of the huge, very precious collection.

The museum, like all early museums, has sections on mineralogy, geology, zoology and botany. These galleries display numerous skeletons of mammals — including one of a 12.3–metre (40–foot) whale, fish, reptiles, birds and the like. There is a gallery of musical instruments, and one housing a stamp collection.

The two most important galleries in this museum are those displaying **sculptures from Amaravati** (in Andhra Pradesh) and the **bronze sculptures** respectively.

The Amaravati Collection

The Amaravati Collection has an interesting history. Back in 1797 a Colonel Colin Mackenzie discovered a ruined Buddhist stupa at Amaravati. On his second visit in 1816, Mackenzie found the stupa almost completely destroyed, as the local landlord had been using stones from it as building material; further stonework had been burnt to produce lime. Whatever Mackenzie managed to save is housed in this museum, with a few other items at the National Museum (New Delhi), the Indian Museum (Calcutta) and the British Museum in London. At the site in Amaravati there remain only the foundations of the stupa, and a small site museum houses finds

Amaravati stupa panel, second century, Andhra Pradesh;
Government State Museum, Chennai

from later excavations at the site which unearthed more sculptures and some crystal reliquary caskets.

In the Chennai museum, the gallery has a **votive slab** from the Amaravati stupa mounted on the wall opposite the entrance, giving some idea of what the stupa may have looked like. Depicted on it is the dome-like stupa itself, surrounded by carved railings and pillars decorated with sculptured panels, flower garlands and festoons.

The stupa, originally 50 metres (162 feet) in diameter, was constructed and renovated between the second century BC and second century AD. Emperor Ashoka is said to have been responsible for its origin. The stupa, we are told, continued to be used for worship till the 11th century. The **sculptures** from Amaravati also extend over two significant eras, the **Hinayana period**, when only Buddha symbols were used in sculpture, and the **Mahaynu period**, when human images of Buddha were made.

The limestone used in the Amaravati stupa is milky white in colour and its texture seems as soft as wax. The delicacy of the stone enabled craftsmen to fashion sculptured panels that are especially fine and sensuous. Ananda Coomaraswamy, writing about these sculptures in his now classic work, *A History of Indian and Indonesian Art*, says that the 'ivory-like delicacy and precision of carving, the languorous accentuated beauty of figures makes the Amaravati reliefs the most voluptuous and the most delicate flower of Indian sculpture'.

The sculptures depict various stories from the *Jataka* tales, describing the earlier incarnations of the Buddha. There are beautiful scenes of the worship of emblems of the Buddha: an empty throne, his footprints and the tree under which he attained enlightenment. The panel showing **women worshipping at the Buddha's feet**, bending and kneeling in obeisance, has some of the loveliest figures of Indian art. Bejewelled, with a variety of hairstyles and a minimum of clothing, they appear joyful and happy, which is how worship should be. It is also interesting to look for historical information in these sculptures: costumes of the period, depictions of what appear to be wooden houses with balconies, chariots drawn by horses, musical instruments like those still used in India today, men and women in their separate occupations and a host of other subjects providing an insight into the life of people 2,000 years ago.

Famous amongst the sculptures is a circular panel which is entitled, **Taming of the Elephant Nalagiri**. This sculpture is set apart at one end of the gallery. It tells the story of a jealous man who let loose a dangerous and violent elephant, Nalagiri, to kill the Buddha. In the panel, you can see the elephant charging through the city gateway; from the safety of their balconies, women are watching the havoc being wrought by the elephant below; a young woman swoons into her friend's arms as the elephant charges past. On seeing the Buddha fearless and standing upright in his flowing robes, the elephant suddenly loses all anger and kneels to worship him. A delightful story-telling technique has been used in this panel full of action and movement, a composition of figures exhibiting contrasting emotions of fear and calm, anger and peace.

The life of the Buddha is depicted in a series of episodes on low-relief sculpture panels. Popular amongst them is the symbolic **Dream of Buddha's Mother, Maya**. She is shown lying on a simple wooden bed, surrounded by attendants; above her, in the frame or ceiling of her bedroom, is the baby elephant that she saw in her dream. This vision was interpreted as presaging the birth of the Buddha. Another episode relates to the Buddha's final departure from his palace. He is said to have left on horseback to travel through the forests, looking for an answer to the riddle of life. Finally, as he meditated under a huge *pipal* tree at the place now called Bodhgaya (in Bihar), he attained *nirvana* (enlightenment). Artists of the **Hinayana period** symbolise this event by depicting the Bodhi (wisdom) tree. After his enlightenment, the stages of the Buddha's life include his further meditation where he is shown seated cross-legged in the lotus position and later, standing, as he walked around the *Bodhi* tree, and then delivering his first sermon, and blessing his disciples.

There are a number of **statues of the standing Buddha** with his right hand raised in the gesture of *abhaya*, or 'protection'. His earthly body has been draped with a fabric that hangs in great folds around him. The Buddha's feet are bare, for he was an ascetic. The artists strive to render the Buddha's face free from all emotion, in control of his thoughts, meditative and always peaceful. One could spend hours, looking at the lovely figures, the lotus designs, the flower pots and stories depicted here in stone.

In Andhra Pradesh other stupas with good quality sculptures can be seen at **Nagarjunakonda** and **Goli**. The museum has some sculptures from these stupas which were contemporary to Amaravati.

This museum also has **stone sculptures of the Pallava, Chola, Hoysala and Chalukyan periods**. As far as Pallava sculpture is concerned, a better, *in situ* display can be visited: the rock-hewn **temples at Mahabalipuram** and from Kanchipuram, the seventh-century capital of the Pallavas, and a thriving cultural centre even today, with its magnificent sculptures and temples, is just a day trip away from Chennai.

The Bronze Gallery

Another important collection in this museum is in the Bronze Sculpture Gallery, which is reached by leaving the main museum and crossing the courtyard behind the theatre to a newly constructed building. South Indian bronzes are renowned for their elegance and beauty, and numerous museums throughout the world have at least a few examples. Temple sculptures in bronze were placed on huge chariots or palanquins bedecked with jewels and flowers and taken through the streets to bless devotees on festive occasions. These movable sculptures were then returned to their respective temples and re-installed in smaller shrines and rooms. The principal temple deity (usually of stone) was never moved. When housed in their own temples, though, the bronze deities do not show up at their best because there they are always covered in jewellery, flowers and sandalwood paste, and have clothes draped around them.

Nataraja, Chola bronze, 12th century

Some knowledge of the technique used in crafting these bronzes enhances an appreciation of their beauty. A model, of exact shape and size and with all details of jewellery, hair, etc, is first made in wax, which when heated slightly has a plastic quality that enables it to be worked by hand to produce the most subtle forms. The whole figure is then coated with layers of clay, ground with charred rice husks, cotton and salt, to form the cast or mould. The coating is then allowed to dry, its interior taking the shape of the wax model. The mould is then heated to a temperature at which the wax melts inside the clay mould and is run out through an opening left for this purpose. Molten metal is then poured in, quickly filling all the spaces within. When cool, the clay mould is broken, and the bronze sculpture is finished with some fine chiselling. South Indian bronzes made by this 'lost wax' (*cire perdue*) process have a special glow and colour, for the metal used is an amalgam of five metals including copper, silver, gold and tin. In the hardness of metal they also retain the 'fluid' quality of the original wax model from which they were made.

The best **south Indian bronzes** are those of the **Pallava and Chola periods** (ninth to 13th centuries), during which the sculptures acquired perfect proportions, exquisitely fashioned with the minimum of decoration.

In this gallery there are numerous **sculptures of Nataraja**, that is, **Shiva performing the 'Dance of Creation'**. These have so impressed our art historians that Ananda Coomaraswamy entitled one of his books, *The Dance of Shiva*, and C Sivaramamurti wrote an entire volume on Nataraja alone.

Shiva is the Lord of Creation and Transformation, and in India the cycle of nature's evolution and transmutation is symbolised as a dance. In many sculptures the four-armed Nataraja holds a drum in one hand, symbolising sound, rhythm and energy, the very origin of life: in another he holds a flame, the symbol of transformation or destruction; and the other two arms are held in the gesture of protection. One foot is usually placed firmly on a dwarf, the demon of ignorance and darkness; the other foot is lifted up in various movements of the dance. Nataraja's hair flows in long tresses symbolising the power of his cosmic dance. A tiny crescent moon balances in his hair, a symbol of the passage of time. The crescent moon is reduced to a mere ornament in Shiva's locks to symbolise his conquest of Time and Death. The poetry and symbolism that accompany each sculpture in India make the art much more meaningful. There is poetry for every movement and philosophical considerations behind every symbol and detail.

In a delightful passage from his study called simply, *Nataraja*, Sivaramamurti quotes from Coomaraswamy's research in Tamil poetry on Shiva's cosmic dance:

> O my Lord, thy hand, holding
> the sacred drum, has made and
> ordered the heavens and earth and
> other worlds and innumerable souls.
> Thy lifted hand protects the
> multifarious animate and
> inanimate extended universe.
> Thy sacred foot, planted on the ground,
> gives an abode to the tired soul,
> struggling in the toils of karma.
> It is thy lifted foot that grants
> eternal bliss to those who approach thee.

Among the other sculptures in this gallery are the **Somaskanda figures** of Shiva seated with his wife Parvati, and their son Skanda. In the *Shiva Purana*, the entire story of the miraculous birth of Skanda (or 'Kumara' or Karttikeya') is described. The story ends with the meeting of Kumara with his parents, for the first time. The *Shiva Purana* describes Shiva and Parvati seated on their thrones, awaiting the arrival of their son:

> On seeing his son, the great Lord Shiva,
> the sole kinsman of the Universe,
> along with the great goddess
> Parvati, was filled with pleasure
> and love.
> Placing Kumara shining with
> brilliant lustre on her lap,
> Parvati shone with glory
> as the greatest among
> women who carried children.
> Kumara, seated on Shiva's lap, played and
> teased Vasuki, the King of
> the Snake Gods that adorned
> Shiva's neck.
> Lord Shiva, sole ruler of the
> worlds, uttered nothing, his
> throat choked with affection.

It is such beautiful passages as this, from the *Puranas* and poetry, that inspired artists to depict their gods in human form, with both tenderness and charm. The ninth-century *Somaskanda*, from Tiruvelangadu (North Arcot district), is exquisite, though unfortunately the little figure of Skanda is missing. Parvati's garment drapes softly over her limbs in gentle contrast to the strength and rigidity of her metal jewellery.

Another outstanding piece is the **Vishapaharana**, from Kilappuddanur (eighth century). It is a sculpture of Shiva seated in deep meditation. In mythology Shiva is also referred to as Nilkantha, or 'Blue Neck', a feature he acquired when, for the protection of the universe, he swallowed all the poisons of the earth. The figure has been carefully created and the body, pulsating with life, is draped in simple clothes and ornaments.

The most renowned group of figures is, of course, that of **Rama, Sita and Lakshmana**, from the Thanjavur district. Rama, the hero of the Ramayana legend and his brother Lakshmana (or 'Laxman') are both holding a bow; and Sita, with one hand raised, is holding a lotus bud. In **Pallava** and **Chola art**, perfection in sculptural proportions was attained by a slight elongation of the lines, to create slender, elegant figures. The artist has captured the slight swelling of the stomach, the gentle curve of the armpit, and the smooth skin quality of the creeper-like arms and fingers. Notable also is the suggestion of movement in the fall of the jewellery and drapery in these three figures. The weight of the body of these sculpted figures is placed on one foot, producing a stance both relaxed and poised. It is in bronze masterpieces like these that the artist was able to transform the human body into godliness, full of quiet power and controlled energy.

There are several masterpiece in this gallery, some sculptures are as much as a metre (over three feet) tall, others as tiny as a few centimetres, but all exemplify the craftsman's achievement and mastery. There are similar high-quality bronzes at the Thanjavur Art Gallery in Tanjore.

The Government State Museum and National Art Gallery,
Pantheon Road, Egmore,
CHENNAI,
Tamil Nadu.

Hours:	10 am–5 pm except on Fridays and holidays.
Admission:	nominal.
Suggested viewing time:	two hours.

Ardhanarisvara, Chola bronze, 11th century; Government State Museum, Chennai

The Fort St George Museum

Fort St George in Chennai has been witness to a number of dramatic events in the history of the East India Company. Trade in the 17th century with India was largely for spices (used for the preservation as well as flavouring of meat in Europe), calicos, gold, gems, drugs, porcelain and ebony. Strong rivalry had developed over the years between the Dutch, Portuguese, Spanish, French and British, for supremacy over trade routes and the establishment of 'factories' and trading centres in India. In December 1600 the British East India Company was granted exclusive privileges to trade in the East by Queen Elizabeth I, who had shares in this enterprise. For the company, the next step was to establish a base on Indian soil.

The first British envoy to the Mughal court, Captain William Hawkins, was there from 1609 to 1611 but failed to get local permission to set up trading posts in India. It was only in 1613 that Emperor Jahangir permitted the setting up of the first British depot — at Surat, in Gujarat, on the west coast. Sir Thomas Roe was appointed as the first British ambassador to the Mughal court, where he served continuously from 1616 to 1618 with fair success, obtaining permission for the establishment of three additional 'factories', including one at Agra, in the Mughal heartland. In south India the rulers were from the outset more amenable to granting rights to British traders. The local raja granted the British Company a lease on Madras, at that time only a small strip of land ten kilometres (six miles) long, where they built Fort St George. They were also given permission to set up a mint there. The British settlement in Madras grew, and by the middle of the 18th century the population had grown to 300,000. Today it is well over four million.

The French East India Company was founded in 1644, and by the 1720s had established several 'factories' along the west and east coasts, including the one at Pondicherry. In 1742 war broke out between Britain and France, primarily over the control of trade routes and colonies in America and Asia. In India, too, this rivalry sparked off several clashes. In 1745 the British captured French ships. In retaliation, in 1747 the French governor-general of Pondicherry, Joseph Dupleix, stormed into Madras and occupied Fort St George. When the war ended a settlement was reached, and Madras was restored to the British.

It was from Madras that Robert Clive sailed to Calcutta, and with the Battle of Plassey (1757) brought Bengal under British rule. The British East India Company then moved its Indian headquarters to Calcutta, where Clive took over as its governor in 1765.

From 18th-century prints it appears that Fort St George was originally built right on the seashore, a welcoming sight for weary travellers from Europe. Today, highways and the broad Beach Road steal some of the domineering elegance of this historic fort. In its heyday, all British trade and commerce were executed within the fort; the Indian population lived outside its limits.

Within the fort, one of the oldest buildings is **St Mary's Church**, which is worth seeing, just to catch some of the flavour of early British India. It was consecrated in 1680, but the tower and steeple were added later. The church is of simple construction — just one large hall with three aisles — and contains numerous items that make it a museum in itself. There are **tombstones** that record the hardships and illnesses of the early British inhabitants; the **altar piece** is a painting of the *Last Supper* (ascribed to a pupil of Raphael's), stolen from French-occupied Pondicherry when the British defeated the French in 1761. It was in this church that Clive was married in 1753. Another important personality married here was Elihu Yale (born in Boston, Massachusetts) who came to Madras from England in 1672. He joined the East India Company as a clerk, but fruitful investments in pepper and shipping soon made him a prosperous, independent merchant. He later became governor of Madras, but was not to live for very long after his subsequent return to England. Yale made donations to the collegiate school in Saybrook, Connecticut which, bearing his name, was later given its charter (in 1745) and grew to become the renowned Yale University.

From the church, the museum of Fort St George is within easy walking distance. It was set up in 1948, just after India won its independence. The museum is housed in a building constructed in 1792 as the fort's Exchange Office — it was here that the East India Company officers would discuss trade agreements.

The museum's galleries house collections of portraits, paintings, prints, arms, coins, medals and documents. A **statue of Lord Cornwallis** (1800), made by English sculptor **Thomas Banks**, has a bas relief of Cornwallis receiving Tipu's two sons as hostages, in accordance with the Third Mysore War Treaty. To appreciate the **portrait gallery** fully, one really needs a *Who's Who* of Indian colonial history. The portrait paintings are mostly of former governors of Madras, and of the kings and queens of England.

The museum also has an excellent collection of **early prints** and a complete set of those produced by **Thomas and William Daniell**, the uncle and nephew team. These 18th-century prints, like the set in the Victoria Memorial Museum in Calcutta, are of views of important sites of India. The Daniells spent seven years in India, between 1785 and 1794, travelling and recording their impressions. The collection also includes some other 18th-century **prints of Fort St George**, as well as of other sites in Chennai like **St Thomas' Mount**, where the early Christian disciple, St Thomas, is said to have been martyred. There are scenes of Tanjore and Tirunelveli, in present-day Tamil Nadu.

The museum has a valuable collection of **documents**, letters and declarations which have been used by historians to reconstruct the history of this period.

The **arms section** has an assorted display of weapons, some belonging to important historical personalities.

The **coin section** reflects the growing wealth of the colonisers. There are samples of British coins, those from the early Indian mints in Bengal and Chennai, and some belonging to the former French and Portuguese possessions in India.

Some porcelain objects and the silver communion vessels of St Mary's Church are also preserved in this museum.

The Fort St George Museum,
Fort St George,
Beach Road,
CHENNAI,
Tamil Nadu.

Hours:	9 am–5 pm except government holidays.
Admission:	free.
Suggested viewing time:	one hour (including a visit to St Mary's Church).

रूपलावण्ये पूर्वमनीषसंश्रमानधावुते च इव्यांद लघुप्रसावेना
यासां प्रत्येबोह्यतैद्यपतापितौरस्मासिरीषा बहूर्नैनि
षि: ८८ स्ठ विरवाच प्रवेछवाषियुकानादेवानो
साबूवीतोःरास्तुभूर्वविदि: स्तुयनेत्का षार्य
अंतळुभेदिप्रनिरक्तै: देवै: समस्तें: समे
नि:स्तामिका कोष्पाकी तिस्त्र मतिज्ञ नोल
षार्वती कालिके तिस्त्रमारख्यल हिमावलकला
ह्म दूर्कचिद्रामुएञ्च्रभतौमुभानिभयो:
प्यालिस्त्रीमहाराजआमयणीहिमाचलम् ८५
लाकाप्य कौदेवी ग्रहनाचातुरस्रर ४६ छीव
निरेष्पेन्ताचवान्द्रष्टुमर्हति ४२ यानित्राणि
तिनेगेह ४८ ऐरावत: समानीनोगभीर्तेपूरुष
अर्कमेनविष्यतितिरुण लेभ्नमिहानीतेयद
रान् किंलल्लिनीन्चेयाच्भिर्मिला मन्त्रान
तेख़ायरूद्दनवलोबूरासीत्पनावेनें ५३

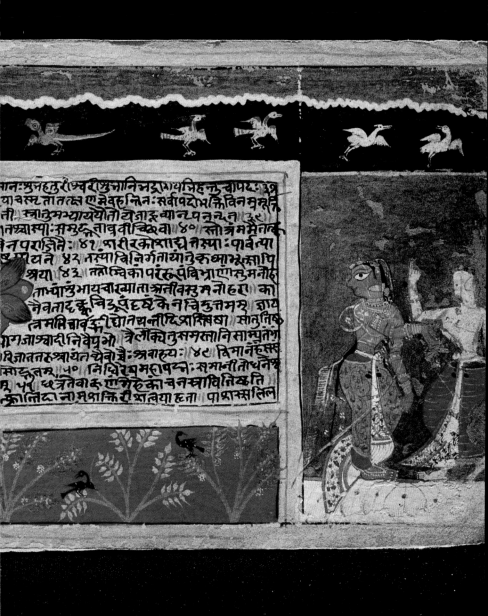

Ahmedabad (Gujarat)

The Calico Museum of Textiles

This is one of India's finest specialised museums. It presents a tasteful display of Indian textiles, in well-kept galleries. It was founded in 1949 and is the brainchild of Ms Gira Sarabhai who initiated the collection of rare, exquisite fabrics from different parts of India. Through their foresight and vision at a time when Indian textiles were losing their traditional excellence and popularity, such pioneers were instrumental in reviving interest in India's rich textile heritage and showing the need to preserve and extend it. Today, thanks to the efforts of both government and private enterprise, the Indian textile industry, especially its handlooms section is second to none in the world.

The state of Gujarat famed for its superior cotton, with Ahmedabad as the old capital, has always been a major area for textile production. It is therefore quite fitting that this museum should have been set up here, giving artists, craftspersons, weavers, scholars and casual visitors the opportunity to study and enjoy the beauty of Indian textiles of different periods and from different places.

Archaeological evidence and literature both indicate that textile production is an ancient Indian art, dating from even earlier than the Indus Valley Civilisation, 5,000 years ago. From paintings at Ajanta and Ellora, from miniatures and manuscripts, we get some idea of how fabrics were worn, their colours and combinations. References in literature speak of muslins and cottons so fine that they were compared to the evening dew, so cool and translucent in the case of the *sherbati* **fabrics** that they were described as 'air woven'.

The aesthetics of textile design followed certain principles. There were special colours associated with festivals and seasons: mustard-flower yellow for spring, and deep brick red and crimson for auspicious occasions. Textiles, like Indian poetry, painting and sculpture, reflected an innate love of nature. Motifs on textiles derived their names from flowers, birds and animals: the peacock's eye, the jasmine bud, fish, running water and other abstract designs are to be found on woven, painted, printed and embroidered Indian fabrics.

The museum in its present, new setting creates a charming atmosphere, with courtyards, gardens, fountains, quiet passages and evocative settings created with the textiles themselves to show how they were used: religious textiles, cloth used in the royal court, etc. This introduction is very well presented and offers an insight into the genius of Indian weavers and the skills and traditions associated with this ancient art.

Textiles can be broadly divided into those fabricated from cotton, wool and silk. Of these, cotton and wool appear to have been used throughout Indian history, beginning from the time of the **Harappan Civilisation**. Indigenous silk was produced by the tribes of the north-eastern states like Assam, and of the Bihar and Orissa regions. These *tusser* and *muga* **silks** are still available in natural hues of gold, and each with their own distinct textures.

There is a legend that a Buddhist monk brought a mulberry tree to India from China, where silk production was a closely guarded secret. There are numerous references in literature to silk garments throughout the medieval period. On a more significant scale, silk was introduced into south India during the reign of Tipu, Sultan of Mysore, in the 17th century, through his 'French connection'.

Any material, including textiles, can be studied according to the techniques involved in their production. For fabrics, the first stage is the preparation of the yarn for weaving: the twirling and twisting (spinning), which provides the initial element of texture to the cloth. Handspun yarn, like that used in *khadi* (handspun and handwoven cloth), lends a delightful uneven texture to the cloth. The colours and dyeing techniques for yarn used are equally important. The best example of these is *ikat*, in which the yarn is tied and dyed in two, three or four colours, so that when it is woven the designs 'assemble themselves' on the fabric. The museum has some outstanding samples of *ikat* from Gujarat, referred to there as *patola*, in which both the warp and weft threads carry 'colour coding', to create intricate, slightly fuzzy-edged motifs of elephants, flowers and birds. This artistic technique is still practised today in Orissa, Andhra Pradesh and Gujarat.

The next step is the weaving, in the course of which warp and weft interact to create sensitive combinations of colours, and an unbelievable variety of textiles. In this range we have elaborate **brocades** in which gold or silver and coloured thread are woven into the fabric to create special motifs and designs.

To set a loom for weaving requires an in-built sense of harmony, mathematics and an uncanny sense of the forms to be created on a two-dimensional surface. **Balushar saris, brocades, the textiles from Paithan in Maharashtra and Kanchipuram silks** are some of the examples displayed

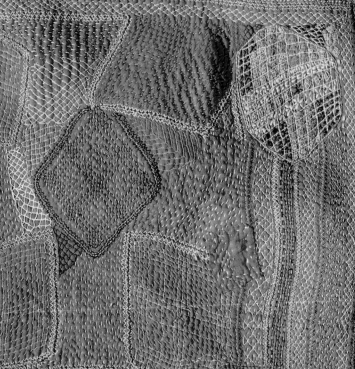

Silk and gold brocade textile, 19th century, Banaras; Museum of Textiles, Ahmedabad

here. The artist not only had to consider technique and colour scheming, but also the functional value of the cloth, and how it would look when draped and worn.

Weaving in silk, cotton, wool and sometimes a mixture of materials was mastered using simple horizontal and vertical looms. In the north-eastern states, the **hip loom**, or **loin loom**, is still common. Use was also made of the **Jacquard loom** and individual bobbins to introduce colours like gold in just the motifs of the fabric.

After weaving, the numerous way in which fabrics can be decorated — painting, tie-dye, embroidery, appliqué — are presented.

The museum has some exquisite samples of printed fabrics, especially those from Gujarat and Rajasthan. Wood blocks carved by hand were used to imprint the design on the cloth. Each block carried only one colour. Extraordinary skill was involved in the creation of one tiny motif, using as many as three or four different colours.

Painting on cloth, called **Kalamkari** ('pen work'), was another popular art and there are examples of temple hangings, and canopies from Gujarat

Quilted textile, Gujarat; Museum of Textiles, Ahmedabad

and south India. A sizeable market was established in Europe in the eighth and 19th centuries for printed fabrics from India, for which the European trader introduced Western designs that the Indian artist was able to transfer on to the cloth, for hangings, furnishings, tableware and garments.

Painted, printed and embroidered hangings were used to curtain off portions of the temple such as the main sanctum, and from Rajasthan, especially Nathdwara, come huge *picchwais* (woven curtains or 'that which hides the deity') with graceful figures in gold and silver against a midnight-blue background, fragrant with flowers falling from the heavens, and the blossoms of trees.

Embroideries range from cotton on cotton cloth, silk, wool, gold and silver thread and sequins, mirrors and beads. The embellishment of fabrics with a variety of embroidery stitches was popular in all regions of India, from the tribal shawls, to those of Kashmir, the blouses and skirts of Rajasthan and Gujarat, and royal attire of the medieval emperors. The museum has some excellent examples of *phulkari* (flower work), including the embroidered *odhanis* made by young brides of the Punjab to cover their heads. A *phulkari* has a veritable 'garden' of abstract, interlocking designs, in brilliant hues of golden yellow, red and brown, on a rich, brick-red base cloth. From Himachal Pradesh, the exquisite *rumal*, or cloth used to wrap gifts and offerings, which are so finely embroidered that one cannot tell the right side from the wrong. Episodes from the epics and myths have been painstakingly transferred onto the cloth and stand out like shadows in a fine mist.

Amongst the woollen fabrics, the most highly prized wools are *pashmina* and *shahtush*, which, though very light and fine when woven, are extremely warm. The Indian shawl, of great variety in weave and design, was one item of male and female costume that captured the imagination of the artist. The shawl is worn loosely over the body, swung around one or both shoulders; it frames the body and head, and can be worn in many ways. The most complex woven shawl is the *jamavar* (*jama* = robe; *yar* = yardage). To prepare this shawl a process not unlike that used in making tapestry is used, with hundreds of tiny shuttles, each loaded with coloured threads, being moved along to link the weft threads of the fabric. Though all Indian textiles use an amazing range and combination of colours, it is in these shawls that a new dimension is added to the art of colour combination. It is said that some 300 tints of vegetable dyes were once used in shawl weaving.

The textile museum has been rearranged, and work is in progress to display the textiles according to their usage. There are so many other extraordinary items in this museum that it is impossible to mention them all here. However, the history of textiles — traced through the representations in ancient paintings, like those from Ajanta and the Lepakshi temple, and through sculptures down the ages — testifies to a long-standing, innate love of textiles in India. Each region and state developed its own technique, skill and style, for which it is famous to this day. At present the battle against synthetic fibres and machine-made products continues, and it is museums like this that capture the essence of a very great artistic tradition of hand-made textile production in this country.

The Calico Museum of Textiles,
Shanti Bagh Area,
AHMEDABAD,
Gujarat.

Hours:	10 am–12.30 pm and 2.30 pm–5 pm except on Wednesdays and government holidays.
Admission:	call to book visit.
Suggested viewing time:	at least two hours.

The Utensils Museum

The credit for this unusual museum goes entirely to the genius of its founder, Surendra Patel. It is a museum exclusively concerned with Indian utensils. In a pretty little village complex, with simple, elegant huts around a courtyard and pond, the display is both indoors and outdoors. Patel, once he conceived the idea, went on an all-India hunt for metal utensils for the museum and has managed to assemble more than 10,000 exhibits.

Metallurgy is an ancient Indian craft, beginning with the Indus Valley Civilisation, 5,000 years ago. The art of production of metal utensils, pots and pans required the preparation of metal sheets that could be welded together and beaten into shape. In rare cases, as in the production of the Kerala *uruli*, huge dishes were cast in a mould.

There are **pots** that are used for the storage of water, a precious item in the desert, and in the dry conditions of Gujarat and Rajasthan. The water pots were used for carrying water from often very distant reservoirs. They were designed to balance on the head, to fit snugly on the hip and to be manageable on long walks. At home the pots were emptied into

Cart, Utensils Museum, Ahmedabad

Duck, Utensils Museum, Ahmedabad

larger storage vessels, kept one on top of another like a pyramid, sometimes suspended in a rope cradle from the roof.

From the shape of the pots, it is easy to identify their functions. Those with long, narrow necks and small openings were for precious items like oil, while larger ones were for the storage of grain. There are boxes with lids that can be locked — for storing money, jewellery and other valuables. In the average village house, there was a minimum of furniture, and storage containers for clothes, money and food were highly treasured items.

The enormous variety of shapes is staggering. Equally interesting is the vast range of techniques used to make and decorate these household items. There are pots made of two or more metals such as brass and copper; there are examples of repoussé work and enamel ware. Among the latter are some beautiful specimens of **Bidri ware**, where the base metal -- usually bell metal — has been engraved with designs, and the pattern filled with silver, and even gold, though rarely, as in the case of a gold-inlaid nutcracker. There are collections of spoons, rolling pins, tiffin carriers and a wide range of cooking vessels.

The museum-village complex also has a restaurant called 'Vishala'. Good, hygienic traditional food of the region is served on leaf-plates, bowls, earthernware glasses and pots in a rustic, leisurely environment.

Utensils Museum,
Vechaar Vishalla Environmental Centre,
AHMEDABAD,
Gujarat.

Hours:	Best to visit the museum and eat at the restaurant in the evening.
Admission:	nominal.
Suggested viewing time:	half an hour.

City Palace; Alwar, Rajasthan

Alwar (Rajasthan)

The Government Museum

Maharajas Jai Singh and Viney Singh were instrumental in setting up this museum, which is housed in a portion of the old city palace of Alwar. It has a representative collection of sculptures of the region, paintings and manuscripts, and a number of articles belonging to the royal family of Alwar, such as textiles, royal robes, turbans and ceremonial gowns. Items from the palace, such as hookah stands, fly whisks, pen holders, plates, boxes and ornamental vases stand witness to the eclectic tastes of 19th-century Indian royalty. The strangest object is a silver dining table with a motor that moves water around it, giving the illusion of it being a floating fish.

The museum has a large display of **arms**, including ornamental and ceremonial shields inlaid with gold and silver. Swords and the *katar* (dagger) with a variety of different types of hilts — some worked with metals, some ivory, even walrus bone, crystal and jade inlaid with precious stones — are on display.

For the lover of traditional Indian art, it is the painting and manuscript sections that are the most interesting. The museum has a copy of the famous *Gulistan* (*The Rose Garden*), written in 1258. The entire manuscript is beautifully illustrated by artists of Alwar.

Paintings from the **Alwar School** of the 19th century include a series of the **incarnations of Vishnu** and a **Ragamala series**, and there are some **late Mughal paintings**, as well as **portraits** of the Alwar royal family.

Another curiosity of the museum is an **illustrated scroll**, written on a single sheet some 80 yards long, of hand-made Kashmiri paper. The extraordinary calligraphy has to be read with a powerful magnifying glass.

Government Museum,

ALWAR,

Rajasthan.

Hours: 10 am–5 pm.

Admission: free.

Suggested viewing time: an hour.

Vadodara (Gujarat)

The Baroda Museum and Picture Gallery

This museum is located in Sayaji Bagh, a garden that is popular with the inhabitants of Baroda (or Vadodara), who picnic and stroll there. The collection in the museum belongs largely to the former ruler of the state, Maharaja Sayaji Rao Gaekwad III. During British rule it was the fashion for Indian rulers to take a keen interest in European art. On their travels and holidays abroad they collected paintings and sculptures as well as acquired many Western habits and customs. The outcome of these royal pastimes was a random collection of strange (often peculiar) art objects from all parts of the world. The palaces of many Indian princes became cluttered with these acquisitions and came to resemble poorly planned storerooms. Simplicity was forsaken for opulence, and the former elegance of Indian royalty was reduced to vulgar display.

This museum was opened in 1921 and additions and changes have been made periodically, but the 'cluttered look' continues to dominate the museum galleries. On the ground floor are rooms with the **European Art** collection, where Greek and Roman sculptures rub shoulders with paintings of a variety of European schools. There are galleries with displays of **Asian Art** from Burma, Sri Lanka, Cambodia, China and Japan — bronzes, ivory and pottery, and a painted gilt wooden statue of the *Bodhisattva*. There are samples of art objects, especially **manuscripts** from Persia, Turkey and Japan.

The **Indian Art** section has one part devoted to **prehistoric artifacts**. Some objects are from Graeco-Roman trading centres in Gujarat, like Broach. A bronze Roman jar of the second century is one of the prized possessions of this museum. The **Indian Painting** Gallery has a noteworthy sample of Indian painted manuscripts from Rajasthan and the Hill schools, portraits of various maharajas, a *Ragamala* series, illustrations to the *Bhagavad Purana* and others. The museum also has special galleries for its natural history, geological and zoological collections.

Baroda Museum and Picture Gallery,
Sayaji Park,
VADODARA,
Gujarat.

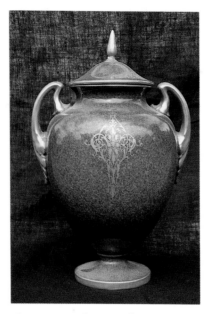

Vase, 19th century; Maharaja Palace Museum, Vadodara

Hours:	10 am–5 pm except on Mondays and government holidays.
Admission:	nominal.
Suggested viewing time:	45 minutes to an hour; can be combined with a walk in the zoo and the surrounding park.

Bhopal (Madhya Pradesh)

The Bharat Bhavan

The Bharat Bhavan, literally 'Abode or Home of India', was conceived and established as a cultural complex in the early 1980s. Since then, this museum-library, theatre and music centre has played a vital role in the contemporary art scene, attracting artists and performers from all over India and abroad.

The low buildings that appear to melt into the landscape were designed by the architect, Charles Correa. The buildings of the complex include the Rang Mandal, the theatre where a repertory company stages plays throughout the year. These plays are often based on innovative themes, but they draw also on India's older theatre traditions for inspiration on style and technique. There is a Music Hall (Anahad), a Poetry Library (Vagarth) and an Art Museum (Roopankar).

The museum specialises in two areas: contemporary art, with paintings and sculptures by various eminent Indian artists, and tribal and regional art forms from the area of Madhya Pradesh.

It is only recently that due honour and importance have been given to folk and tribal art, bronzes, terracottas, toys and ritual objects. The art of everyday life in India, as it were, is especially interesting, for there is a freshness and spontaneity about it that anyone can enjoy. Madhya Pradesh, one of India's largest states, has many regions like Bastar, Jhabua and others still inhabited by tribes.

The Bhavan regularly organises special exhibitions, programmes and 'happenings' that may interest the visitor. So look out for their programmes when you are in Bhopal.

Bharat Bhavan
BHOPAL,
Madhya Pradesh.

Hours:	10.30 am–5pm except on Sundays and government holidays.
Admission:	50 paise.
Suggested viewing time:	an hour at least.

Palm-leaf manuscript, Usha Vilasa *illustrations, 18th century;*
Orissa State Museum, Bhubaneswar

Bhubaneswar (Orissa)

The Orissa State Museum

When Bhubaneswar became the capital of Orissa, the museum was moved from Cuttack to its present location. The collection of the museum centres on the arts of the region. Orissa has one of India's oldest and most artistic traditions, ranging from Buddhism, Jainism to Hinduism, including the building of the magnificent **temples of Bhubaneswar** and the **Sun Temple at Konarak** in the 13th century. There are several galleries devoted to sculptures from these temples, though many would prefer to see the reliefs *in situ*, in the nearby temples themselves.

Like the temples at Khajuraho in Madhya Pradesh, Tanjore (Thanjavur) in south India and Modera in Gujarat, those in Orissa reached their apogee between the tenth and the 13th centuries. Sculptural works of fine quality and restrained ornamentation were prepared to adorn parts of the temple. The sculptured panels of musicians, elephants and deities such as Mahishasuramardini are noteworthy.

The museum is also well known for its vast collection of **palm-leaf manuscripts**. Palm leaves were dried, and with a stylus the writing was incised into the leaf. It is said that the script of Oriya has a predominance of rounded letters, formed from writing on palm leaves which would have split if the letters had been too angular in relation to the horizontal line of the leaf. The leaves were then blackened with charcoal and wiped so that the incised letters stood out in black. There are several painted and incised drawings and illustrations on the manuscripts. These paintings, like the stone sculptures, follow a style that is particular to Orissa. Well-developed figures, wearing heavy jewellery and patterned clothing are depicted in the scenes. Elaborate hairstyles, plaited braids with jewels, long earrings and long accentuated eyes are characteristic features of this style. The details of the scenery in these paintings are quite remarkable — a tree signifies a forest, a flowering bush, a garden, a few waves with lotuses symbolise a pond. Architectural structures are included to depict houses, palaces and jungle hamlets. The sky is strewn with flowers when the occasion is auspicious.

One of the earliest palm-leaf manuscripts (1690) is of the *Gita Govinda*, a devotional poem written by **Jayadeva** in the 12th century. The painting is in primary colours: red, yellow and blue, with shades of green.

Palm-leaf manuscript illustrations, 18th century; Orissa State Museum, Bhubaneswar

This manuscript has 80 folios, with drawings on both sides. The museum's copy is signed by the artist **Dhananjaya**. There is a translation of one verse from the Gita Govinda that speaks of Radha's longing for her divine lover Krishna:

> She ornaments her limbs
> when a leaf quivers or falls;
> suspecting Krishna's arrival,
> she spreads out the bed;
> making her bed of ornaments and fantasies,
> she evokes a hundred details of you;
> she will not survive
> tonight without you.

Here the artist, on this small scale, has attempted to convey universal concepts, ideas that could fill the world.

Orissa State Museum,
Jaydev Marg,
BHUBANESWAR,
Orissa.

Hours:	10 am–4 pm except on Mondays and government holidays.
Admission:	free.
Suggested viewing time:	an hour.

Goa

The Archaeological Museum, Old Goa

Old Goa is just nine kilometres (six miles) from Panaji, the capital of Goa. At this site are numerous churches that date from the 16th century onwards. Ancient Goa was once in the mainstream of India's history. There is evidence of its association with the Mauryan Empire. The land was later ruled by a number of dynasties: the Satavahanas, the Bhoja and the Chalukyas of Badami till the 13th century. In the 11th century the Kadambas of Goa moved their capital to Goapur or Goa Velha. Trade by both sea and land flourished, and Hinduism and Jainism were patronised. This land was then conquered by generals of the Delhi Sultanate, following which it formed part of the Vijayanagar kingdom. The Adil Shahis of Bijapur held sway in the 15th century and evidence of their occupation remains in the **Gate of the Palace of Adil Shah**, not far from the church of St Cajetan in Old Goa today.

Vasco da Gama, the Portuguese explorer opened the gates of Goa for trade with India after his arrival in Calicut in 1498. In search of a foothold on Indian soil, with little interference from local rulers, the Portuguese set up base on the idyllic shores of Goa in 1510 when Alfonso de Albuquerque succeeded in driving out the forces of Ismail Adil Shah. The natural harbours and the lush landscape afforded an appropriate site for a permanent settlement. Under the governorship of Nino da Cunha, the Portuguese extended their hold inland and along the coast. It was time now to build and make more stable arrangements on Indian soil.

Fortress walls and administrative buildings were put up, and beautiful churches were erected in the European style, with Doric and Corinthian columns, huge archways and elaborately adorned altars. Missionaries and members of religious orders, such as the Carmelites and Jesuits, followed the traders and made their home in Goa. The church of **St Cajetan** was modelled after St Peter's in Rome. The **Basilica de Bom Jesus** contains the mortal remains of the patron saint, St Francis Xavier. The decoration of the churches, following the Gothic tradition, was elaborate painted stucco work, with wooden statues and plenty of gold, silver and jewel-studded items that were used in the church services. Painted wooden panels and frames adorned the interiors of the churches, along with stone and wooden statues

Infant Jesus, Ivory, 17th century; Goa

of saints, the Virgin Mary and Christ on the cross (Bom Jesus Basilica display area). Those statues that were made in India strove desperately to imitate the traditions of Western art, coping samples that were brought to India from Portugal and Spain.

The **museum** housed in the lovely old **convent of St Francis of Assisi** has exhibits from different periods of the history of Goa. The **key gallery** has statues belonging to the Hindu period — sculptures of deities such as **Uma-Mahesa**. There are a number of *sati* (sutte) **and hero stones**. These stone slabs were erected in memory of a warrior, often to mark the place of his untimely death. The stone slabs have inscriptions and a small panel with relief sculpture depicting some aspect of the associated legend of the warrior-hero.

There are large **paintings** of the Portuguese explorer Vasco da Gama and founder Alfonso de Albuquerque. The painted portraits, yellowing with age, give us some idea of these fearless travellers, explorers and empire builders. Dressed in the fashions of their homeland, they look almost regal with their determined, self-assured expressions. On the first floor there are a number of portraits of Portuguese governors.

There is a large **coin collection** that traces the chequered history of Goa and its occupation by various rulers, including the Portuguese.

The courtyard or enclosed garden of the convent is well maintained. An air of peace and tranquility still surrounds the churches, each one of them now virtually a museum in itself, recording the history of Goa.

The Archaeological Museum,
OLD GOA,
Goa.

Hours:	10 am–5 pm except on Fridays and government holidays.
Admission:	Nominal.
Suggested viewing time:	at least half an hour, visit to the churches a whole day.

Guwahati (Assam)

The Assam State Museum

This museum was founded in 1940 with a nucleus collection assembled by the Kamarupa Anusandhan Samiti (Assam Research Society). The museum's collection is largely archaeological, with sections devoted to epigraphy, numismatics and iconography. The sculptures from the Assam region fall into four principal categories — stone, wood, metal and terracotta.

Assam's neighbours, Bengal and Bihar, had historical links with the Sino-Tibetan Burmese lands. It is through Assam that the mighty Brahmaputra River flows to India. The history of this region stretches far back into the Stone Age, and its rich and fertile lands offered a home to several tribes. In ancient inscriptions of the **Gupta period** Assam was referred to as Kamarupa· Shiva is said to have carried the dead body of his wife Sati and danced in rage and sadness. Her body was scattered throughout the land by the force of the dance. Her *yoni* (female sexual organ) fell at the place where the **Kamakhya Devi Temple** now stands, on a hill near Guwahati — the present capital of Assam, on the banks of the Brahmaputra.

Hunter, Terracotta, 17th century; Assam State Museum, Guwahati

Devi, Pala period; Assam State Museum, Guwahati

Worship in this temple continues even today, with blood sacrifices of animals to appease *Shakti*, the powerful female principle. Apart from mother goddess worship, a strong *Vaishnava* cult also grew in Assam and many **sculptures** in the museum reflect the multiple strands of the culture of this region. The **Bust of the Devi** (ninth century) and the figures of lovers in the Assam museum reflect one aspect of the tradition of *Shakti* worship. The figures in sculpture carry marked Assamese features: high cheekbones and rounded faces, with long, often slanted, eyes.

With the conquest of Assam in 1288 by the Ahoms, a tribe of Thai origin, the influence of Indian art reached more distant regions, and in turn developed a new synthesis of cultures. The mighty Ahom rulers prevented the Mughals from conquering their territory and influencing their art. During British rule, like the rest of India, Assam came into administrative and cultural contact with Britain.

Assam State Museum,
GUWAHATI,
Assam.

Hours: 10 am–4.30 pm except on Mondays and government holidays.

Suggested viewing time: half an hour.

Hyderabad (Andhra Pradesh)

The Salar Jung Museum

In the mid-19th century, the Nizam of Hyderabad appointed a prime minister to whom was given the title of Salar Jung. His son, Salar Jung II, and grandson Salar Jung III, were also selected as prime ministers by later rulers. It was these three men who contributed to what is now called the **Salar Jung Collection** in this museum.

Mir Yousuf Khan, Salar Jung III, was a passionate collector of art objects. He died in 1949, a couple of years after India became independent, leaving no heirs. On his death, the administration of the collection was entrusted to a special committee that placed the collection on display in the palace of Salar Jung III, turning it into a museum. It was only in 1958 that the collection was donated to the Government of India, and in 1968 the museum was transferred to its present, poorly designed building.

The museum possesses a vast collection of art objects, but only a small portion is on display. There is also an enormous library of rare books and manuscripts. The three Salar Jungs collected objects from Europe, the Middle East, the Far East and India. The items were purchased on foreign trips and through dealers. During the colonial period many rare items such as the collection of swords, daggers and other antiques were taken away from the country. It is fortunate that some of these art objects have found their way back into this collection. The museum is famous for its European art collection, though in fact, the Indian art selection is far superior, not only in size, but also in variety and quality. There are excellent collections of **jade, weapons, textiles and metalware**, which are significant as they provide a glimpse into post-Mughal court life and are suggestive of the grandeur and wealth of rulers in days gone by.

The present museum building is not the best example of modern Indian architecture, but the collection is very representative of all that was in vogue in the late 19th century among powerful families of the state of Hyderabad. The museum is still being reorganised, and the abundance of objects is being sorted for display in some sort of coherent way. The building is constructed round a courtyard with a verandah leading into the exhibition rooms, on both the ground and first floors.

The first room on the ground floor is devoted to a selection of **Salar Jungs' personal belongings**: their clothes, household goods, books and furniture, along with gifts and photographic documentation of their lives and times. The rest of the ground floor is devoted to **Indian arts** and **crafts.**

Room 3 has a collection of **textiles** and **bronzes.** The textiles, particularly those from Masulipatam and Kalahasti in Andhra Pradesh, are especially relevant as they continue to be produced even today. Cotton **screens** used in temples or homes are on display. There are larger screens on which are painted sequences of illustrations from particular religious stories. These are painted in a technique called *Kalamkari, kalam* meaning 'pen' or 'stylus', and *kari,* 'work' or 'craft'. The entire screen, often three-five metres (ten-15 feet) long, is hand-painted using vegetable dyes in subtle shades of brick red, olive green, white and blue.

The *Patachitra,* as they are called, were carried in scroll form by itinerant storytellers to accompany their narration of the epics and myths, and the recitation of popular ballads. Using an iconographic symbolism familiar to the villagers, the illustrations were presented in sequence as the narrative proceeded, accompanied by music, verse and song. The scrolls in this gallery reflect some of the vitality and dramatic effect of the art of storytelling.

The Textile Gallery
This gallery has an assortment of Indian textiles in cotton, silk and wool, and a display of **glass objects** (an odd combination). The best items in the collection are the **brocades,** in which real silver or gold threads were woven into the fabric. The **shawls of Kashmir** are equally gorgeous, and it is difficult to find this quality of workmanship nowadays. Among the embroidered items, the gold thread or *zari* **work** is still popular, and Hyderabad has some excellent mastercraftsmen in this area. *Phulkari* **embroidery** from the Punjab is also easy to recognise. A rich, deep brick-coloured cotton cloth serves as the background on which the embroidery is done. Silk threads in subtle shades of yellow, green and orange are woven into the ground fabric like tapestry, till the background almost disappears. Abstract *bagh* designs of squares and blocks of colour represent gardens.

One way to enjoy this gallery is to see it after you have seen the Indian **miniature** painting gallery. The paintings show how the clothes were worn and how colours were matched according to the fashion of the period.

The Ivory Room

This room is a fascinating one. Ivory was much coveted in India during the British colonial period. This led to an alarming fall in India's wild elephant population. Today the elephant is protected, and production of artifacts in ivory is now carried out on only a very limited scale and export is prohibited. The old state of Mysore (now Karnataka) and Kerala were the traditional homes of ivory carving. Today bone often substitutes for ivory, but this material can never attain the dull lustre and creamy white quality of genuine old ivory.

The *nawabs* of yesteryear, however, faced no such restrictions and entire tables and chairs were constructed of intricately inlaid and painted ivory. Since ivory is hard, very fine, almost lace-like carving of it was possible. On display are chess sets, images and painted objects. What always seems to fascinate visitors are the objects made using the **cutaway technique**. Here the ivory is first carved with a lacy surface design. The space behind it is cut away till the design shows up like a screen, and further carving continues at deeper levels of the ivory. The object then acquires a trellis-like exterior case, and the forms within forms are created out of a single piece of ivory.

A few ivory objects from Japan are also on display.

The Metalware and Arms Gallery

Room 17, with its display of Indian metalware and weapons, is quite special. In India, the metalworker experimented with several techniques: repoussé, embossing, engraving and enamelling. However, the Hyderabad region became most famous for the technique called Bidri. Bell metal with a dull sheen is blackened chemically and inlaid with silver or brass motifs. The **Bidri ware** on display here, mainly hookah stands, trays and plates, is very ornate, the dull grey-black offsetting the floral patterns and geometric designs in the sparkling white of silver.

The arms exhibited here are of various types: swords, daggers and guns. It is not only the weapons that are interesting but also the workmanship on them. On the handles of swords and daggers, and the area where handle and blade meet, one sees some of the finest engraved and inlaid metalwork to be found anywhere. Some swords have miniature decorations on their blades of hunting scenes, with rather gleeful, tiny lions hunting deer.

Perfect in form, function and design, almost with a touch of

tenderness, are the **gunpowder boxes** in various shapes, the one showing a **fleeing deer** being the most famous.

Ceremonial swords with gilt embellishments are displayed here, along with swords with jade handles encrusted with gold and gems. There are also the personal swords of heroic Indian rulers like Tipu Sultan, Jahangir, Aurangzeb and Salar Jung I and the diamond-studded, ceremonial *darbar* sword of Salar Jung III.

The Jade Room

It is difficult to find anything to match the delicacy of jade. Jade in all its many hues — soft, translucent, white, pink and shades of green — has been carved into **handles for small daggers**, the top of the handles exquisitely fashioned into the head of a camel, horse, goat, a bejewelled parrot or a lion. Other **jade objects** to be seen in the gallery are wine cups, bowls and plates, mirror frames and book stands.

Jade is not found in India, and it is presumed that the stone was brought to Indian courts and crafted there by Indian artists. It was in the **Mughal period** that the emperors seemed especially to favour jade art. There are numerous references in contemporary Mughal literature to gifts of jade being given to the emperor, or by him to his brothers, family and friends.

The small daggers with jade handles, or jade and precious stone inlay, would really have served as ornaments, to be tucked into the broad belt, or *kamarband* (cummerbund), worn over the tunic. This fashion is often depicted in Mughal paintings, examples of which may be seen in the Miniature Indian Painting Gallery (No 18).

The beauty of the **jade wine bowl** on display lies in the thin, almost translucent, quality of the entire object. This was achieved by the difficult and time-consuming task of wearing down the sides of the object with abrasive instruments, till the walls of the bowl were fine and smooth. The bowls were fashioned to fit perfectly in the palm of the hand, as that was how it was held for drinking. There was a belief that jade changes colour if the liquid in it is poisoned. The shapes of the wine cups were often inspired by nature to match the organic form of leaves and flowers. In doing so, the artist sought to capture the fullness of a flower, the twist of the stem, the web of the veins and the gentle curve of the edge of the leaf. It is not difficult to imagine such a light jade cup poised in an emperor's

Portrait of the Nizam of Hyderabad, 20th century; Salar Jung Museum, Hyderabad

palm. Why the artist chose to give the wine cup a leaf shape is a matter of conjecture. There is an ancient as well as contemporary Indian tradition of fashioning a shallow cup by joining several leaves together which is to be used for eating or drinking purposes.

The tiny **jade plates** could have been used for a variety of purposes. We are told that the royal menu at every meal consisted of so many dishes that the king would merely taste them, as a connoisseur would. These precious plates may have carried delicate condiments for the emperor.

The **book stands** were opened up and laid on the floor, to serve as a low table. The *Quran* or other precious manuscripts would be opened on it, the sides propped up by the stand so that the book never really lay flat, thus avoiding damage to the tightly bound spine. To read the book, one would have to sit on the floor and turn the pages, never holding the book in one's hand. Since reading or recitation from religious books went on for several hours, a book stand was essential. It also minimised damage from constant handling. It must be remembered that books in the period before printing was invented were all handwritten, often beautifully illustrated, and were therefore very precious. A bejewelled jade book stand would thus be an appropriate support for the treasured manuscripts of royalty.

The Miniature Painting Gallery

The Indian painting section should be seen for a number of reasons. It has a collection representative of different schools and styles, beginning with **Jain palm-leaf miniatures**, followed by paintings on paper from the Deccan, Malwa, Mewar and Kangra regions. *The Prince and the Hawk* is a lovely 17th-century painting that shows the high level of sophistication this art had reached during the **Mughal period**. There is another painting, of the same period, of the *Madonna and Child*. Christian missionaries and ambassadors from Britain had visited Mughal emperors like Jahangir and presented them with gifts of paintings and other offerings. This must have influenced the Indian artists, who did not hesitate to render foreign themes in their own style.

Of the **Deccani School**, the museum has a fine collection, for this is the region of their origin. In the collection are a few paintings that utilise a special marbling technique. The paint was floated on a liquid in which it would not dissolve or mix. The colours were then carefully worked on, to create tiny zigzag patterns and designs, the paper slipped under the paint to lift the design off the water and on to the painting.

Another interesting technique came from the Sholapur region of Maharashtra. On the paintings, if closely observed, will be seen thin layers of gold foil which the artist has finely worked with punched and embossed designs. There are many paintings on themes from Hindu mythology, such as *Manmatta and Consort* (late 18th century). In the examples of the **Rajasthani School** of painting one can see an illustration of the story of *Laila and Majnu*, a popular and tragic love story very similar to that of Romeo and Juliet. In this painting, the artist has shown all of nature mourning with the lovers; pairs of animals and birds commiserate with the human beings, in the sadness of love, at the loss of the beloved.

This is also a good museum for the study of **Indian manuscripts** illustrated with paintings in a variety of techniques and styles. These constitute a rich source of information on life in the medieval court.

The Western Art Section

This section attracts numerous visitors, especially to see a **cuckoo clock**, in front of which hundreds gather at each hour and half hour to watch the miniature toy figures trooping in and out. The section displays marble copies of **classic sculptures** of Greek and Roman gods, but the pride of the Salar Jung Museum is the *Veiled Rebecca* by **G B Benzoni** (1876), bought by Salar Jung I while on a visit to Italy. A courtesy visit to the **European Statuary Gallery** is, therefore, called for.

The Western art galleries also contain a collection of **glass** from Venice, Bohemia and England, and **European porcelain**. The paintings gallery has a collection of copies of Western masters, and some oil paintings attributed to **Turner**, **Constable** and **Chardin**.

There is also a collection of **carpets** from West Asia, and an assortment of objects from China, Japan, Nepal, Tibet and elsewhere.

The Salar Jung Museum,
HYDERABAD,
Andhra Pradesh.

Hours:	10 am–5 pm except on Fridays and government holidays.
Suggested viewing time:	one hour at least.

Jatayu attacking Ravana, the ten-headed King of Lanka, to save Sita from abduction, scene from Ramayana, *Pahari, 18th century; Bharat Kala Bhavan, Varanasi*

Jaipur (Rajasthan)

The Maharaja Sawai Madho Singh Museum

This museum is divided into three main sections: the Textile Gallery in Mubarak Mahal; the Arms Gallery; and the Art Gallery in the Diwan Khana.

In the first courtyard, as you enter, stands a charming little square structure called the **Mubarak Mahal**, the guesthouse built by the royal family in the late 19th century. The carved stone and marble archways are in a style reminiscent of Mughal architecture, with a combination of Hindu and Islamic designs. This is a two-storeyed building: the ground floor is for administrative offices, and the first floor, approached by a narrow staircase to one side, contains the Textile Gallery.

The Textile Gallery

In the first room is a display of **brocade garments** of the Jaipur royal family. Coloured silks with woven silver and gold motifs were used to make tunics for the men, held at the waist by a cloth sash or belt called a *kamarband* (cummerbund). The combination of the colours of the tunic, sash, turban, pyjamas and embroidered slippers was a matter of aesthetic style and personal taste. Most popular amongst this collection is the oversized garment, the *atamsukh* of **Maharaja Sawai Madho Singh I** (reigned 1750-68), who, as the guides will tell you, was seven feet (two metres) tall and four feet (1.23 metres) in circumference (around the tummy). He must have weighed a good 500 pounds (230 kilograms).

The most famous region for the production of fine delicate **silk brocade** was and still is Varanasi (or Banaras) in Uttar Pradesh, and a lot of the samples displayed here come from that region. Each individual motif was woven into the silk warp and weft of the cloth by the introduction of gold threads to create the design. When the golden motif was complete, the thread was given a knot, and cut, and the silk-thread weaving continued till the next gold motif had to be introduced. This required careful planning of the design of the cloth and intricate, painstaking work; it sometimes took the master weaver months to complete one assignment. Look carefully for details of each motif, for the weaver often combined gold and silver threads along with other silk colours, adding to the complexity of the weave and the intricacy of the design.

In two of the rooms in the textile gallery there are displays of cotton hand-printed **fabrics from Sanganer**. The town of Sanganer is 16 kilometres (ten miles) south of Jaipur, and is still the centre for delicate **wood block-printed cloth**. The art of printing on cloth in India is ancient, but 'Sanganeri prints', as they have been called, are particularly famous. Wooden blocks are carved in different sizes, one side forming the handle, the other carved in relief to a depth of five millimetres (a fifth of an inch) or more. The design created on one block will carry only one colour of the motif. If the printed cloth has two, three or more colours, it means that there were individual wooden blocks for each additional colour. The more intricate the colour combinations, the more difficult the process of printing on the cloth became. The cloth was then washed in the waters of Sanganer village, which were said to be excellent for 'fixing' the dye on to the cloth. The printed cloth samples on display are of excellent quality, with clear, minute motifs as decoration.

Sanganer red and black are especially beautiful colours, and the characteristic small flower, creeper and leaf designs are placed in geometrical symmetry to create pictures of gardens on the cloth.

Gujarat and Rajasthan are the two states of India that have a thriving embroidery tradition. You can see anything from brightly coloured embroidery with a myriad different hues of silk thread, to embroideries of white thread on white cloth and pale shades that appear to melt into the very fabric. This is perhaps an important feature of Indian art, for in every endeavour the entire range of possibilities has been explored -- from the depths of subtlety to the heights of gaudy brilliance. Among the **embroidered items** are samples worked with gold, with silver thread, with sequins and ribbons.

Zari is gold, and *zari* work refers to the gold-thread embroidery that was popular with the ruling classes in north India. The workmanship on the huge flowing skirts and head covering (*dupatta*, or *odhani*) is superb. A favourite specimen is a midnight-blue cloth covered with gold star-shaped designs — like the night sky studded with a million stars — perhaps used to cover the tiny head of a little princess.

There is a sad, rather dusty diorama of a palace room full of women dressed in Rajasthani attire — long skirt full of gathers, embroidered *odhani*, blouses and jewellery — which gives us some idea of how a variety of prints, brocades and embroidered items were worn together, to produce a rich and dazzling ensemble.

Amid the textiles are a few cabinets containing samples of glassware, hookah bases, rose water sprinklers, bowls and cups. The glass, often coloured, is decorated with hand-painted designs that cast flickering images of dancing light on the walls.

The Arms Gallery

At a corner of the courtyard in which the textile gallery stands is the gallery of arms. This gallery is always bright and shiny, perhaps because the weapons are so well polished and cared for. There was a time when 'arms made the man', and a certain pride and honour were associated with the weapons that an individual carried or was allowed to carry, like an award or title given by the ruling king. In the gallery, the cabinets and displays are clearly marked.

On display is the *katar* a two-sided blade with a grip handle that was sheathed and then hitched to the waistband or cloth sash worn by men over their tunics. In some of the Rajput paintings in the Art Gallery you can see how the *katar* were worn as part of formal attire by courtiers and princes. On the daggers, swords and *katar*, the joins where the hilt is fixed to the blade are often intricately carved. Engraved designs and scenes are inlaid with gold and silver. There are figurative scenes of gods and goddesses and hunting scenes of men pursuing animals. Other decorative designs are floral, with creepers and flowers weaving into one another to form an almost woven texture. There are daggers with ivory handles, in which the hard, creamy brown surface is carved into different forms — a parrot, an animal's head or a flower, for example.

There are other **daggers with jade hilts**, in hues of green and white. The jade was carved into hilts with animal motifs, often bejewelled with inlaid precious stones and gold. Such ornamental daggers, with elaborate handles, were worn formally, with ceremonial costumes. Each one has a story behind it, as they were often gifts or presentations from friends and rulers.

The Indian artist never left anything without embellishment, and royalty never used anything that was not beautifully crafted, so even the **gunpowder containers** are interesting objects, of artistic merit. Gunpowder containers were usually horn-shaped. Their original form was perhaps derived from the animal horn from which they were ordinarily made. Here, there are horns decorated with mother-of-pearl, there are gunpowder containers made out of shell, wood and ivory, one ornate than the next.

The museum rooms have lovely painted ceilings, and walls decorated with all kinds of weapons, shields, swords, spears, daggers, knives and other beautiful but deadly instruments of aggression and destruction.

The Art Gallery

In the middle of the second courtyard, past the royal gateway, there is a raised, pillared platform. On display are two **large silver jars** that have gone down in the *Guinness Book of Records* as 'the largest single pieces of silver in the world' (height 1.6 metres or five feet three inches, circumference 4.5 metres or 14 feet ten inches, with a capacity of 9,000 litres or 1,980 gallons each). Maharaja Sawai Madho Singh II had these vessels made to carry water from the River Ganga (called *Gangajal*), for religious and drinking purposes, when he went to England in 1902. Fortunately, he travelled by ship!

Towards the right of the hall containing the silver jars is the **Art Gallery.** The gallery is unfortunately very poorly lit, and the display very crowded, for it is housed in the painted *Diwan Khana* of the palace complex. The roof has painted decorations, and the walls are adorned with a collection of old **Mughal and Indo-Persian carpets.** The carpets, by themselves, are beautiful, but it is difficult to appreciate their size, colours, or effect in the present display.

On the central raised platform of the Art Gallery are some **palanquins** and *haudahs* (howdahs), the seats that were mounted on elephants' backs. Around the raised platform are glass cabinets containing paintings, manuscripts, and books. There are **palm-leaf** and **paper books** that were not bound but were held together in painted covers of wood. There are also **scrolls**, with religious texts, some so tiny that they could quite easily fit into a pocket. There are also bound books with illustrations of texts both Hindu and Islamic — on astronomy, falconry and other subjects.

In the main hall, the first glass cabinet of paintings (as you enter and walk clockwise around the room) has some interesting art of the **Mughal School.** A painting entitled *Lovers at Night* (Mughal, c. 1725) is an unusual piece. In order to depict the quiet of the night, the artist has restricted his use of colours to black and white and a few dull shades of silver, gold and ochre. White flowers, the white of the marble architecture, and clothes glimmer in the moonlight. The lovers are being led and followed by attendants carrying fans and other requisite items as they move into an enclosed garden, walking quietly, holding their breath so as not to give away the secret meeting of the lovers they have helped to organise.

There is an interesting painting — *The Madonna with Her Child* (Deccani School, 1627) — in which the figure of Joseph is executed in a purely European style, his face full of concern, and his gestures evoking those of Renaissance masterpieces. The Madonna, however, is more Indian especially in the way the cloth drapes over her head, in the style of her features and expression. The portrayal of the Infant Jesus is even more confused, for it is neither Western nor Indian, but a combination of both. The mango tree behind the holy family is entirely Indian, along with the hungry parrot who is shown pecking away at the mangoes. One recalls the introduction of Western painting to India during the period of Jahangir, and the many attempts by Indian artists to reproduce Western themes in their work.

Of interest also is the portrait of *Sawai Madho Singh I on a Boat* (Jaipur, 1750-67), for it is the artist's vision of this great ruler of Jaipur. The lakes and palaces are the artist's view of what this region must have looked like in days gone by.

Jaipur is a city of many beautiful palaces and royal pavilions. In order to recreate a picture of how these buildings and gardens were originally used, it is interesting to look closely at a few paintings in particular: the *Princess on the Terrace* (Mughal School, early 18th century), *Jahangir and His Courtiers* (Mughal, 1750), the *Princess and Musicians* and *Lady on a Swing* (Amber, 1675–1700), for example. There are terraced gardens with flowers and fruit trees, fountains and water channels. Cloth pavilions have been erected on platforms with carved stone railings. People sit and lie on huge cushions and mattresses, listening to music, talking and enjoying themselves, out in the open, taking in the cool evening air which is filled with moisture and the fragrance of the flowers.

There are some strange paintings too, such as the one with figures of women that combine to form the body of an elephant — *Nari Kunjam* (Jaipur, 1770–1800) — and others of the *Ragini series* (Jaipur, 1770–1802).

On one wall, high above eye level, are four large, very softly coloured paintings of the **Baramasa series**, reflecting the changing moods of each season of the year. The *Lady with a Crane* is a lovely example of this romantic school of art (Hyderabad, 1728–40).

The Maharaja Sawai Madho Singh Museum,
JAIPUR,
Rajasthan.

Hours: 9.30 am–4.45 pm except on government holidays and during Dussehra-Diwali (October-November, please check the dates).

Admission: Different rates for adults, and children. Concessional rates on a few special holidays.

Suggested viewing time: An hour or more.

Silver vessel; Maharaja Sawai Madho Singh Museum

Khajuraho (Madhya Pradesh)

The Archaeological Museum

Near the sleepy, deserted village of Khajuraho in Madhya Pradesh stand some magnificent temples, the pride of Indian architecture. From an estimated 84, only 22 temples remain, some of which are Hindu, others Jain. The temples are quite special, exemplary of what is usually called the 'Central Indian Style' of temple architecture.

Khajuraho was once the city of temples of the **Chandellas**, under whose patronage the Jain and Hindu temples were built during the tenth to 12th centuries. A distinguishing feature of this style of temple architecture is the high platform on which the temples were constructed. The profile of the temple against the sky symbolises the range of mountains where the gods are said to reside — the range of Mount Kailash, in the Himalayas. The temples are lofty and distinguished in appearance, often rising 31 metres (100 feet) above the ground. The main exteriors have ribbons of sculpted bands right around the temple. Walking on the platform, one can see sculptures of deities, female figures in various poses, the flying *apsara* or divine, heavenly dancers with musical instruments and garlands celebrating worship at the temple. The quality and standard of the sculptures are excellent, for each individual block of pale yellow sandstone has been worked to perfection, and they can be viewed either as part of the temple or separately. The undulating wall space of the temple breaks the natural light into shadows and sunlit passages, the walls teeming with sculpture breathing life into the stone monuments.

The main group of Hindu temples referred to as the 'western group' includes the **Lakshmana Temple** (AD 954) and the **Visvanatha Temple** (dated AD 999), the **Chitragupta Temple** and, the most splendid of them all, the **Kandariya Mahadeo Temple**. Amongst the Jain group of temples, the **Parsvanatha** and the **Adinatha temples** have sculptured panels of a very high order of artistic excellence.

In 1910 the local British Agent of the territory, W E Jardine, collected the sculptures that had fallen from the temples and placed them in an enclosure adjoining the western group. You can still see the open-air store, fenced off with high boundary walls. The present museum building lies across the road from the western group of temples. It has a neat,

Dancing Ganesh, Chandella period, 11th century; Archaeological Museum, Khajuraho

uncrowded display of a few of the sculptures salvaged from the site around Khajuraho. A visit to this museum is well worthwhile, for it offers an opportunity to look at the sculptures at eye level and to study them in detail. There is, of course, one difficulty. The artists of Khajuraho, in planning to place the sculptures *above* eye level, made necessary adjustments in the figures to compensate for the distortion created by distance. On viewing the masterpieces in the museum, you therefore often encounter this perspective 'correction' that makes the figures look slightly out of proportion when viewed at eye level.

At the entrance to the museum are seated **two lions** with thick curly manes and what appear to be welcoming grins. Inside the museum, the galleries have been divided according to the type of sculpture. There are sculptures of Shiva, his consort and family in the **Shiva Gallery**, of Vishnu in the **Vaishnava Gallery** and the **Jain sculptures** are in another gallery with an assortment of panels and bracket figures.

In the entrance hall stands a colossal sculpture *Dancing Ganesh*. In the Khajuraho temples, there are several depictions of this deity, but this sculpture surpasses them all. This elephant-headed god is the son of Shiva. Nataraja is the form adopted by Shiva in the 'Dance of Creation'. In Indian sculptures Shiva's son is often seen imitating his father in the cosmic dance, or assisting him with an accompaniment of musical instruments. Here, Ganesh is dancing; his tiny mount, the rat, also prances on its hind legs to show that it too is 'in the mood'. A few drummers manage to squeeze themselves into the scene and are shown holding long horizontal drums that are struck on both sides. The *pakhawaj* or *mridangam*, from the south, is also a horizontal two-sided drum that is still used today for dance recitals. Ganesh's dance pose is also very typical: the straight body is flexed at the hips and at the base of the neck to create an S curve called a *tribang* (three bends or curves). Ganesh wears the minimum of jewellery — a waistband and dangling bells that sway with his movements. Ankle bells are necessary in some Indian dance styles, to echo the rhythmic beat of the drums in a very complicated pattern of footwork.

In this sculpture, Ganesh has been given three pairs of arms, each arm carrying one iconographic emblem. In one hand he holds a bowl of *laddu* (round sweetmeats), as he was said to have quite a sweet tooth. Even while he dances his trunk has found its way to the *laddus*, and it looks as though he is going to sustain his dancing with a surreptitious bite or two. No wonder he has such a lovely round, well-proportioned paunch. Ganesh is also the deity of prosperity and good fortune, and it is appropriate that you meet him first.

In this museum is the figure of *Hari Hara*, a curious example of Hindu iconography. In Hindu philosophy, there is a belief that God is One, but the All-encompassing Being who creates and sustains the world appears in different forms: as Shiva, Vishnu, Devi the goddess and a host of others. In this sculpture, the artist has created the figure of one male deity which, on closer viewing, can be seen to depict Shiva and Vishnu fused together. In the hairstyle, the right-hand side is different from the left, Shiva's hair is bunched up into a high top-knot, and Vishnu wears a crown. In one hand Shiva carries a trident, which is his symbol, and Vishnu carries a disc with many spokes. On Vishnu's side, the small figures that frame the panel depict his various incarnations — on the top, the boar-headed Vamana, lifting the Mother Earth out of the primeval floods. Near his feet is a small figure of a warrior mounted on a horse. This is Kalki, the incarnation of Vishnu that is yet to come, at the destruction and dissolution of this world.

The figure of the **seated Buddha** in this museum is said to be the only one of its kind to be found in Khajuraho. The Buddha is in what is called *bhumisparsa mudra* (the earth-touching pose). There is an important story behind this *mudra*. When the Buddha was meditating in Bodhgaya, under a *pipal* tree, he was continually harassed by the demon Mara. The Buddha paid no heed to the noise, thunder and lightning. Mara's daughter then came to try and seduce him back to normal life, reminding him of his forsaken palace, wife and son. Still the Buddha remained unmoved. As the tension builds, the meditating Buddha lowers his right hand and touches the Earth, to call her as witness to his single-minded pursuit. The Earth is said to have responded to his touch, and the Buddha achieved his goal — enlightenment.

In this sculpture, the Buddha is seated on a many-petalled lotus. He is in the *padmasana* position, a yogic pose for meditation in which both feet are placed sole upwards on the lap. His youthful body is covered in a fragile garment of unstitched cloth. His face is peaceful, carrying just a hint of a smile, as if in recognition of this moving moment in his life.

In the Vaishanava Gallery there are several sculptures of different manifestations of Vishnu, the most beautiful one being that of **Bhu Varaha**. Vishnu, in one of his incarnations, assumes the form of a giant boar (*varaha*). The story has it that once, when the world was engulfed by a

Girl playing with a ball, Chandella period, 11th century;
Archaeological Museum, Khajuraho

flood (like the biblical one, perhaps reflecting the prehistoric event recounted in myths the world over), Vishnu in the form of a boar rose out of the water and rescued the earth. The sculpture here shows a large boar-headed man raising a tiny (by comparison) seated woman, who is the personification of Mother Earth. The might of Varaha is exaggerated in contrast to the gentle way he is lifting, Bhu, the Earth. She, in turn, places a hand on his snout for reassurance. Unfortunately, her face has been badly damaged, but her body is beautiful. It is as though she is fidgeting, a little nervously, in all the movement and excitement that surrounds her. The water goddess and other gods help Varaha by offering a lotus footrest, as others look on at this dramatic event. Varaha, as the boar incarnation, carries the customary symbols of Vishnu: the conch shell, the discus and the standard. If you look carefully, you can see the subtlety of the artist's skill in his portrayal of the human body of the Earth Goddess and the slight swell of the stomach of the Varaha. It is the artist's human touch that makes this sculpture especially endearing.

Unfortunately, the museum's beautiful **image of Lakshmi Narayana** is badly damaged; only a portion of the chest and head remains. Vishnu and his consort, Lakshmi, hold each other in a light embrace. Their jewelled faces and sensuous torsos do not detract from their loving expression. The artist has striven to express an important notion in Indian philosophy: that male and female principles, though opposite, are meant to be one; a fused, harmonious, wholesome entity. In this sculpture, the magnetic power that draws these two opposites together is almost obvious. The artist has accentuated the maleness and femaleness of the figures: the goddess has large, well-developed breasts, a slim waist and torso, in comparison with the broad shoulders of her divine lover. Rodin's sculpture *The Kiss* and this one of Lakshmi Narayana must be the world's most sensuous tributes to love.

There are some interesting **sculptures of Surya**, the Sun God, in this museum. In one of them, the figure of Surya stands straight, as he rides on his chariot drawn by seven horses in the colours of the rainbow. In Surya's hands there would have been two lotuses, but unfortunately they have been broken. The sun's daily movement across the sky is heralded by Dawn, Aruna, and around him, the gods are full of praise. Another sculpture of Surya depicts sunset; in this image he wears a grim expression, knowing it is time to go to bed.

In the Gallery to the right of the main entrance are sculptures, panels and miscellaneous items. Among them are two lovely figures of women: the *Surasundaris*, as they are called, who inhabit every nook and cranny of the Khajuraho temples. These tall, slim figures are dressed in a garment that covers only their lower torso, their lull breasts and upper body being covered only by heavy jewellery and a flowing sash, or *dupatta*. One sculpture is of a woman playing ball. She stands with her back to you but twists round so that you can see her profile. In one hand she holds the ball, while another ball is seen falling halfway down her leg. The artist, unable to show the movement of the ball, has solved the problem by showing two balls in different positions, so that one knows exactly what is happening. The creeper-like limbs and the twist of the body with one leg bent to show the sole of the woman's foot make this sculpture fluid and graceful. There is another sculpture of a woman with a child held high in her arms.

In the Jain Gallery there are a few **sculptures of Jain *Tirthankara*** in different poses. It is quite clear that Hindu and Jain sculptures have much

Lakshmi and Narayana, 11th century; Khajuraho

in common in style, composition and the techniques of portrayal of the figures though their content and subject are so dissimilar.

Archaeological Museum,
KHAJURAHO,
Madhya Pradesh

Hours: 10 am–5 pm. Closed on Fridays.

Admission: Same ticket for entry to the monument and the museum, free on Fridays.

Suggested viewing time: half an hour, at least.

Mathura (Uttar Pradesh)

The Government Museum

Mathura and Brindavan in Uttar Pradesh are approximately 150 kilometres (94 miles) from Delhi. The former two cities are inseparable from the legend of Lord Krishna. This is the area where it is believed that Krishna was born, and it was on the banks of the River Yamuna (Jamuna) that he played his mischievous pranks, and where he met the beautiful Radha.

> He calls your name on his sweet reed flute. He cherishes even the breeze-blown pollen that must have touched your fragile body. In the woods swept by the wind on Yamuna's banks Krishna, in wild flower garlands, awaits.

The sentiments of the 12th-century lyrical verses of the *Gita Govinda* of Jayadeva are echoed by hundreds of Indian love poets, singing in praise of Krishna. He is worshipped as an important incarnation of Vishnu; as the 'Child God', he is adored as an offspring would be adored by its parent; as a young lover, he inspires passion and devotion; as a cowherd, he appeals to all the agricultural communities of India; and as Krishna, the spokesman of the *Bhagavad Gita*, in the epic *Mahabharata*, he provides philosophical guidance to millions of Indians.

The story of Krishna has, by some, been compared with that of Jesus Christ, not without some foundation. For example, there is the episode of Krishna's birth, when the reigning king orders his parents to be locked up in a jail following a prophecy of the birth of a child that would threaten and defeat him; and there is the spiriting away of Krishna, on the night of his birth, in a basket across the rising waters of the Yamuna. Stories of his childhood and growing years are full of pranks like those of any child, along with miraculous deeds that single him out as one endowed with godly powers. These legends have been the inspiration of many painters and poets throughout Indian history.

Miniatures from Rajasthan and Kangra and many other schools of painting include numerous renderings of Krishna's life and of the 'woods on the bank of the Yamuna'. In Indian dance and theatre, in stories enacted year after year, century after century, artists never seem to tire of giving their interpretations of Krishna's life in Mathura and Brindavan.

For the historian and archaeologist, Mathura occupies a special place. Its mounds, and plains have yielded hundreds of sculptures and icons that

Young Yakshi, with mournful Youth in the balcony, second century;
Government Museum, Mathura

establish the antiquity and status of the Mathura of yesteryears. Not only
for Hindus but also for Buddhists and Jains, Mathura is a city of great
religious importance. Legend records that the Buddha visited here; during
Mauryan rule, Emperor Ashoka (third century BC) built many stupas here.
The **Sunga dynasty** that followed the Mauryans continued to patronise
Mathura, till it was taken over by the **Greek rulers** in the last few
centuries before the birth of Christ.

In the first century, Mathura became an important centre of the
Kushana empire during the rule of **Emperor Kanishka**. An imposing statue
of this remarkable ruler is a major attraction of the Mathura Museum,
where it was installed after its discovery by an Indian archaeologist, Rai
Bahadur Pandit Radha Krishna, in 1912. **Kushana coins** and further
excavations in the region confirm the historical importance of Mathura
during the first centuries of the Christian era. Historians suggest that
during this period Mathura became the workshop for Buddhist art.
Sculptures made in Mathura were exported to other places of importance to

Terracotta, Mauryan period, second century BC; Government Museum, Mathura

Buddhists. The characteristic pinkish sandstone with white spotted markings and the style of the Buddhist art of Mathura are easily identified, even when found hundreds of miles away. The **Gupta empire** later absorbed the city, and sculptures and coins of this period have been preserved in the Mathura Museum.

Excavations in Sonkh and the surroundings of Mathura have revealed centuries of continuous occupation of this region from prehistoric times. The story continues till the marauding Muslim armies of Sultan Muhammad Ghazni entered the northern Gangetic plain and destroyed cities and temples, including those at Mathura. For centuries after that Mathura sank into relative insignificance, and it was only in the 16th century that the city culture revived again under the so-called liberal policies of the Mughal emperors, Akbar and Shah Jahan. Today Mathura is a busy little town; temples have sprung up everywhere, and on festive occasions like the birthday of Krishna, Janmashtami, in August-September each year, the streets are filled with thousands of pilgrims from every corner of India.

The museum at Mathura was established in 1874, simply as a storehouse. Selections of the better sculptures were made and removed to larger, more important museums like the Indian Museum in Calcutta, the museum at Lucknow and, of course, the British Museum in London. A new museum, in the present location, was built in the 1930s, and the sculptures installed are to some extent in chronological order. The present museum building is constructed from the characteristic pink sandstone of Mathura. The building is octagonal, almost ring shaped, in plan, with an internal courtyard garden.

As you go past the reception area, two **monumental sculptures**, the prize possessions of the museum, greet you. On the right is the **figure of King Vima Kadphises** seated on a lion throne. Though headless, it is a very imposing representation of the Kushana ruler of the early years of the Christian era. The inscription at the base, in the space between the feet, mentions the name of the ruler, referred to as 'the son of the gods', the 'king of kings' who ordered the construction of a garden, temple and well. Even if you cannot read the inscription, you can be in no doubt that this is indeed a king of kings, sitting proud and upright on his throne. The royal seat has two rather stylised lions, one on each side. Kadphises wears large boots, indicative of his foreign origin. Indian kings rarely wore shoes (because they are proscribed by religion and are unsuitable for the climate), and the depiction of footwear in Indian sculpture is even rarer. The soft felt boots are embroidered with vine creepers and bunches of grapes, lending a delicate touch to this majestic statue.

Opposite, on the left-hand side, is the magnificent standing **figure of King Kanishka**, who succeeded Kadphises. During his reign, the Kushana empire grew even more powerful, and centres of trade and Buddhism at Mathura and in Gandhara covering the north-western region, parts of Pakistan and Afghanistan, flourished. This statue is the only representation of Kanishka left, apart from the coins of his reign. It offers a striking image of a great statesman. He is clothed in a thick, stiff coat worn over a thin tunic, and on his feet are large heavy boots. In one hand he grasps a sword which is beautifully carved, and in the other a mace. Both are intricately decorated with borders and animal figures. The king's feet point outward, with the huge boots indicative of his impressive size and stature. The tunic under his coat is held fast with a metal belt which causes pleats and folds to ripple down the body of the figure. The inscription in Brahmi script mentions that this is the great king, the king of kings, Kanishka. It is a pity that the head is missing; it would have been very interesting to see what kind of face was supported on those powerful shoulders.

To the right is one section of the **Gallery of Sculptures**. Attention must be drawn to one particular panel of relief sculpture at the far end of the gallery, on the right-hand wall. It is a vertical **panel depicting a Buddhist stupa**. The panel has an inscription, translated for visitors on the identification label, which informs us that the stupa was donated by the family of a courtesan, Vasu, daughter of Ganika Lavana Sobhika. The railings around the hemispherical mound were adorned with sculptures and what you see in this gallery are the remains of the railing pillars, posts and beams that once formed part of stupas. Unfortunately, the stupas were not properly or systematically excavated, and most of the sculptures of the Mathura Museum were unearthed without the exact location and positioning of the finds being recorded. Therefore the position in which they belonged in the plan of the stupa is not known. In stupas belonging to the **Hinayana period** of Buddhism, the Buddha is represented only symbolically, for example, by a *pipal* tree, which is the tree under which the Buddha attained enlightenment, or by a stupa, as on the vertical panel mentioned above.

Beyond the gallery is a small room containing **terracotta sculptures and metalware from Mathura**. Clay figures for worship were produced for many centuries, alongside those carved in stone. These clay objects were prepared using a variety of techniques. The soft clay was either pressed into a mould or hand modelled. Ornamentation, rosettes and jewellery were punched onto the soft clay surface using a carved stick, before sun-drying or baking. What is fascinating is the profusion of decoration, the hair styles and the costumes on these tiny terracotta figures.

There are figures that date back to the fourth century BC, including specimens from the **Mauryan, Sunga** and the **later Gupta** periods. These include sculptures of women with enormous coiffures and playing musical instruments, lovers in embrace, chariots, religious figures of the goddess Lakshmi being bathed by two elephants and so on. (A fine collection of ancient Indian terracottas can also be seen at the museum in Patna.)

On the right-hand side of the gallery is a niche that contains **sculptures from Gandhara.** In front of this niche is the famous sculpture of the so-called **Bacchanalian Figures.** The sculptured panel, in high relief, depicts a huge pot-bellied man sitting with one leg up on a cushion. In one hand he holds a huge wine cup, and the other hand is clenched and shown resting on his leg; his expression is one of concentration and determination. An attendant rushes towards him, perhaps to refill his glass, while three other figures look on. This, and the **sculptures of the Buddha and a** *Bodhisattva* placed in the niche, show a marked Graeco-Roman influence. This can be traced back to the settling of a number of the generals from the army of Alexander the Great of Macedonia, in the north-western region of India.

In J P Vogel's article, 'The Mathura School of Sculpture', in the Archaeological Survey of India's *Annual Report for 1906-7*, the author made an interesting observation that sparked off decades of debate in India, regarding the origin of the human images of the Buddha. After citing his reasons, Vogel wrote:

> It follows that both the Buddha and *Bodhisattva* images of Mathura are imitations by Indian sculptors of the prototypes created by the Hellenistic artists of Gandhara. The process of deterioration of those types can be traced in Gandhara itself where the work of foreign sculptors was continued by their Indianised descendants or successors.

Yet it is this very Indian element that makes these sculptures unique.

On the opposite side, to the left of the main entrance, the sculpture gallery continues, with pillars from stupa railings, sculptures and figures of Hindu deities such as **Surya,** the Sun God, on a chariot. The range of artistry displayed is quite remarkable. The same pinkish sandstone railings have been carved to create both sublime and meditative figures of the Buddha, and voluptuous, sensuous figures of woman, as well as of the Hindu gods of later periods.

A particularly charming sculpture is the **bust of a Naga Queen of the Serpents**, dating from the second century. From a central column, five female heads emerge as though from the multi-headed hood of a snake. Worship of the *Naga*, or deities of the waters, was and still is common in India, and the Buddhists too adopted and adapted the practice. The back of the sculpture, instead of being plain as would be expected, is carved with a tree, in relief, with long, tapering, tender leaves that appear to swell and curl in the breeze. Along the tree's branches runs a squirrel with a bushy tail and alert little eyes. It is in details such as this, at times humorous, at times majestic and powerful, that the vitality of the Mathura School of sculpture can best be experienced and understood.

Government Museum,
Museum Road,
Dampier Park,
MATHURA,
Uttar Pradesh.

Hours: 10 am–5 pm except all government holidays.

Admission: nominal.

Suggested viewing time: an hour.

(overleaf) The State Museum, Patna, Bihar

Patna (Bihar)

The State Museum

This museum was established in 1917 and was moved to its present building in the 1930s. The building is a hybrid of European, Mughal and Rajput architectural styles. The structure is absolutely unsuitable as a museum and lacks adequate ventilation and dust-proofing. The collection of the museum, however, is so outstanding that it is worth a visit, despite the poor display and upkeep.

The region of Bihar, particularly the area around Patna, constituted the centre of the **Mauryan empire** around the third century BC. There is also material evidence of the antiquity of the inhabitation of the region, from even earlier times. The Mauryan empire, under Emperor Ashoka, was able to bring a large portion of what is present-day India under its influence. Emperor Ashoka, on his conversion to Buddhism, gave generous patronage to the arts, for the building of stupas in different parts of India, along with funds for the building of roads to link pilgrimage centres for the convenience of travellers. It was during his reign that trade links and cultural contacts were established with present-day Sri Lanka, Nepal and countries further to the east. The wealth amassed from his large empire is reflected in the rare art objects and sculptures attributed to the period of his reign. Contemporary travellers have recorded descriptions of the fabulous wooden palaces of Pataliputra. Unfortunately, none of them remains today, most probably having been lost in fires, or perhaps destroyed by subsequent rulers.

In this museum there is an excellent collection of **stone and terracotta sculpture** of the Mauryan and subsequent periods.

On the ground floor are the **sculpture galleries**. The most important and significant sculpture is the **Yakshi from Didarganj**. She is a large, buxom woman, more than life-size, carved out of a yellowish sandstone which was obtained from the mines of Chunar in Bihar. She is an attendant figure, or *chauri* bearer (with a fly whisk), carved in the round. The Yakshi wears a fine lower garment, held in place by a belt of many chains. Her huge anklets, bangles and earrings are not unusual in design, and similar jewellery in silver is still worn by women in many parts of India. The kind of fly whisk she holds was traditionally made from the hair from a horse's tail. The glossy sheen of the sculpted surface is quite spectacularly beautiful, a characteristic feature of most Mauryan sculpture.

Terracotta figurines, Patna Museum

The Didarganj Yakshi is over 2,000 years old, and the lustrous finish of the stone remains soft and shiny even today. This exquisite Yakshi is a well-travelled lady, having been taken to many Indian exhibitions abroad, and it would be a pity if you missed seeing her.

The galleries upstairs exhibit bronzes and terracottas. The **bronze gallery** has many famous examples of early Buddhist figures, the standing Buddha, *Bodhisattva* and others.

The **terracotta collection** is very special. The pieces on display were uncovered during excavations at Pataliputra, Kosambi, Gaya and other important centres of the **Mauryan** and **Gupta empires**. The terracottas are of several varieties, made using differing techniques, and for a wide range of functions. There are charming baked clay **toy animals** and **figurines** of women, couples and deities, all prepared from moulds.

The most characteristic quality of clay is that it is very 'impressionable' and records even the minutest of details. These clay figures were made by hand, modelled with features pinched and patted into shape by the artists' fingers. Punched designs for jewellery and ornaments have been worked on to the surface of the soft clay with a design stylus or stick. The figures were then sun-dried, and some were baked in a kiln. The variety of terracotta objects records the sensitive observation of nature by the artists. They only confirm the brilliance of the artists of this region so many centuries ago. Even today, in village fairs and *melas*, clay toys and figurines are sold, a sign of the continuity of tradition in the ancient arts of pottery-making and sculpting terracottas.

State Museum.
Budh Road,
PATNA.
Bihar.

Hours: 10.30 am–4.30 pm except on Mondays and government holidays.

Admission: nominal.

Suggested viewing time: at least an hour.

Pune (Maharashtra)

The Raja Dinkar Kelkar Museum

There are few museums in India that are as inspired as the Kelkar Museum. The museum contains the collection of a dedicated lover of Indian art, the late Dinkar Kelkar. He has spent almost 60 untiring years travelling and purchasing objects from the remotest villages and towns of India. Kelkar's passion and sense of humour are reflected in every item of the collection, and his contribution to the study and preservation of art has already become a legend.

The Kelkar Museum confines its collections to the **arts of everyday life**: pots, lamps, containers, nutcrackers, pen stands and the like — objects that one would find in the homes of the village landlord, the farmer, the merchant and shopkeeper. It is fascinating to see how things used in the home were designed perfectly to suit their function and use. The artist's touch on simple utility items, in both decoration and design, made the objects unique for the owner. These everyday arts can he classified according to the materials and techniques with which they are made. There are a variety of things made out of wood, from **carved doors** to **toys**. One can also look at objects according to their function, to study the diversity of forms and the ingenuity of the artists from different parts of India. Here there is an assortment of **oil lamps** in a variety of media from clay to brass, each with its own form and shape. Both these approaches, material and function, provide an exciting entrée to the museum.

Woodcarvings

The Kelkar Museum is fitted with some splendid wooden **doors** and **windows** from Rajasthan, Gujarat and south India. The entrance, or doorway, to a house or to the inner sanctum of a temple has a significance not only in India but everywhere in the world. It is the door that welcomes, the door that opens into the home, the door that the public encounters, and hence its special significance. The horizontal beam above the door, under which you pass, often carries the figure of a deity, the most auspicious being Ganesh the elephant-headed god, and Lakshmi the goddess of wealth who brings prosperity and blessings to those who pass through the portals.

The carving of wood in India was undoubtedly the forerunner of stone carving. Many of the early Buddhist stupas and Hindu temples almost imitate woodwork in the more permanent material of stone, such as in the recessed doorway, the pot bases for pillars, and even in joints. Today it is still possible to see carved and painted doors and windows in Rajasthan and Gujarat. Those of Karnataka and Kerala are different in style, and have a solid elegance with the minimum of carved detail.

In India, there are a variety of trees available that are excellent for carving. The range of wood runs from dark, warm brown or rose-wood to the pale biscuit colour of sandalwood and from the hardest of wood types to the softness of pith. Wood that can be preserved by oil and polish is left to acquire its own sheen, and other wooden objects are decorated with paint to make their surfaces both more durable and cheerful. Other items fashioned out of wood are chests, decorative spice boxes (imagine the colour of the spices in them), toys, cradles and walkers for the young. The joy of such crafts is that very often the craftsmen knew the clients and fashioned each item according to their specific needs.

Metalware

The range of metalware — from locks, to ink pots, ritual bowls, hookah stands (hubble-bubbles), nutcrackers and lamps is quite remarkable.

Lamps in India can be broadly divided into two categories those used for ritual purposes ('*arati*' is 'worship with light') and those used purely functionally, to provide illumination in the home. Light in India has a very powerful religious and philosophical significance. Light is the dispeller of darkness and ignorance, and all lamps, even the simple ones of clay, have some motif or figure that sanctifies the object that is the bringer of light. The lamps are usually small open containers, often made very shallow to contain the oil or ghee, and the wick that was made from rolled cotton. The light of a flickering lamp playing on other objects, casting agile shadows, adds to its beauty. Sacred emblems like the peacock, the goddess Lakshmi, elephants and birds are the most common decorations. There are also hanging lamps, that were suspended on heavy (often ornate) brass chains, and standing lamps used in the temple and the home.

The collection of **locks** includes some humorous, rather playful locks in the form of dogs, horses and even a scorpion. These locks were used on doors and trunks, and had ingenious locking mechanisms and keys. It was as if the artist was striving to make each object more endearing to the owner, however mundane the function of the item may have been. There are also **nutcrackers** embellished with impossible figures of embracing couples, goddesses, riders on horseback and many other designs — some quite bizarre, others quite elegant. With the traditional customs of betel-nut chewing and *pan* (betel leaf) eating came the **boxes and intricately** designed containers for these leafy digestives. Perforated boxes (to keep the leaf fresh) gave the craftsmen scope for unlimited experimentation in form and embellishment, and a generous sample of these boxes is on view at this museum.

Dinkar Kelkar had many dreams. One of them was to add a representative sample of Indian textiles, puppets and musical instruments to the museum collection. He started the collection with household objects, and through his efforts has given us a sense of pride in things that in India were always taken for granted — the simple elegance of articles to be found in the traditional Indian home which today is being inundated with mass-produced industrial goods and kitsch.

There is also an interesting collection of the **Chitrakathi paintings** of Maharashtra. These scroll paintings were used by the village storyteller, to the accompaniment of music and song. The pictures are bold and very graphic. The scrolls were held up before the audience during the narration, to illustrate various scenes and episodes from the story. Regional variations of the *Mahabharata* and the *Ramayana* epics also formed part of the repertoire of the storyteller. Something of the leather puppet traditions of Karnataka and Andhra Pradesh is reflected in these Chitrakathi paintings. The dazzling colour scheme of red, blue and black, and the pale, off-white background must have produced a dramatic effect in the village lamplight, or in the fading sunlight at a village fair, where the storyteller was able to assemble his audience. The clear, dark outlines, the high profiles of figures with their large eyes, and the easily identifiable character portraits must have assisted the narrators greatly in the relating of the story. The pictures are just one facet of the whole art of storytelling, which played an important role in Indian village life. Each region of the country has its own narrative style, handed down from generation to generation — large repertory of myths and religious legends. Into the myth the storyteller wove issues that concerned the life of the audience, political comment, satire, references to change and the present day. It was this aspect of culture that was dynamic, in the true spirit of Indian philosophy, keeping the arts always in pace with the times.

Raja Dinkar Kelkar Museum,
PUNE,
Maharashtra

Hours: 10 am–5 pm except government holidays.
Admission: nominal.
Suggested viewing time: half an hour.

Sanchi (Madhya Pradesh)

The Archaeological Museum

In 1818 General Taylor of the Bengal Cavalry chanced upon a discovery that brought to light the **stupas, temples and monasteries of Sanchi Hill**, 68 kilometres (42 miles) from Bhopal, the capital of Madhya Pradesh. The earliest explorations and subsequent excavations by Sir John Marshall, recorded in the work, *The Monuments of Sanchi*, describe in detail this flowering of Indian sculptural art under the Buddhists and Hindus over a period that stretches from the third century BC to the 13th century. The sculptured panels of the Sanchi stupas I and II have no parallel in the world. They were conceived as didactic sculptures to inform the devotee visiting the stupa of the life and work of the Buddha in his many incarnations. The sculptures are full of vitality, abounding in detail of animals and birds, rivers and trees. The charming figures of royalty, and tree, nymphs, processions, street and forest scenes speak of a joy and a harmony brought about by the gentle teachings of the Buddha. In a later Mahayana period, the figure or human form of the Buddha was portrayed seated in meditation or standing to offer protection and blessings.

The collection of broken and damaged sculptures found around this site needed to be stored and preserved. This is why the **site museum at Sanchi** was established and now stands at the base of the hill. The collection can be divided broadly into: excavated tools, implements, pottery and coins; caskets and containers which were once enshrined in the stupas; and sculptures of the **Hinayana, Mahayana and Hindu periods**.

It is believed that Emperor Ashoka of the **Mauryan dynasty** first constructed a brick stupa here which was renovated later with stone. Throughout his kingdom Ashoka erected pillars with sculpted animal capitals. On these columns were engraved Ashoka's celebrated edicts, directing citizens to the way of the Buddha and enunciating the laws of the empire. In the museum is a **lion capital of an Ashokan pillar**, with four lions facing in the four cardinal directions. They stand on a base with a pattern of geese and plants, and below is the huge upturned lotus, like a bell, that was placed on top of the free-standing pillar. The celebrated lion capital found at Sarnath in Uttar Pradesh is similar to this one, with only

Eastern gateway to Stupa No. 1, Satavahana period, second century BC;
Sanchi, Madhya Pradesh

some minor variations in design, and the latter now serves as the emblem of the Indian Republic.

There are other **early sculptures**: parts of the railings and gateways of the stupas. The **Yakshi figures**, of young women with one raised arm that holds on to a branch of a tree, must be Sanchi's most beautiful and sensuous sculptures. The softly swelling contours of the female body, the graceful relaxed stance, the suggestive clothing and jewellery make these statues memorable.

Further, in the galleries are **figures of the Buddha seated** in meditation, in the *dhyana mudra* (pose). The deep folds of his garments have an almost decorative quality. The artist, struggling to find the appropriate facial expression for the Buddha, has given him a happy little smile. There are other **figures of the Buddhist pantheon**, too: **Padmapani** and **Vajrapani**, both *Bodhisattava* or 'Buddhas-in-the-making', one holding a lotus and the other the *vajra*, or thunderbolt.

Among the **early medieval Hindu Sculptures** there are figures of deities like Vishnu, Ganesh, Mahishasuramardini, Gajalakshmi (Lakshmi, the Goddess of Prosperity, being bathed by two elephants) and many others.

The museum issues publications, including a guide to the museum collection.

Archaeological Museum,
SANCHI,
Madhya Pradesh

Hours:	10 am–5 pm everyday except on Fridays.
Admission:	nominal, Rs5 (same ticket for the site visit and the museum), free for children.
Suggested viewing time:	half an hour

Seated Buddha from Archaeological Site Museum, Sanchi

Sarnath (Uttar Pradesh)

The Archaeological Museum

There is something very beautiful and moving about a visit to Sarnath, like visiting the garden of Gethsemane in Jerusalem or Mount Sinai where Moses received the Ten Commandments. It is not difficult to imagine a quiet, peaceful, shady forest grove here, where deer roamed freely and birds went about their noisy business. Over 2,500 years ago, the Buddha, after years of penance and meditation, attained enlightenment in Bodhgaya and travelled to the Deer Park at Sarnath where he delivered his first sermon, teaching his first disciples his doctrine of peace.

Excavations at Sarnath have revealed the establishment of monasteries and the erection of stupas that brought hundreds of thousands of Buddhist pilgrims to the place where the Buddha discussed his philosophy and set up the first order, or *sangha*, of monks. Sculptures and artifacts from this site have been stored in the museum at Sarnath, and in their stony silence they commemorate the acts of faith and devotion of successive rulers and patrons of Buddhism, from the **Mauryan period** (second century BC) to the 13th century.

The first sculpture to be encountered in the museum is the huge **lion capital** (2.31 metres or 7.5 feet in height) that was adopted as the emblem of the Republic of India. This capital once surmounted a pillar and is said to have been erected by the Mauryan emperor Ashoka (second century BC) to mark the site where the Buddha preached and started the first monastic order of Buddhism. The capital is made of a pale yellowish-grey sandstone, with soft black speckles. The entire sculpture has been burnished and the surface still glows today. The capital comprises four lions facing the cardinal directions, each with a tidy mass of thickly curled mane, and a mouth that curls in a snarl (or grin) to ward off evil. Below, on the abacus, are four wheels, the symbols of the law of *dharma*, progress and movement. Separating the wheels are a bull, an elephant, a lion and a horse — symbols of devotion, strength, power and speed respectively. Below the abacus (the flat upper part of the capital), a huge inverted lotus bulges out to join the pillar below. Emperor Ashoka is also said to have built a stupa here — the brick construction of this shrine is at the core of the **Dhamekh Stupa** at Sarnath — to commemorate the place where Buddha sat to deliver his first lesson.

*Buddha with hand raised in abhaya or protection, Gupta period,
fifth century; Archaeological Museum, Sarnath*

Towards the left-hand wall of the entrance hall are two seated figures of the Buddha, one of which, entitled **Buddha Preaching Law** (fifth century), sums up the historic events of Sarnath. The Buddha is seated, his hands in the gesture of the 'turning of the wheel of law'. Below his seat is a wheel, together with some of his followers and early disciples, and some deer to indicate the Deer Park of Sarnath. The wheel of law — the *dharma chakra* — became a symbol for the Buddha's teaching. The Buddha's body is framed by an ornate halo, reflecting the designs to be found on the **Gupta stone renovations** of the Dhamekh Stupa at Sarnath.

Two colossal statues frame the lion capital, one of which is a *Bodhisattva* of the first to second centuries. The sculpture is massive, in the style of early Kushana art. The figure is draped in a fine toga caught at the waist by a sash; the moving body is clearly visible under the fabric, and between its legs is a tiny little lion.

Around the room and along the gallery to the right are several **figures of the Buddha**, standing with one arm raised in the gesture of *abhaya* (protection, reassurance and blessing). It is as though during the **Gupta** period, when Buddhism received royal patronage, a craft centre developed here at Sarnath, akin to a factory, producing a number of similar figures of the Buddha for widespread distribution. Each of the figures is well proportioned, slim and elongated. The **Gupta style of carving**, having mastered the technique, brought to the Buddha's youthful face an expression of peace and inner tranquility. The tight curls on his head, and the topknot, arched eyebrows, the half-closed, meditative eyes, the perfect nose and unselfconscious mouth are carved in perfect proportion, so as not to suggest even the slightest glimmer of action or loss of control. It is the face of peace, that reflects a tranquil mind and a gentle philosophy.

Also on display at the museum are several fragments of Hindu sculptures, parts of the decorated buildings and monasteries, tools and implements, and terracottas excavated from the site.

The Archaeological Survey of India has some publications on Sarnath that are inexpensive and very reliable. These can be purchased at the ticket office, at the entrance gate of the museum.

The Archaeological Museum,
SARNATH,
Uttar Pradesh.

Hours:	10 am–4.30 pm every day except on Fridays and government holidays.
Admission:	same ticket for the museum and site.
Suggested viewing time:	an hour, including a walk around the excavations at Sarnath.

Srirangapatnam (Karnataka)

The Tipu Sultan Museum

It is in memory of a remarkable historical personality, 'Sahib Tipu', the Sultan and hero of Mysore, that one must mention this museum. Tipu's father, Hyder Ali of Mysore, fought bravely against the advancing British armies in an effort to protect his kingdom. In 1782 Hyder Ali died, leaving his throne to his son, Tipu Sultan. Battle after battle followed, and the 'Tiger of Mysore' held his own, while all other rulers in the region surrendered to British pressure and made alliances with the foreign rulers. Wellesley, the British governor-general, sought to buy control over Indian territory through his policy of subsidiary alliances, which enabled him to subordinate the Indian states to the authority of the British East India Company. British forces were stationed in these states, and the puppet rulers paid them for their protection.

Tipu Sultan refused to comply with this policy. 'Better to die like a soldier than live as a miserable dependant on the infidels,' he said, and tried to strengthen his position through an alliance with France. The British army attacked, storming Tipu's fort at Srirangapatnam, in 1799. There are paintings in the museum of this campaign. It was at the fort in Srirangapatnam that Tipu met his end, fighting heroically as a soldier should, on 4 May 1799. His exemplary courage in the battles against the British will always be remembered. Arthur Wellesley, the future Duke of Wellington, wrote about the massacre that followed:

> Nothing therefore can have exceeded what was done on the night of the 4th. Scarcely a house in the town was left unplundered, and I understand that in camp jewels of the greatest value, bars of gold ... have been offered for sale ....

A simple gravestone marks the place where Tipu was wounded and found dead. But it was in happier days that Tipu Sultan had built the **Summer Palace** called the Dariya Daulat ('Splendour of the Sea'), near the Srirangapatnam fort, in 1784. Laid out in a vast, formal garden, the palace, a neat charming structure, stands in the centre. The palace walls have been elaborately painted with panels and decorative motifs. On one wall there is a mural painting of a procession with Hyder Ali and Tipu on horseback.

The museum housed in the *Dariya Daulat* contains many **items and personal belongings of Tipu and his family**. There are articles of furniture, some of French origin, and rich tapestries and coverlets. Upstairs there are more galleries, and from here one can get a good view of the ornate interior of the palace. There are several portraits of members of Tipu's family, including his young, handsome but unfortunate sons. There are paintings and prints done by British artists of the army, and others, who documented the tragic events of *The Storming of Srirangapatnam* and the *Fall of Tipu and the Imprisonment of His Children*. There are several articles of clothing said to have belonged to Tipu, including some of his swords and shields used both in battle and for ceremonial purposes.

Coins and documents fill in the rest of the picture puzzle that make up the story of Tipu. Though the paintings and the historical recording of events were done by the British, the image of Tipu Sultan always stands proud, dignified and firm, as that of an exemplary hero.

Tipu Sultan Museum,
Summer Palace,
SRIRANGAPATNAM,
Karnataka

Hours:	10 am–5 pm except government holidays.
Admission:	nominal, Friday free.
Suggested viewing time:	one hour. The garden area is a lovely place to sit and relax.

Daulat Dariya, *Tipu's Summer Palace, Srirangapatnam*

Thanjavur (Tamil Nadu)

The Thanjavur Art Gallery

A remarkable collection of **south Indian sculptures and paintings** is housed in the old palace buildings at Thanjavur (Tanjore). Thanjavur has been an art centre of great importance throughout almost the entire history of Tamil Nadu. During the **Chola period**, two magnificent temples were built in this region, the **Brihadeswara Temple** and the **Gangaikondacholapuram Temple** (tenth to 11th centuries). Today, the town is a flourishing centre for bronze sculptures, stonework and paintings.

The palace was originally built by the Nayak rulers of Tamil Nadu. It was this dynasty that added to and enlarged many of the temples, with ornate and often huge sculptures. The palace building, set within a large compound, also contains the Saraswati Library and the Sangeetha Sabha, or Music Hall.

Within the museum there is a gallery with a representative collection of **stone sculptures from the Pallava, Chola, Pandya** and **Nayaka periods**.

Another gallery contains samples of the characteristic **glass paintings of Tanjore**. There are two principal traditions in this style of painting of south India, especially Thanjavur. Every Hindu home is supposed to have a prayer room, where the family deity is installed after the house is built. These household images of gods and goddesses are in bronze, silver or clay or are painted pictures. The paintings are done on wood, using a variety of colours, and to enhance the pictures, details of jewellery and clothing are added by attaching gold leaf, paper, semi-precious and precious gems. The stones are stuck on to the painting, adding colour, highlighting areas of sparkling light and giving the painting an almost three-dimensional depth. Another later tradition is of producing paintings on glass, which is more durable than cloth or paper. A sheet of glass is cut to size, and tempera colours are used along with gold paper and stones to 'construct' a painting.

Gradually even secular art was produced in this latter style. Since these works were produced for a larger audience (than, for example, bronze sculptures), the content and form were adapted to the interests of lay viewers. The Tanjore paintings are, therefore, full of bold forms in bright colours, where the artists' attention has been focused on evolving striking

Frescoes from Daulat Dariya

outlines accentuated by jewelled earrings, necklaces, bangles, armlets and anklets.

This museum is however best known for its **bronze sculpture collection**, of rare artistic quality. It is, of course, impossible here to describe all the 400 or more pieces, but mention will be made of a few outstanding works which, if you are lucky, will be in this museum and not travelling in exhibitions around the world. The **Kalyanasundaramurti** (Tiruvengadu district, early Chola), the **images of Shiva and Parvati at the time of their marriage**, is truly a masterpiece, one of India's finest bronzes of all time. In this sculpture, Shiva stands regal and tall, with one arm around his young wife Parvati. The proportions of the two figures are perfect and the artist has delicately captured the slight swelling of the tummy above the garments, the weight of Parvati's breasts, and the slim, elegant limbs that carry the figures. In the creation of textures, the artist has taken great pains to render with immense clarity the limpness of cloth, the natural curve and fall of ribbons and bands, and the hard, metallic quality of the jewellery, which contrasts so dramatically with the smoothness of the skin textures. It is also a very romantic sculpture, for in Hindu mythology the marriage of Shiva and Parvati was a great event in which all the other gods participated. Parvati the beautiful 'daughter of the Himalaya', undertook an arduous period of penance to attract and hold the attention of Shiva. As an ascetic and thinker, Shiva had no desire to be married, or to be interrupted in his meditation. Parvati persisted, and the other gods insisted, and eventually Shiva agreed to marry. At this marriage, Shiva appeared for the first time, so it is said, as a prince, and he is portrayed as such in this sculpture. Usually, he is the 'wild one', an ascetic not caring what he wears, which was often next to nothing, his body covered with ash and dust. Parvati, his equal in strength and magnificence, is shown here as a young girl, almost shy, her petite frame standing beside the towering figure of Shiva. Tile sculptures glow like burnished copper and gold, an effect created by an alloy specially made of five metals considered to be an auspicious combination for ritual bronzes.

Another sculpture — the **Bhikshatanamurti** — is of Shiva in a different mood. *Bhikshu* means 'mendicant', and in this sculpture Shiva is shown standing wearing little else but wooden sandals, jewellery and a snake wrapped around his waist. Beside him is the pretty form of a dancing deer, which stands on its hind legs to reach up to Shiva's outstretched arm. In the other hand Shiva carries a shallow bowl-like object which is the cause of his predicament.

Brahma, the old god of creation, is said to have lusted after his own daughter. In anger, Shiva struck him, cutting off one of his five heads, and this skull of Brahma's head gets attached to Shiva's palm, like a begging bowl. Shiva becomes a mendicant, going from place to place, like Lady Macbeth trying to get rid of the stain of murder, it is only when he bathes in the Ganga River at Banaras that he is absolved of the 'sin' of murdering a Brahmin and a god. This is why that spot on the river at Banaras is sacred to the Hindus, who flock there in their thousands to take a dip absolving them of sin, and even to die and be cremated there, to end the cycle of rebirth into lives of sin and misery. In this sculpture, Shiva's face is austere and serious, and his hair is wild and filled with symbols of his power — the crescent moon, the skull, the *datura* flower and the snake, for he is conqueror of Time and Death.

Another brilliant sculptural piece is the **Vrishabhantika with the Devi**. Shiva here has one arm raised and bent, as if he were leaning on his bull, Nandi. The Devi, also part of this piece, is an individual sculpture of great beauty and elegance.

Thanjavur Art Gallery,
Palace Buildings,
THANJAVUR,
Tamil Nadu.

Hours:	9 am–1 pm; 3–6 pm except government holidays, especially those of importance in south India.
Admission:	Nominal.
Suggested viewing time:	An hour at least.

Thiruvananthapuram (Kerala)

The Government Museum

This museum was founded in 1857. The area around it has been laid out as a park and **zoological garden**. The museum has a fine collection in its natural history section.

The art collection covers aspects of Kerala's rich heritage in sculptures of stone, wood and metal. Though succeeding periods of Kerala history brought this region under several different rulers, Kerala developed a unique style of craftsmanship in the visual and performing arts. The **gallery of bronzes** shows the marked style of Kerala as quite clearly distinct from that of the **bronzes of Tamil Nadu** where, under the **Cholas**, bronzes tended to be tall and almost unnaturally slim. The Kerala bronzes of the same period are shorter and stockier, with characteristic physical features — squarish jaws and sharp eyes and nose; they also tend to be more ornate, with heavy jewels and elaborate clothing. **Vishnu Srinivasa** (ninth century, Kerala) is one of the oldest pieces in this museum. Later

Shiva the Mendicant, bronze, 12th century,
Government Museum, Thiruvananthapuram

figures of **Nataraja**, various devis and others follow in the same style, with conspicuous jewellery and other elegant details.

Wood sculptures for the adornment of temples in Kerala are also common. Here the majority of temples are slightly different in plan and design from other temples in India. The plan is often circular for the main shrine, and wooden beams, pillar brackets and tiled roofs are favoured in the wet tropical climate of Kerala. Wood was also used to make huge carved chariots for temple processions, too convey carrying the deity through the streets. The **wooden chariots** displayed in the museum are richly carved with sculptures and decorative motifs. Kerala still produces some of India's most valuable and handsome wood for carved furniture and sculpture.

Government Museum,
TIRUVANANTHAPURAM,
Kerala

Hours:	8 am–6 pm except government holidays.
Admission:	Free.
Suggested viewing time:	An hour or more. Also, include a visit to the zoo.

Varanasi (Uttar Pradesh)

The Bharat Kala Bhavan

The city of Varanasi (or Banaras), evokes a thousand vivid images. It is one of the oldest cities in the world, most ancient pilgrimage centres for Hindus, and the Ganga River, on the banks of which it is located, is believed to absolve all the sins of those who take a ceremonial dip in its holy waters, even those of gods like Shiva. Within the environs of Varanasi is Sarnath, an important place for Buddhists, for it was here that the Buddha preached his first sermon after gaining enlightenment, or *nirvana*. In **Mughal times** and thereafter, Varanasi, or Banaras as it is also called, continued to play a crucial role in Indian history, as a centre of learning, philosophy, religion and art. The craft tradition is still strong here, and Varanasi is famous for its exquisite **silk weaving, brocades, pottery** and **metalware.** Located within the city is the famous Banaras Hindu University, with its sprawling campus of buildings and shady avenues. It is here that the Bharat Kala Bhavan is situated; a museum with an outstanding collection of Indian sculpture, painting and textiles. The museum originated with the private collection of a single individual, Rai Krishnadasa. After it was transferred to the university in 1950, donations from others enriched the collection.

The museum is fairly well maintained; the labelling is adequate, and there is space enough to view the objects comfortably. You may, however, have to ask the attendants to switch on the lights as you enter the galleries, as they seem keen on conserving energy, and rightly so!

Indian Sculptures
Since the objects in this museum tend to be moved around quite a bit, it is best to classify and describe them in a manner that makes identification possible wherever they might he placed. The sculptures can be grouped in three broad categories: (1) terracotta and clay figures (2) stone sculptures and (3) bronze and cast metal objects.

The museum has a fine collection of **ancient Indian terracottas**, some found in excavations in and around Varanasi itself. Most of them date back to the **Mauryan, Sunga** and **Gupta** periods; a few belong to prehistoric times, unearthed at the Indus Valley sites. **Indus Valley**

(overleaf) Scene from Bhagavad Purana, Pahari, 18th century, Bharat Kala Bhavan, Banaras

terracottas have a special charm; they are often tiny — only two or three centimetres (an inch) in height. Other larger ones belong to the Gupta period.

Terracotta figurines were produced in a variety of ways. Some were modelled by hand, with the application of decorative motifs and punched designs; others have clearly been impressed with designs from a mould, the soft clay pressed onto the mould taking a reverse impression of the mould design. The designs of the terracotta figurines range from charming animal figures, such as the elephant and rider, and horses, to others of women and deities — like the powerful **Head of Shiva**, with its flowing locks adorned with the crescent moon and scenes from everyday life. The elaborate detail on each tiny terracotta figurine is quite astonishing, especially in the jewellery and costuming of the figures and the rendering of musical instruments, hairstyles and facial expressions. Terracotta sculptures served different purposes — as religious offerings in temples, as objects of worship and as toys for children — for in India clay has retained its original philosophical associations as a symbol for Mother Earth throughout the ages.

There is an entire gallery of Indian terracottas on the first floor and some objects are also displayed on the ground floor, in glass cabinets.

On the ground floor, one entire gallery is devoted to **stone sculptures**, a collection of masterpieces of different styles and from various periods of history. Just past the entrance to the gallery, to your right, the wall space has been divided into niches, each containing a sample collection of items illustrating one style of Indian sculpture. The earliest ones are Buddhist. There are a few relief sculptures in red sandstone from Bharhut, dating back to the second century BC. There was once a huge stupa at Bharhut which fell into ruin; fragments of the sculptured railings and relief panels were rescued and are preserved in the Indian Museum, Calcutta (see the section on it in this book). In this gallery there are two interesting objects from this source. One is a **Yakshi on an Elephant Mount**, a tall figure carved onto a vertical railing post. The yakshi's height gives an indication of the massive proportions of the railing and the stupa, that no longer exist.

The yakshi figures of Bharhut, in relatively low relief, are characterised by a style of carving in which great care was taken to refine representation of the female figure, and in providing every detail of jewellery, hairstyle and texture of fabric worn by the guardians of the stupa.

Along the crossbars of the railing, the artist decorated the stone beams with rosettes, lotus medallions and circular narrative panels depicting the *Jataka* tales. The *Timingila Jataka* (Bharhut, second century BC) is depicted here in stone. The story is similar to that of Noah's Ark. The circular panel is packed with narrative details. The upper half shows a boat with just the heads of people peeping over its side. The lower half of the circle is filled with the crescent-shaped body of a giant fish, with mouth opened wide as it swallows the boat and all those on board. The artist, in a lively, almost comic style has reduced the story to its bare essentials and the cause, effect, the first scene and the last, are all shown in one panel.

There is one beautiful and rare sculpture from Amaravati of the first century entitled, **Buddha Taming the Mad Elephant, Nalagiri**, in which the figure of the Buddha is shown standing straight and fearless on one side, while the elephant that was running riot stumbles to the ground to render obeisance to the Buddha, who miraculously quietens his rage.

There are two elegant sculptures of the **Kushana period** (second century) in this museum. These also formed part of a railing for a Buddhist stupa, but in size they are very much smaller than those from Bharhut. One, entitled **Toilet Bearer**, is from Mathura. It depicts a woman carrying a jug of exquisite proportions, with elaborate carving, in one hand; in her other hand she carries a wicker basket, with a conical cover, overflowing with trinkets. The figure of the woman is delicately carved, adorned with jewellery, with belts of many loops and chains worn round her waist to support the lower garment that falls gracefully, clinging to her lovely legs. Her arms and legs are covered with bracelets and anklets, and one can almost hear them jingling as she walks away to complete her toilet.

The second Kushana sculpture is from the first century (Mathura). It is a rather mischievous one of a **Lady Riding a Griffon**, in which the woman, with an elaborate hairstyle, sits on a griffon that grimaces in an effort to free himself from the control of the woman who pulls firmly on the bit in his beak.

The next alcove has some interesting sculptures from Gandhara, the north-western region of India that was a famous Buddhist area. In the sculpture of what is called **Sundari and Nanda** (third century, Gandhara), the scene is set in a room with distinctive Corinthian pillars that mark the **Graeco-Roman influence** on this region. The figures centre around a seated man (possibly Nanda) who is contemplating whether to join the Buddha and his monastic order.

Beside him is his gorgeous wife, appropriately named Sundari ('the beautiful one'), who is the cause of Nanda's predicament. Whether or not he can leave her and become a monk is the dilemma posed in this story. Sundari is shown seated, with an attendant combing her hair. It is a masterpiece, almost theatrical in detail, and important because it shows how Indian and foreign influences were synthesised in the **Gandhara School**.

There are some damaged, sculptured **heads of the Buddha** that are almost skull-like, depicting a stage in Buddha's meditation during which he practised severe penance in search of the path to truth and enlightenment. The Buddha (fortunately) found that neither extreme asceticism nor extreme hedonism led to happiness and knowledge, and he therefore preached that the Middle Path and a balanced life lead to true wisdom and joy.

There are many sculptures of **Surya, the Sun God**, whom art historians believe was a deity adopted from foreign lands, for he is the only Hindu god shown wearing boots in sculptures. One such sculpture of Surya, belonging to the Gupta period (sixth century), has a distinctly Persian or Zoroastrian appearance. Surya is shown standing, his tunic held in place by an ornate metal belt with a very interesting buckle, and his hair is in ringlets and layered curls.

From central India of the tenth and 11th centuries come a few outstanding sculptures of which this museum has reason to be proud: **Hara Gauri** (Chandella period, 11th century, from the Banaras region); **Brahma** (11th century, central India) seated on his vehicle the *Hansa*; and **Mahishasuramardini Durga** (11th century, Banaras), the powerful goddess slaying the demon bull Mahisha, whom she has caught by his hair, her multiple arms full of energy; her body swaying diagonally, her foot resting on her companion tiger, as she inflicts the fatal blow of destruction on evil.

Among the **Shiva sculptures** on display, the one entitled **Ravana Nugraha Murti** (tenth century) is the most poetic. The story narrated here is of Ravana, the ten-headed king of Lanka, who, in his ego clouded by ignorance dared to threaten the gods. The lower portion of the sculpture shows Ravana shaking the Mountain of Kailash where Shiva and Parvati are seated. The mountain forms a wavy line marking off the lower half of the composition. Above, Shiva is sitting relaxed, one of his hands holding a trident, his elegant fingers unperturbed by Ravana's efforts to shake up his kingdom. One hand is in the *abhaya mudra*, the gesture of protection and reassurance.

So unperturbed is Shiva, despite all the commotion, that the *naga* or snake that Shiva wears like a piece of jewellery around his body has taken

*Marriage of Shiva Parvati, Chandella period, 11th century, Khajuraho,
Bharat Kala Bhavan, Banaras*

time off to sniff the flower that Shiva holds in one hand a touch of creative
humour by an anonymous but great artist. Shiva's arm also reaches out to
embrace Parvati who is obviously disturbed. She seems to have almost
slipped off his lap, in fear, one hand touching Shiva's leg as if to make
him aware of the terror aroused by Ravana. On her lap is one of her sons,
and her other son Ganesh (the elephant-headed one) sits below them to
one side, his little baby head turned to look at his parents for help. It is a
sculpture full of imminent action, for the story has it that Shiva, merely by
the pressure of his toe, put an end to Ravana's disturbance and crushed
his ego as well. It is the little details — the gesture of a hand, the tilt of a
head, the positioning of minor characters — that make this sculpture so
remarkable.

Another interesting piece depicts the **Marriage of Shiva and Parvati**
(Pratihara school, tenth century, Etah, Uttar Pradesh). This sculpture, the
stances are a trifle, captures the scene of the marriage ceremony that
commemorates the great love of two major deities, the perfect male and
female ideals. For some reason, one will always remember their toes. In
India there is a saying that if your second toe is longer than your big toe

you will dominate your spouse. In this sculpture both Shiva and Parvati have second toes that are longer than the big ones, and one wonders who wins the arguments in their marriage! Perhaps the artist is trying to convey to us that they are both equals, and that their marriage endures for numberless aeons.

Rarely in north India (though often in south India) does one come across a beautiful, solitary sculpture of **Karttikeya**, a son of Shiva and Parvati. There is a **Gupta sculpture** of the fifth century, from the Varanasi region, of the young chief of Shiva's army sitting astride a peacock whose glorious tail spreads out like a canopy behind him. The peacock and its rider, Karttikeya, appear to blend into one another, reflecting the perfect harmony between the deity and his companion.

There is an equally outstanding sculpture of Lord Ganesh, Shiva's other son, in this museum. The **Dancing Ganesh** (Pratihara school, ninth century, Kannauj) is poised for movement, his foot ready for action. The little figure of the Elephant God is surrounded by many pairs of arms that once carried symbols of inconographic importance. Ganesh is dancing to the accompaniment of music played by lively musicians -- even his *vahana* (vehicle), the rat, is dancing to the music -- and the snake that Ganesh wears like a belt has slithered off through the vigour of his rhythmic movements.

The museum has one lovely sculpture from Khajuraho (11th century, Chandella period) which must be the most photographed female figure in the gallery. **Alasa Kanya** is a languorous woman, yearning with desire. Need one say more? With her fingers locked together, she stretches her arms above her head, her young firm breasts and taut body quivering with sensuous longing, filled with the lazy charm of one who knows she is beautiful.

The Museum's Paintings

In the first gallery room as you enter, there is a colossal statue of **Krishna Holding Mount Govardhana** (Gupta, fourth century, Varanasi) and in the painting gallery, towards your left, are two paintings that depict the same story. One is from Kishangarh (18th century, Rajasthan) and the other from Mewar (18th century). This story is of the supersession by Lord Krishna of the older, Vedic god, Indra, the Lord of Thunder. Indra was incensed that the inhabitants of Govardhana (a hillock near Mathura in Uttar Pradesh) were paying more respect to Krishna than to him, so he brought about a huge, terrifying storm. Krishna came to the rescue of the people by raising the hill with one hand and holding it like an umbrella over their heads, to protect the cowherds and the cows. In the paintings, the people crowd under the mountain, sheltered and safe from the storm.

In the painting from Mewar, Indra, astride his magnificent white elephant amidst the rolling clouds, watches the scene of his humiliation. The mountain lifted by Krishna is peopled by animals, sages and hermits. The painting from Kishangarh, in a style very characteristic of this school, has elegant, elongated figures, with stylised faces, long tapering eyes and straight, almost bridgeless noses. The sky, dark with clouds, carries Indra's dramatic and flamboyant signature of lightning and his noisy thunder.

In the Gupta sculpture, of Krishna Holding Mount Govardhana, many of these painted details have been eliminated, and Krishna's youthful body is larger than life as he carries the mountain of rocks and boulders on one hand. His face is calm, the gesture effortless; his long flowing locks are undisturbed, the chain with tiger claws unmoved by the dramatic action implied in the episode. Each of the three renderings of this story is unique, in its own way, and a comparative study such as this offers an insight into Indian art. Bound together though it is by common myths and religious themes, the creative genius of the artist, separated both in time and space, gives to each work a quality that is entirely distinctive.

The most ancient paintings displayed in the gallery are Buddhist in origin. The illustrated text *Astasahasrika Prajnaparamita* is a **Buddhist manuscript** of the 12th century, which has well-composed pages with handwritten text and illustrations of episodes from the life of the Buddha. The long, tapering pages are beautifully designed, broken into sections, with elegant calligraphy and lively paintings in reds, yellow and blues.

From the **Mughal School**, there are some exquisite examples such as the **Scene of an Assault on a Fort**, from the *Hamzanama* (Mughal, Akbar period 1567–82). The style of painting associated with the 'ateliers' of Akbar's court has a distinctive quality and charm. The compositions are bustling; later styles, favoured in the time of his son and his grandson Shah Jahan, are more restrained, with fewer people and less robust action. The '**Akbari Style**' also uses architectural details as a woven pattern in the composition and not as a separate entity. The people are dressed in vibrant hues, patterned garments combining many motifs and colours, with a marked Persian influence in style; even the shields are colourfully decorated. The drama of action and composition of colours is slowly replaced by more subdued hues and subtler shades in subsequent Mughal art. Here in Akbar's period, the art, like the emperor, is strong and dramatic, forthright, and sometimes even cruel.

This museum is known to have a remarkable and famous collection of paintings from the regions of Rajasthan and Kangra, and the other hill states. Unfortunately, only a portion of the vast collection can be displayed.

From the **Pahari–Guler School** of the 18th century, there are some lovely paintings depicting **Radha with Krishna**, their love-making, their trysts and of Radha waiting for her lover to arrive. These paintings have a backdrop of green that represents the forest, shady groves, flowering scented trees, birds and a river rippling by. The sounds evoked in the paintings are poetic, the mood always charged with love. The delicate flowers, like gems, appear to glow, and a certain timeless quality pervades the scene. Radha, ever youthful and eager, though dressed in the most elegant of clothes — her flowing veil, her billowing gathered shirt — is exquisite for the beauty of her face. The artist provides her with an alabaster cream complexion that contrasts beautifully with the bluey-grey of Krishna's body; her gestures are always soft, while his are forward and demanding. The colour of Krishna's *dhoti*, a sunlight mustard yellow, in contrast to his skin tones, highlights his beauty and strength. The couple together, or each alone, are lost in their thoughts, forever young, and forever in love.

The *Approaching Storm* is a very moving painting, full of grace and feeling despite its tiny scale. The composition is simple and quite abstract. Half the painting is filled with huge clouds that appear to be pursuing the young lover. Radha is dressed in most dramatic colours, white and saffron orange, that stand in direct contrast to the grey of the cloud. The colours of the clouds evoke the image of Krishna, who is said to be of that blue-black hue of rain-laden clouds. Krishna, like the rain, brings change and prosperity, growth and joy. Has the artist used the clouds as a metaphor for love? There is something simple yet sensuous about this painting. The strong movements, billowing garments, the forces of nature and the imagined fragrance of rain as it mingles with the parched earth leave a lasting impression.

One of the most maligned characters of Indian history is the Mughal emperor Aurangzeb, the not-so-favourite son of Shah Jahan. Aurangzeb inherited a relatively impoverished treasury from his father, who spent a great deal of money on extravagant building projects including the Taj

Laurak helping Chanda to escape, illustration from the manuscript of the love story of Laur Chanda, pre-Mughal style, circa 1475, Bharat Kala Bhavan Museum, Banaras

Mahal, the new capital in Delhi and the Red Fort. Aurangzeb, in reaction, placed restrictions on art and on expenditure on monumental buildings, and chose instead to lead a simple, pious life, for which history has often condemned him as being 'anti-culture' and a Muslim fanatic. However, at least one indication that he may have been misrepresented can be found in this museum: a *farman* (royal decree) of Aurangzeb's, in beautiful calligraphy, and signed and sealed, proclaims that

> ... therefore, in accordance with the Holy Law, we decided that the ancient temples of Varanasi shall not be overthrown but that new ones shall not he built.
>
> No person will disturb Brahmins and other Hindu residents in those places so that they remain in their occupation and continue with peace of mind to offer prayer. For the continuance of our God-given empire that is destined to last for all time ... you are instructed to follow this decree immediately.

Textiles

The museum has a sizeable and exquisite collection of textiles of which a small sample is on display. The fabrics range from simple cottons, silks and wools to complex woven, embroidered and printed samples. There are some excellent examples of **Banaras silks and brocades** with delicate gold- and silver-thread work. In the collection of **embroidered shawls from Kashmir** are all the colours of the rainbow, creating subtle patterns and designs on the delicate woollen fabric. There are also some good examples of *Chamba rumal*. These richly embroidered cloths carry designs of stories and scenes, often from the life of Krishna. They were used for wrapping ceremonial gifts and offerings.

On the first floor, there are a few galleries dedicated to donors who have given their private collections to the museum. Mention must be made among these of Alice Boner, an old friend of India and scholar of Indian art, whose, research work to the day stands like a beacon for those in the field of art history. She has left some of her own paintings (though these are not very good) and some items from her personal art collection to the museum.

The museum has an attractive set of postcards of miniature paintings for sale, as well as some folios and research monographs.

Krishna saving Gopies from Agha, the demon python, scene from
Bhagavad Purana, *Pahari School, late 18th century,*
Bharat Kala Bhavan Museum, Banaras

Bharat Kala Bhavan,
Banaras Hindu University,
BANARAS,
Uttar Pradesh.

Hours :   11 am–4.30 pm (July–April); 7.30 am–12.30
                                     pm (May–June) except on Sundays and
                                     university holidays.

Suggested viewing time: one hour, at least.

(overleaf) Entrance to the Government State Museum, Chennai

Reference Section

A STATEWISE LIST OF MUSEUMS

[*Museums outlined in this book.]

- All archaeological site museums are closed on Fridays and government holidays. Entrance fees are often the same for the site and the museum.
- Most state museums are closed on Mondays or Fridays. Entrance fees are nominal.
- Most museums are open from 10.30 am–4.30 pm on working days.

ANDHRA PRADESH

Amaravati, Archaeological Museum: A site museum near the remains of the Buddhist stupa (2 BC–AD 2). Sculptures in marble, caskets and other objects related to the site.
Hours: 10 am–5.30 pm. Closed Friday and government holidays.

Hyderabad, Jagdish and Kamla Mittal Museum of Indian Art: Collection of miniatures, bronzes, terracottas and ivory.
Hours: By appointment.

*Hyderabad, Salar Jung Museum: Indian textiles, wood, bronze, jade, armoury, Indian paintings, European sculpture, paintings, Chinese and Japanese art.
Hours: 10 am–5.30 pm. Closed Friday and government holidays,

Hyderabad, State Museum, Public Garden: Good collection of sculpture from Buddhist and Hindu period. Decorative arts, copies of paintings from Ajanta.

Nagarjunakonda, Site Museum: Remnants of exquisite sculptures and architectural details from ancient Buddhist stupa.
Hours: 10 am–5 pm. Closed Friday and government holidays.

ASSAM

*Guwahati, Assam State Museum: Art, sculptures of the region.
Hours: 10 am–4.30 pm. Closed Monday and government holidays.

BIHAR

Bodhgaya, Archaeological Museum: A site museum, near the place where Buddha attained *nirvana*. Objects unearthed in archaeological excavations, sculptures in stone and bronze especially of Pala period.
Hours: 10 am–4.30 pm. Closed Friday.

Nalanda, Archaeological Museum: At the site of the ancient and famous university area of Nalanda. Fine collection of terracotta figurines, pottery, sculptures from Gupta to Pala period.
Hours: 10 am–5 pm. Closed government holidays.

Patna, Department of Ancient Indian History and Archaeology: A good collection of archeological objects.
Hours: (Summer) 6.30–11.30 am; (Winter) 10.30 am–5.30 pm.
Closed on university holidays.

*Patna, State Museum, Budh Road: Exquisite terracottas from Mauryan to Gupta period. Bronze Buddhist sculptures and others including the Didarganj Yakshi, the Mauryan *chauri* bearer.
Hours: 10.30 am–4.30 pm. Closed Monday and government holidays.

Vaishali, Archaeological Museum: A good collection of terracottas, pottery, seals, coins, sculpture and antiques. A library and guide service is also available.
Hours: 10 am–5 pm. Closed Friday.

Stone railing with lotus medallions, Bodhgaya, Bihar

DELHI

Archaeological Museum, Red Fort: Objects connected with history of the fort.
  Hours: 9 am–5 pm. Closed Friday.
Crafts Museum, Pragati Maidan: Village complex, village houses of India.
  Demonstrations by craftspersons. Exhibitions, sale of craft objects made at the
  exhibition.
  Hours: 9.30 am–5 pm. Closed Monday and government holidays.
*The Gandhi Memorial Museum, Raj Ghat
*The Gandhi Smriti Museum, Birla House, Tees January Marg.
  Hours: 9.30 am–5.30 pm. Closed Monday and national holidays.
International Dolls Museum, Nehru House, Bahadurshah Zafar Marg: Dolls from all
  over the world.
  Hours: 10 am–5 pm. Closed Monday and national holidays.
National Museum, Janpath: Indus Civilisation, Mauryan, Gupta period sculptures.
  Medieval sculptures from different schools and parts of India. Excellent bronze
  sculptures and painting gallery. Collection from central Asia and the America.
  Collection of textiles, decorative arts, jewellery, coins. Special exhibitions.
  Hours: 10 am–5 pm. Closed Monday and government holidays.
National Gallery of Modern Art, Jaipur House: Modern art sculptures and paintings
  from the post–1857 period. Sculpture garden.
  Hours: 10 am–5 pm. Closed Monday and government holidays.
National Museum of Natural History, FICCI Building, Barakhamba Road: Special
  galleries on botany, zoology, collections and dioramas of birds, animals, butterflies, etc.

Gallery on environment, ecology, living cell. Special discovery room for children.
Hours: 10 am–5 pm. Closed Monday and government holidays.

*Nehru Memorial Museum and Library, Teen Murti House, Teen Murti: Photo-documentation of National Movement, life and works of Jawaharlal Nehru, India's first prime minister.
Hours: 10 am–5 pm. Closed Monday and government holidays

Rail Transport Museum, Chanakyapuri: Wonderful collection of vintage locomotives, princely saloons, models and photographs. A must for railway fans.
Hours: 9.30 am–5.30 pm. Closed Monday and government holidays

GOA

*Archaeological Museum, Old Goa: Objects related to the history of Goa. Portraits of Vasco da Gama, etc.
Hours: 10 am–5 pm. Closed Friday and government holidays.

GUJARAT

*Ahmedabad, Calico Museum of Textiles, Shanti Bagh Area: Wonderful collection of Indian textiles.
Hours: 10 am–12.30 pm, 2.30–5 pm. Closed Wednesday and government holidays.

Ahmedabad, Gandhi Smarak Sangrahalaya, Harijan Ashram: Life of Mahatma Gandhi.
Hours: 9 am–12 pm; 2.30–7 pm.

*Ahmedabad, Utensils Museum, opposite Vasana toll naka: Collection of Indian utensils -- an assortment of metal pots.
Hours: 10 am–5 pm.

Vadodara, Maharaja Fateh Singh Museum, Laxmi Vilas Palace: Visit to the palace of the Maharaja of Baroda -- the royal collection of art objects from India and abroad.
Hours: 10 am–5 pm. Closed Monday and government holidays.

Vadodara, Museum and Picture Gallery, Sayaji Park: Indian paintings, archaeological artifacts. Art from Japan, China, Nepal, Tibet and Europe.
Hours: 10 am–5 pm. Closed Monday and government holidays

HIMACHAL PRADESH

Chamba, Bhuri Singh Museum: Fine collection of Pahari and other paintings, bronzes, copperplates, historical letters, wood carvings, arms, ornaments, old photographs, coins and manuscripts.
Hours: 10 am–5 pm. Closed Monday and government holidays.

JAMMU AND KASHMIR

Jammu, Dogra Art Gallery: Pahari paintings, armoury, etc.
Hours: 10 am–4 pm. Closed government holidays.

Srinagar, Sri Pratap Singh Museum, Lal Mandi: Miniature paintings, decorative arts, manuscripts and textiles.
Hours: 11 am–4 pm. Closed Friday and government holidays.

KARNATAKA

Badami, Archaeological Museum: Stone sculpture of medieval period.
Hours: 10 am–5 pm. Closed Friday.

Bangalore, Karnataka Government Museum: Archaeology, prehistory, sculptures from Hoysala Chola, Chalukyan period. Paintings, traditional arts of Mysore.

Bijapur, **Archaeological Museum:** A good collection of armoury, porcelain, chinaware, coins, miniatures, manuscripts, carpets and stone sculpture.
Hours: 10 am–5 pm. Closed Friday.

Hampi, **Archaeological Museum:** A site museum with objects unearthed and preserved from the Hampi excavations. Sculpture, coins, etc from Vijayanagar period.
Hours: 10 am–5 pm. Closed government holidays.

Mysore, **Folklore Museum, University of Mysore:** Remarkable collection of arts of Karnataka, especially leather shadow puppets, masks, toys, etc.
Hours: 11 am–5 pm. Closed Sunday.

*Srirangapatnam, **Tipu Sultan Museum, Summer Palace:** Collection associated with Tipu Sultan and family. Paintings, historical documents, prints, textiles, coins, etc.
Hours: 9 am–5 pm. Closed government holidays.

KERALA

Kochi, **Archaeological Museum:** Fine collection of ornaments, dress, weapons and paintings.
Hours: 10 am–5 pm. Closed Friday.

*Thiruvananthapuram, **Government Museum and Art Gallery:** Paintings — Indian, Indo-European, others from China, Japan, etc.
Hours: 8 am–6 pm. Closed government holidays.

Thiruvananthapuram, **Napier Museum:** Arts and crafts, ivory, lamps, musical instruments and paintings.
Hours: 8 am–6 pm. Closed Monday and special holidays.

Thiruvananthapuram, **Shri Chitra Art Gallery:** Collection of paintings, miniatures and copies of mural paintings.
Hours: 8 am–6 pm. (Wednesday) 8 am–1 pm. Closed Monday and a few holidays.

Thrissur, **Archaeological Museum:** Exhibits from Harappan Civilisation, Gandhara sculpture. Archaeological artifacts from Kerala pottery, tools from megalithic sites, sculptures in wood and metal.
Hours: 10 am–5 pm. Closed Friday and government holidays.

MADHYA PRADESH

*Bhopal, **Bharat Bhavan, Shamla Hills:** Tribal arts and contemporary work.
Hours: 10.30 am–5 pm. Closed Sunday and government holidays.

Bhopal, **State Museum:** Collection of sculpture, paintings, objets d'arts and coins.
Hours: 10 am–5 pm. Closed Monday.

Gwalior, **Archaeological Museum:** Sculptures, sati stones, terracottas, etc and paintings.
Hours: 10 am–5 pm. Closed government holidays.

Gwalior, **H H Maharaja Jayaji Rao Scindia Museum, Jai Vilas Palace:** Collection of royal family.
Hours: 11 am–4 pm. Closed Monday and government holidays.

*Khajuraho, **Archaeological Museum:** Masterpieces from temples of Chandella period (tenth-12th centuries) of the vicinity.
Hours: 9 am–5 pm. Closed Friday.

*Sanchi, **Archaeological Museum:** Sculpture, coins, tools, etc found during excavations at this famous Buddhist pilgrimage centre.
Hours: 9 am–5 pm. Closed Friday.

(overleaf) Nayika waiting for her lover with the bed and room prepared, illustration to the Rasamanjari, Basohli, 17th century, Dogra Art Gallery, Jammu

Vidisha, District Museum: Collection of sculpture, inscriptions, terracottas, coins and earthern ware, plaster casts.
Hours: 10 am–5 pm. Closed Monday.

MAHARASHTRA

Mumbai, Bombay Natural History Society: 1750 specimen (human and a few animal specimen) mounted in jars.
Hours: 9.30 am–4.30 pm. Closed Sunday and state holidays.

Mumbai, Dr Bhan Daji Lad Museum (Victor and Albert Museum): Fine collection of armoury, sculpture, pottery, leather work, ivory, manuscripts, paintings, fossil, minerals.
Hours: 10.30 am–5.20 pm. (Sundays) 8.30 am–5.20 pm. Closed Monday and eight important public holidays.

*****Mumbai, Prince of Wales Museum, Mahatma Gandhi Road:** Indian sculpture — Indus Valley Civilisation, Gandhara, different medieval schools. Indian miniature paintings are superb. Tibetan and Nepalese art. European paintings and decorative arts from the Far East.
Hours: 10 am–5 pm. Closed Monday and government holidays.

Nagpur Central Museum: An old museum, with collections from archaeological excavations, Indus Valley Clivilisation. Paintings, epigraphy, numismatics, armoury sections.
Hours: 10 am–5 pm. Closed Monday and government holidays.

Pune, Museum of Deccan College: This college has conducted several excavations. Manuscripts, artifacts, paintings, armoury, etc.
Hours: 11 am–5 pm. Closed Sunday and government holidays.

*****Pune, Raja Dinkar Kelkar Museum:** Superb collection of Indian everyday crafts. Lamps, woodwork, sculpture, textiles, etc.
Hours: 10 am–5 pm. Closed government holidays.

ORISSA

*****Bhubaneswar, Orissa State Museum, Jaydev Marg:** Arts of the region. Sculptures from nearby temples, and palm-leaf manuscripts.
Hours: 10 am–4 pm. Closed Monday and government holidays.

Konarak, Archaeological Museum: At the site of the famous Temple of the Sun, with sculptures from the ruins.
Hours: 9 am–5 pm. Closed Friday and government holidays.

Ratnagiri, Archaeological Museum: Collection of sculpture, pottery, inscriptions, seals, beads and coin.

PUNJAB

Amritsar, Central Sikh Museum: Paintings regarding Sikh history, coins, old arms and manuscripts.
Hours: 7 am–7 pm; (Mondays) 8 am–6 pm. Open on all days.

Chandigarh, Government Museum and Art Gallery, Sector 10/c: Excellent collection of Gandhara sculptures, especially the *Bodhisattvas* paintings from Mughal, Basohli and Kangra schools.
Hours: 10 am–4.30 pm. Closed Monday and government holidays.

Patiala, Arms and Chandeliers Gallery: A collection of arms and chandeliers.
Hours: 10 am–5 pm. Closed Monday.

Patila, Art Gallery: Collection of arts and crafts.
Hours: 10 am–5 pm. Closed Monday.

Patiala, Medal Gallery: Medals, coins and decoration on display.
Hours: Open on request.

RAJASTHAN

*Alwar, Government Museum, City Palace: Paintings, armoury, decorative arts from the Raja's collection.
Hours: 10 am–5 pm. Closed Friday and government holidays.

Bharatpur, Government Museum: Sculptures from the region. Armoury and other crafts.
Hours: 10 am–5 pm. Closed Friday and government holidays.

Bikaner, Ganga Golden Jubilee Museum: Paintings, manuscripts and crafts of the region, see especially textiles of Mughal period.
Hours: 10 am–5 pm. Closed Friday and government holidays.

*Jaipur, Maharaja Sawai Madho Singh Museum, City Palace: Textiles, armoury, paintings and manuscripts.
Hours: 9.30 am–4.30 pm. Closed government holidays.

Jaipur, Government Central Museum, Ram Niwas Gardens: Stonework from regional architecture, metalware, ivory, armoury, paintings, etc.
Hours: 10 am–5 pm. Closed Friday and government holidays.

Jodhpur, Mehrangarh Fort: Exhibits the heritage of the Rathores and Marwar in arms, costumes, paintings, elephant howdahs and palanquins.

Jodhpur, Sadar Museum: Excellent collections of paintings from school of arts in Rajasthan. Armoury, textiles and pottery.
Hours: 10 am–4 pm. Closed Friday and government holidays.

Udaipur, Government Museum, Palace complex: Collection of sculptures and paintings.
Hours: 10 am–5 pm. Closed Monday and government holidays.

TAMIL NADU

*Chennai, Port St George Museum, Beach Road: Armoury, portraits, coins and manuscripts relating to East India Company days and British colonial rule.
Hours: 9 am–5 pm. Closed Friday and government holidays.

*Chennai, Government State Museum, Pantheon Road, Egmont: Sculptures from Buddhist stupa at Amaravati, south Indian stone sculptures, musical instruments, natural history section, south Indian bronzes -- one of the best collections in India.
Hours: 10 am–5 pm. Closed Friday and government holidays.

Madurai, Sri Meenakshi Sundaresvara Temple Museum: South Indian bronzes, paintings, musical instruments, decorative arts and jewellery.
Hours: 10 am–5 pm.

Padmanabhapuram, Palace and Museum: Palace, amazing wooden architecture and sculptures, furniture and other articles. Museum with coins, stone sculpture and assortment of crafts.
Hours: 10 am–5 pm. Closed Monday.

Pondicherry, Pondicherry Museum: Collection of findings at Arikamadu, bronzes of Chola period, armoury, coins and handicrafts.

Pudukottai, Government Museum: Archaeological sections, sculptures, epigraphy and numismatics, other galleries of geology, zoology, etc.
Hours: 10 am–5 pm. Closed Monday.

*Thanjavur (Tanjore), Thanjavur Art Gallery, Palace Building: Exceptional collection of Chola bronzes.
Hours: 9 am–1 pm, 3–6 pm. Closed government holidays.

UTTAR PRADESH

Agra, Archaeological Museum: Collection of paintings, sketches, *farman*, mosaic works and manuscripts.
Hours: 10 am–5 pm. Closed Friday.

Allahabad Museum: Rich collection of sculptures, terracottas (from Bharhut, Khajuraho, Gandhara, Kausambi), coins and archaeological objects. Paintings from 15th century onwards form a good collection, including works of the Mughal, Pahari and Basohli schools.
Hours: 10 am–5 pm. Closed Wednesday and government holidays.

Allahabad, Anand Bhawan: Personal belongings of Jawaharlal Nehru and other members of the family. Picture gallery.
Hours: 9.30 am–5 pm. Closed Monday and government holidays.

*****Banaras, Sarnath Archaeological Museum:** Site Museum, with an excellent collection of early Buddhist sculpture.
Hours: 10 am–4.30 pm. Closed Friday and government holidays.

*****Banaras, Bharat Kala Bhavan, Banaras Hindu University:** Superb collection of Indian sculpture and paintings. Textiles, and other arts.
Hours: Summer (May–June) 7.30 am–12.30 pm; Winter (July–April) 11 am–4.30 pm. Closed Sunday and all university holidays.

Lucknow, State Museum, Banarasibagh: Excellent collection of Buddhist and Jain sculptures. Hindu stone sculptures of importance. Paintings, manuscripts and rich coin collection.
Hours: 10 am–5 pm. Closed Monday and government holidays.

*****Mathura, Government Museum, Dampier Park:** Excellent collection of Buddhist sculpture, Kushana art, terracottas and coins.
Hours: 10 am–5 pm. Closed Monday and government holidays.

WEST BENGAL

Calcutta, Academy of Fine Arts: Rabindranath's paintings and personal belongings, letters, manuscripts, sculpture, old miniature paintings, lithographs and engravings.
Hours: 3–8 pm. Closed Monday.

*****Calcutta, Ashutosh Museum of Art, University of Calcutta:** Terracottas from Vishnupur, Sena sculpture, arts of Bengal.
Hours: 11 am–5 pm. Closed Sunday and university holidays.

Calcutta, Marble Place Art Gallery and Zoo: Fine collection of marble, bronze, wood work, paint, glass and porcelain.
Hours: 10 am–4 pm. Closed Monday and Thursday.

Calcutta, Rabindra Bharati Museum: Collection of Tagore's paintings, photographs, personal effects, books, journals, tapes and disc records.
Hours: 10 am–5 pm, (Saturdays) 10 am–1.30 pm. Closed Sunday, government holidays and university holidays.

*****Calcutta, Indian Museum, 27 Jawaharlal Nehru Road:** Bharhut Buddhist sculptured railings, sculptures from medieval schools. Textiles and other arts. Mineralogy, zoology and anthropology sections.
Hours: Summer (March–November) 10 am–5 pm, Winter (December–February) 10 am–4.30 pm. Closed Monday and government holidays.

*****Calcutta, Victoria Memorial Hall, Queen's Way:** Sculptures, paintings, portraits, prints of the British colonial period. Armoury and personal belongings of Queen Victoria.
Hours: 10 am–4 pm. Closed Monday and government holidays.

Pillared Hall, Temple at Madurai, Tamil Nadu

Indian Iconography and Glossary of Terms

Once in the museum, you are bound to see much more than has been described in the previous chapters. To assist you in recognising some of the objects, a brief description of a few major iconographic details has been given below for your reference.

There are a few points to remember in understanding Indian iconography.

The relevant *Shastras* provide minute instructions of how iconographic details have to be included in creative work. The size of the figures, the length of the eyebrows and fingers, types of hairstyle and so forth are all specified. The creativity of the artist is in the interpretation of these instructions which you will easily discern.

Indian deities are based on a concept of wholeness and the absolute. The gods and goddesses have countless attributes all rolled into one. In icons, the artist is advised to present the deities in one of their many forms, such as their terrifying and commanding aspect or their pacific attitude. This allows for a range of forms of each deity, for example, Shiva acquires the form of Bhairav, the awesome one that quelk fears, and Dakshinamurti, the ascetic teacher. Vishnu acquires the form and incarnation of Narasimha, the lion-headed man devouring an evil demon, and in the role of Rama, the ideal gentle hero of the Ramayana. These diverse forms are employed in art to show the devotee the range and the potential power of the deity. The devotee is asked never to forget that these forms are mere fragments of the entire concept of divinity.

That is why I have classified all the forms, incarnations and representations of one deity under a single heading — for example, Devi: Uma, Parvati, Kali, Durga, etc — to maintain this synthesised concept of Hindu philosophy. Icons, images and paintings are said to have been produced for the lay and ignorant devotee. It was believed that the wise and well-initiated follower had no need for images to evoke the gods. This is quite true as Hindu philosophy is very abstract. Take for example this creation hymn from the Vedas.

> Then even nothingness was not, nor existence.
> There was no air then, nor the heavens beyond it.
> Who covered it? Where was it? In whose keeping?

It was for the temples and worship at home that images were then created to translate abstract philosophical ideas into tangible forms. Therefore, when looking at these forms, the philosophical ideas have to be re-evoked.

Objects of worship

Abhaya The hand gesture of protection.

Agni Lord of Fire. Depicted in human form surrounded by flames, or just as a flame worshipped as part of all major Hindu rituals, as the purifier of the world, the keeper of the hearth, etc.
One of the chief deities mentioned in Vedic literature.

Ananta The infinite. A term applied to Vishnu and others.

Apsaras Celestial nymphs, seen flying above the gods, showering flowers, carrying umbrellas, garlands, etc.

Ardhanarisvara See Shiva.

Arjun One of the five Pandava brothers. See Mahabharata.

Avalokitesvara *Bodhisattva*. See Buddhist art.

Avatars **of Vishnu** See Vishnu.

Balakrishna Baby Krishna. See Krishna under Vishnu.

Balrama Brother of Krishna, worshipped beside Krishna.

Bhagavad Gita Song of the Divine One. Part of *Mahabharata* epic. Philosophical discussion between Arjun and Krishna contains the essence of Hindu philosophy.

Bhumidevi See Vishnu.

Bhumi Personification of the Earth.

Bhudevi Wife of Vishnu.

Bodhi tree See Buddhist art.

Bodhisattva Potential Buddha, renounces *Nirvana* to preach for the benefit of humanity.

Bhagavad Purana Puranic literature devoted to Vishnu with details of the story of Krishna. Often illustrated with paintings.

Bhairava See Shiva.

Buddhist Art

Hinayana Period Third–first centuries BC. The Buddha in this period is given no human form. His presence is represented by the following symbols.

The *pipal* tree Ficus religiosa. A large tree with spreading branches and heart-shaped leaves. It was under this tree that the Buddha attained enlightenment or *Nirvana*; also called *Bodhi* tree.

The empty throne Symbol of honour.

Footprints The presence of the holy one in Buddhist or Hindu iconography is symbolised by footprints with auspicious markings.

Stupa After the Buddha died his body was cremated and the remains divided into portions. A stupa, or funerary mound, was built over the remains, in different parts of the country. It was an object of veneration and a pilgrimage place for Buddhists.

Dharma chakra The Wheel of Dharma. The word dharma has many meanings: duty, the way, the path, action and ideal. The wheel is used to suggest concepts of movement, time, progress and change.

Adoration of the Bodhi *tree, pillar from railing, Bharhut, second century* BC, *Indian Museum, Calcutta*

Some of the incarnations of the Buddha The Buddha appeared in several forms in his previous lives, gradually acquiring the strength and moral stature to attain Buddhahood or enlightenment. These stories are narrated in the *Jataka* tales.

Chadanta Jataka A white elephant with six tusks — and two wives. To his jealous wife he willingly sacrificed his tusks and died.

Mahakapi Jataka In the form of a monkey the Buddha willingly sacrificed his life to save his companion.

Mriga Jataka A golden deer who through his bravery was able to convert the hunter to the path of non-violence, or *ahimsa*.

The life of the Buddha To commemorate the Buddha's life on earth, a few important events that often appear in Buddhist narrative sculptures have been identified.

Maya's dream The Buddha's father was Suddhodana, the raja of Kapilavastu, a state in modern Nepal. His mother Maha Maya had a dream of a white elephant, which was interpreted to mean the birth of a 'gift to humankind' — either a great king or saint. Mother Maya is often portrayed lying on a bed surrounded by attendants, with a tiny elephant hovering above.

Birth of the Buddha In sculptures, mother Maya is shown standing near a tree, from her side the baby Buddha appears. According to the story, Maya desired to go to her father's home for the delivery. On the way there, they came to a grove of sal trees, named Lumbini. Stopping for a rest, she went into labour, and the Buddha was born.

Yasodhara and Rahul Gautama (Buddha) married Yasodhara, and had a son, Rahul. After attainment of *Nirvana*, they too joined his religious order.

The Buddha sees the cruelties of life Gautama's father strove hard to prevent his son from leaving the palace fearing that he might become an ascetic. Gautama managed to leave the palace in his chariot and in the streets of the city encountered illness, poverty and death. He then resolved to find the meaning of life and the path to end the cycle of human misery.

The Buddha leaving his palace In sculpture this scene is depicted by a horse, Gautama's faithful steed Kantaka, leaving the palace. Divine beings carry an umbrella over the horse (in Hinayana sculpture the horse is shown riderless, but the umbrella symbolises the Buddha's presence), others carry the feet of the horse, so that no one in the palace can hear and stop the Buddha in his resolve to renounce the world and all his earthly possessions.

Nirvana Gautama wandered for many days and months, visiting teachers and scholars and searching for the answer to the riddle of life. He understood that mere learning or asceticism will not provide an answer. At Bodhgaya in Bihar he meditated. He is tempted by Mara, and rain and thunder try to disturb his concentration. Beautiful women, the daughters of Mara, remind him of his palace, wife and son, but he perseveres.

Seated in the yogi posture for meditation, the lotus pose, or *padmasana*, the Buddha finally attained enlightenment. In sculpture he is shown seated in *padmasana* with his hands placed on his lap, one palm above the other in the *dhaya mudra*.

Mahaparinirvana The great and final liberation of Buddha from the cycle of incarnation.

Bhumisparsa mudra Buddha in meditation, tempted by Mara, reaches out with one hand and touches the ground, calling Mother Earth to witness the magical moment of his conquest of temptation and desire. Buddha is shown seated with one hand touching the earth. Below him, Mara and Mother Earth are usually personified.

Bodhisattva Potential Buddha is shown often as a prince wearing a diadem.

Avalokitesvara *Bodhisattva* A being who is capable (*isvara*) of enlightening insight (*avalokita*). In the legend we are told that he renounced the attainment of Buddhahood out of compassion and will continue to preach till the last being has been brought to enlightenment. He is often shown in sculpture, supported by a lotus stand, wearing jewels and rich attire. His face is however, lost in quiet meditation.

Avalokitesvara Padma Pani (or *Bodhisattva* Padmapani) He stands holding a lotus.

Bodhisattva **Vajrapani** In one hand he holds a *vajra* or thunderbolt, often like a rod with two small spheres at each end.

Maitreya Buddha The Buddha who is yet to come.

Chand The personification of the Moon.

Chamunda See Devi.

Churning of the Ocean Often depicted in painting and sculpture, this refers to an episode at the beginning of time when the ocean was churned (like milk); ambrosia and all goodness appeared, and the gods and demons fought to attain such powers. See Kurma *Avatar* under Vishnu.

Dakshinamurti See Shiva.

Dharmachakra Wheel of Dharma, see Buddhist art.

Devi A general term for the female principle, female goddess (Shakti, the power). It is in the union of male and female, of two opposites, that the wholistic concept of Hindu philosophy is to be understood.

Devi stands on a lotus pedestal, carrying a lotus in one hand. In her benign and terrifying form she may have a number of arms relaying her various attributes.

Seated Devi, Government State Museum, Chennai

Durga The inaccessible one. Devi is seated on a lion, having killed the demon Durgama.

Chamunda The goddess here too has a terrifying appearance. She is the destroyer of evil and wears a garland of skulls. She has a posture of an ascetic and has starved herself in her meditation and penance. Snakes, scorpions and the like adorn her emaciated body. The goddess, we are told, was created by Durga to encounter the demons Chanda and Munda from whom she derives her name.

Kali Bhadrakali and Mahakali are the forms that the Devi assumes to destroy evil. Her form with many arms, weapons of war and her terrifying expression scares away her opponents and evil-doing enemies, and which also destroys the fear of her devotees.

Mahishasuramardini Devi is created with all the powers of the gods to slay the demon bull Mahisha. She is often shown with several arms, beheading Mahisha, who transforms himself from a bull into the form of a man but is finally killed.

Uma, Parvati The wife of Shiva carries a lotus in one hand, and is often seated or standing next to Shiva.

Ekadanta See Ganesh.

Ganga Personification of goddess of the sacred River Ganga. The saint Bhagiratha prayed for her presence on earth to wash away the sins and ashes of the dead. Ganga with all her force descended, and Shiva took the weight of her mighty river on his head. The waters are said to have become lost in his curls, subdued by his presence. The river flows from the northern Himalaya, through the central plains of India, to the east where it meets the Bay of Bengal.

Ganesh (or Ganapati, Vighnesvara or Vinayaka) The remover of obstacles and the son of Shiva and Parvati.

Shiva Purana Parvati created Ganesh from dirt off her body. He served as her guard. On one occasion, Shiva attempted to enter Parvati's bathing area and was stopped by Ganesh. Unknowingly, Shiva cut off the head of his son. Parvati, in her fury, demanded the return of her son's life, and Shiva replaced Ganesh's head with that of an elephant's he obtained from a herd nearby.

Ganesh has two wives, Buddhi and Siddhi, personification of wisdom and attainment of desire respectively.

Ganapati The Lord of the *gana*, or chief of the army of the gods. He is also said to have aided Vyasa in the composition of the *Mahabharata*.

Ekadanta Ganesh's elephant head is represented in iconography with one broken tusk.

Garuda, the celestial bird mount of Vishnu

Hanuman, the loyal monkey friend of Rama of the Ramayana epic

There is a story that the Moon (*Chand*) looked down at the elephant-headed baby and began to laugh. Ganesh snapped his tusk and hurled it at the Moon who began to lose his brightness. Ganesh stopped the process, but the curse had been given, and forevermore the moon will wax and wane.

Eka is one, the only supreme being. *Danta*, tusk or tooth, is a symbol of strength and power. Hence Ekadanta is the all-powerful one. Among India's most popular deities, he is worshipped at the commencement of every activity and venture.

Ganesh is shown standing, sitting and dancing. Due to his belly, he is rarely in yogic posture but on a seat or throne. Ganesh's trunk turns towards the left (very rarely to the right). Apart from jewellery, Ganesh, like his father Shiva, wears a snake tied as a belt around his waist or across his chest, like the holy thread of caste Hindus. Ganesh has as his companion vehicle, or *vahana*, a rat that aids him in finding a way past all obstacles.

Garuda Mythical bird. This companion *vahana* (vehicle) of Vishnu is shown carrying him or with human arms folded in prayer.

Govardhana Mountain that Krishna lifted. See Krishna under Vishnu.

Gopies Cowherd women and wives who sport with Krishna.

Hanuman Monkey chief, the faithful companion and devotee of Rama in the *Ramayana*.

Hari Hara See Shiva.
Hinayana Period See Buddhist art.

Indra Lord of the firmament and sky, thunder and lightning, he holds a *vajra* (thunderbolt) in one hand. He rides on a huge white elephant resembling a white cloud. This Vedic deity was superseded by Krishna and others in later periods.

Jataka tales A collection of 500 tales relating to the previous incarnations of Buddha.
See Buddhist art.

Jain (Mahavir Jain or Gomateswara) born of princely family, like the Buddha, he leaves his home and takes to a life of severe asceticism. His teachings revolve around the notion of life as a continuous stuggle against desires. He spreads the message of peace and *ahimsa* (non-violence) as the path of deliverance from the cycle of life.

Kalki *Avatar* of Vishnu. See Vishnu.
Kali See Devi.
Kaliya Serpent that Krishna subjugated. See Krishna under Vishnu.
Kalyanasundara See Shiva.
Karttikeya See Skanda.
Krishna *Avatar* of Vishnu. See Vishnu.
Kurma *Avatar* See Vishnu.

Lakshmi The goddess of wealth emerging from the ocean and bathed by two elephants (Gajalakshmi). She represents all goodness. She appears in all Vishnu's incarnations as Sita, wife of Rama, as Rukmini, Satyabhama and Radha beside Krishna, etc. She carries lotuses, a pot of ambrosia and other emblems as well.
Linga Phallic symbol of Shiva. See Shiva.

Mahabharata See page 55-56.
Mahishasuramardini See Devi.
Maitreya Buddha who is yet to come.
Matsya *Avatar* See Vishnu.

Naga, Nagadeva A race of sacred serpents who rule the underworld, they represent the waters, the earth and all the treasures derived from the earth. As snakes are crucial to farmers in loosening the soil and destroying rats who eat the grain, snake worship is common in almost all parts of India. They are portrayed alone, often with hoods and jewellery or entwined as couples (*naga* and *nagini*) and along with other deities like Shiva, Ganesh, etc.

Often seen with human heads and arms and snake-like bodies, they are said to be immortal, having tasted the ambrosia from the 'Churning of the

Ocean' story (see above). They bring prosperity, marriage and offsprings to their devotees.

Nandi Bull. Companion (*vahana*, or vehicle) of Shiva.

Narasimha *Avatar* of Vishnu. See Vishnu.

Narayana Epithet of Vishnu.

Nataraja See Shiva.

Natesa See Shiva.

Parasurama *Avatar* of Vishnu. See Vishnu.

Pasupati Shiva, lord of all creatures. See Shiva.

Pipal tree See Buddhist art.

Radha Krishna's young lover. See Krishna under Vishnu.

Rama *Avatar* of Vishnu. See Vishnu.

Ravana King of Lanka, who kidnapped Sita and was defeated by Rama in the *Ramayana*. Depicted with ten heads, he is described in literature as a brave and well-read man. Unfortunately, his weakness (lust) was the cause of his downfall.

Rukmini Wife of Krishna. See Krishna under Vishnu.

Saraswati Goddess of learning and of all knowledge and wisdom. Her symbols are a book (palm leaf), holy beads, a *vina* (stringed musical instrument) and the lotus. She is assigned to Brahma as his companion.

Satyabhama Wife of Krishna. See Krishna under Vishnu.

Sesha The serpent that floats on the sea of eternity. See Anantasesha under Vishnu.

Skanda (Karttikeya or Subrahmanya) Shiva's son and the lord of Shiva's army, Skanda rides on a peacock. He was born of Shiva's seed, carried away by Agni (lord of fire) and brought up by Ganga (the river). (This is one version.)
He is described as a youthful, handsome boy, who is as radiant as the Sun.

Shiva An important deity, one of the trinity of Vishnu, Brahma and Shiva, conveying the symbols of preservation, creation and reabsorption, and recreation (achieved sometimes through destruction).
There are several manifestations of Shiva:
(i) Without form, the Supreme Being with no beginning and no end.
(ii) The luminous pillar or *linga* (phallic symbol), the emerging form that is limitless in its power.
The pillar appears in a story, from the Shiva Purana, when Vishnu and Brahma contest on who is the greatest. Shiva turns into a never-ending luminous pillar, Brahma and Vishnu strive to find the end of the pillar but fail to do so, hence stating Shiva's greatness.

Nataraja, tenth century, Madhya Pradesh, Archaeological Museum, Gwalior

The *linga* rests on a *yoni* stone, symbolising the female principle. The *linga* is often rounded or faceted; in rare examples a face or many faces appear on the side of the *linga*.

(iii) The third form that Shiva assumes for the benefit of his devotees is of a human.

Shiva is described firstly as an ascetic wearing the skin of a tiger or a simple loincloth. Snakes wind round his wrist and neck, like jewels, for he is also Lord of the underworld. In his hair Shiva wears the crescent moon as a jewel to symbolise this aspect as 'conqueror of time and all that changes'. He wears a *datura* flower in his matted sage-like hair. As in all depictions of deities, Shiva has many forms and many arms, limbs and heads to show his various attributes.

Nataraja Shiva dancing the dance of creation. He often stands with one leg lifted up, the other trampling on Apasmara, the symbol of ignorance. He is often shown with four arms: one carries a name (destruction), the other a *damru* (a little drum that beats out the rhythm of creation), one hand in *abhaya mudra* (protection) and the other pointing to his foot (denoting salvation from ignorance). His hair spreads out in waves, and there is often a halo of fire around his twirling form.

Pasupati Lord of all creatures, Shiva usually has his trident in one hand and a deer in the other.

Gangadhara Shiva is said to bear the weight of the great River Ganga as it falls down on to the earth. Ganga is depicted as a female goddess often perched in Shiva's hair, much to the annoyance of Shiva's jealous wife Parvati.

Tripurantaka In reference to a legend when Shiva, with his bow and arrow, destroyed the three cities of the demons.

Kalyanasundara Shiva as a handsome prince at the time of his marriage to Parvati.

Bhairava The 'terrible' form of Shiva, with an awesome expression, as an ascetic with little clothing accompanied by a dog.

Vishapaharana Shiva with a blue throat. He saved the world by swallowing the poison of the ocean. This stained his throat, hence *nilkantha* (*nil* means blue, *kantha* means throat).

Dakshinamurti The ascetic and teacher Shiva is seated in yogic position, surrounded by animals and devotees.

Shiva–Parvati Seen often as husband and wife, seated with their two children, Ganesh and Karttikeya, and their animal companions (Nandi, Shiva's bull, Parvati's tiger, Ganesh's rat and Karttikeya's peacock).

Hari Hara Partly Vishnu and partly Shiva.

Ardhanarisvara A composite figure, half-man and half-woman, Shiva and Parvati united to symbolise the reconciliation of opposites to create a wholistic entity.

The male half wears a different headdress, clothing and jewellery. The female side curves gracefully, relaxed and in repose.

Somaskanda Shiva, Parvati and son Skanda. See Skanda.

Stupa Buddhist funerary mound.

Subrahmanya See Skanda.

Surya The lord of the sun rides across the sky on a chariot drawn by seven horses (the seven colours of the rainbow). He usually carries two lotuses in his hand. He wears high boots, and the breastplate over his chest has given rise to a belief that his image is of foreign origin. He is accompanied by his charioteer, the lame Aruna. The women companions or handmaidens include Rajni, Usha and Chhaya — radiance, dawn and shade respectively. Usha and Pratyusha drive away the darkness with their bows and arrows.

Tara Buddhist goddess of compassion·

Tirthankaras There are ten regions of the universe, each with 24 Tirthankaras in each of the three ages — past, present and future. They take the part of teachers who, by their example, lead the way to salvation. Mahavir Jain was one such saintly person.

Tripurantaka See Shiva.

Trinikrama See Vishnu.

Uma See Devi.

Vajra Thunderbolt.

Vajrapani *Bodhisattva* with the thunderbolt. See Buddhist art.

Vamana *Avatar* of Vishnu. See Vishnu.

Varaha *Avatar* of Vishnu. See Vishnu.

Venugopal Krishna, the flute player.

Vinayaka See Ganesh.

Vishapaharana See Shiva.

Vishnu From ancient lore, where Vishnu was one amongst the Vedic deities, he emerges to form part of the trinity of Brahma, Shiva and Vishnu.

Vishnu is shown in three positions, standing, sitting and reclining. When he is standing with one hand raised in the *abhaya* hand gesture, he is offering protection to his devotees.

In one hand Vishnu carries the *Shankh*, or conch, used to blow the battle signal, the sound of salvation. In his other hand is the *chakra*, or disc, the symbol of protection, a circular wheel with spokes that is flung at the enemy, cutting off their heads and arms. He also carries the lotus of creation and a wooden club, the symbol of destruction. Vishnu's consorts are Lakshmi, who sits to the right, and Bhumidevi, on the left. They are the attributes of wealth and the prosperity of the earth, and they carry a lotus and a lily.

Anantasesha The reclining Vishnu lies on the serpent Sesha that floats on the

Episode from the Childhood of Krishna, Bhagavad Purana, *Basohli style at Mankot, 18th century, Government Museum and Art Gallery, Chandigarh*

sea of eternity. Lakshmi is seated beside Vishnu, and Bhumidevi is often shown pressing his feet.

The serpent Adisesha has a hood of one or more heads, with a body that coils to provide a bed or seat for Vishnu. Brahma is said to have emerged on a lotus from the belly of Vishnu.

The *vahana* of Vishnu is Garuda, identified with the Brahminy kite, a large beautiful chestnut-coloured bird found in India.

Incarnations or *avatars* of Vishnu In every cycle of decadence Vishnu is said to come to earth to save her from destruction. Vishnu is seen sometimes surrounded by his ten *avatars*.

Matsya *Avatar* Vishnu appears in the form of a huge fish, or half-fish and half-man.

The legend tells of a sage who caught a small fish and put it in a bowl. The fish grew too big for the bowl, and the lake, and had to be taken to the sea. This fish saved the universe that was overwhelmed by a deluge.

The fish *avatar* is also said to have saved the Vedas and boly hooks from the floods.

Kurma *Avatar* Vishnu appears as a tortoise that served as a gigantic pedestal in the episode referred to as the 'Churning of the Ocean'. The gods and demons churned the ocean at the beginning of time as one churns milk to make butter. By churning the ocean, the good and evil came to the top of the ocean, and ambrosia — the formula for eternal and youthful life — was brought forth from the waters. In order to churn the mighty ocean, the gods needed a churning stick. For this they used a mountain, and Vishnu as a tortoise provided the support to hold the stick in place.

Varaha *Avatar* From the deluge, at the origin of the earth, Vishnu in the form of a giant boar lifted up the earth (goddess) out of the waters of creation.

Vishnu's form is often shown as half-man with the face of a boar, that has picked up the earth Bhu, personified as a little goddess (Bhuvaraha).

Narasimha *Avatar* Vishnu appears with a lion's head and human body, usually with the evil man, Hiranyakasipu, who is being torn apart and devoured, on his lap. The story has it that Hiranyakasipu obtained many boons from the gods and declared himself infallible. No one, neither man nor beast, could kill him, no weapon could injure him, neither by day nor at night, outside or in the house. Perturbed by his power, the gods requested Vishnu to destroy Hiranyakasipu. Vishnu assumed the form of half-man and half-lion, and at dusk, at the threshold of the house (neither inside nor outside), he tore the demon to pieces.

Vamana *Avatar* (**Trivikrama**): In sculpture and paintings Vamana, or Vishnu, is usually depicted as a dwarf or small man who is receiving a gift from Bali the king. In order to teach Bali a lesson, Vamana asks for a gift of three paces.

Varaha, the Boar incarnation of Vishnu, Basohli, 1765,
Government Museum and Art Gallery, Chandigarh

How much land can the dwarf take in three paces thinks Bali and agrees to make this gift. Vishnu steps out of the Vamana form and places one foot to conquer the earth, another that stretches from earth to heaven, and looks for a third place. Bali, realising Vishnu's greatness, offers his head, acknowledging his defeat. In sculptures Vishnu is shown stretching out his leg to take the three steps (*tri* meaning three plus *vikrama* meaning victory). The repentant Bali was then made lord of the underworld.

Parasurama Very rarely to be seen, Vishnu in human form holds a *parasu* (battleaxe), in one hand. Born as a Brahmin, he took to the ways of a *kshatriya* (warrior), and slayed his mother for her lustful ways.

Rama This *avatar* of Vishnu is the hero of the epic *Ramayana* and, with his wife Sita and brother Lakshmana, is depicted in sculptures and paintings. Rama usually holds a bow, Sita stands to his right, and Lakshmana, a little shorter than Rama, often carries a bow. Hanuman the monkey lord is often shown with this group.

Krishna

Venugopal An *avatar* of Vishnu as the boy cowherd, Venugopal — Krishna as the player of the *venu* (flute) — plays music, luring his followers, the cowherds and cows.

In order to free the world from oppression, Krishna was born to kill the wicked King Kansa. This king had imprisoned Devaki, prophesied to be the holy mother. Her child was smuggled out at birth and given to Yasodha to look after. This scene is depicted as a stormy night, with a child being carried away in a basket. King Kansa is dashing a child to the ground, attempting to kill all infants he thinks might destroy him.

Balkrishna Baby Krishna dancing with a butter ball, crawling and playing.

Kaliyakrishna and Goverdhana Krishna's childhood as a cowherd is described in many scenes: with his mother Yasodha killing the demon horse, conquering the serpent Kaliya, breaking away from the cart and mortar, stealing butter, dancing with a butter ball, playing with the *gopis* and girls of the village, lifting up Mount Goverdhana to protect cows and humans from the storm sent by Lord Indra.

Krishna is usually depicted with the attributes of Vishnu, the conch and the disc. He wears a peacock-feather crown, a flaming yellow *dhoti*, garlands and flowers. His skin is said to be dark like the blue-black rain clouds, symbolic of his goodness.

His lover as a cowherd was Radha. Krishna's chief wives are Rukmini and Satyabhama. From his childhood in Mathura and Brindavan (UP), Krishna went to live in Dwaraka (Gujarat).

Krishna reappears in the *Mahabharata* story. He plays the charioteer and philosopher–guide to Arjuna during the great battle to explain the *Bhagavad Gita* (song of the Divine One) which contains the essence of Hindu philosophy.

Buddha Also considered to be an *avatar* of Vishnu (incorporated in the medieval period).

Kalki The *avatar* of Vishnu that is yet to come, at the end of this *kaliyuga* (time

Vishnu carrying the disc and conch, Chandella period, 11th century,
Archaeological Museum, Khajuraho

Chronology, Historical Sites and Related Museums

Approximate Chronology	Historical Period	Historical Sites	Related Museums
	Stone Age	Bhopal Shymala Hills, Bhimbetka, 35 kms from Bhopal (Madhya Pradesh).	National Museum of Man, Bhopal; National Museum, New Delhi.
	Neolithic Age	Excavations in progress.	
2500 BC	Harappan Civilisation	Kalibangan (Rajasthan); Lothal (Gujarat); Others.	National Museum, New Delhi; Lothal Site Museum; Indian Museum, Calcutta; Prince of Wales Museum, Mumbai.
800 BC	Iron Age	Excavations at various places.	National Museum, New Delhi; others.
	Birth of the Buddha; Birth of Mahavira	Lumbini, Nepal; Bodhgaya (Bihar); Sarnath (Uttar Pradesh).	Bodhgaya Museum, Sarnath Museum.
327 BC	Invasion of Alexander From Macedonia		
c. 315 BC	Visit of Megasthenes From Greece		
Fourth–Second centuries BC	Mauryan Rule	Pataliputra, Patna (Bihar); Sarnath (Uttar Pradesh); Sanchi (Madhya Pradesh).	Patna Museum, Patna; Site Museum, Sarnath.

Yakshi, eastern gateway, Stupa No 1, second century BC, Sanchi, Madhya Pradesh

Second–first centuries BC	Sunga	Bharhut (Uttar Pradesh); Bodhgaya (Bihar).	Indian Museum, Calcutta; Lucknow Museum (Uttar Pradesh); Mathura Museum, (Uttar Pradesh).
second BC–AD second centuries	Satavahana	Sanchi (Madhya Pradesh); Rockcut caves (Maharashtra); Amaravati Stupa, (Andhra Pradesh).	Sanchi Museum; Government Museum, Chennai (Tamil Nadu); Site Museum, Amaravati; National Museum, New Delhi.
	Indo-Graeco-Roman	Taxila, now in Pakistan, etc. North-western region, Mathura (Uttar Pradesh).	Indian Museum, Calcutta; Chandigarh Museum; National Museum, New Delhi.
c. first century	Mission of St Thomas to south India		
first–second centuries	Kushana		Indian Museum, Calcutta; Prince of Wales Museum, Mumbai.
second-third centuries	Ikshvaku Shakas Vakataka	Caves of Ajanta (Maharashtra).	
third–fifth centuries	Visit of Faxian Gupta	Deogarh, Nachna, Sanchi (Madhya Pradesh); Udaigiri (Orissa).	National Museum, New Delhi; Indian Museum, Calcutta; Site Museum, Sanchi (Madhya Pradesh); Patna Museum, Patna (Bihar) etc.
630–44	Visit of Xuan Zang		

fourth–ninth centuries	Pallava	Mahabalipuram and Kanchipuram (Tamil Nadu).	Government Museum, Chennai (Tamil Nadu); National Museum, New Delhi.
Sixth–eighth centuries	Western Chalukyas	Aihole, Badami and Pattadakal (Karnataka).	Government Museum, Chennai; National Museum, New Delhi; Prince of Wales Museum, Mumbai.
eighth–ninth centuries	Rastrakuta	Ellora (Maharashtra).	
seventh–11th centuries	Eastern Chalukya	Vengi, Vijaywada (Andhra Pradesh).	
eighth–13th centuries	Eastern Ganga	Temples of Bhubaneswar and Konarak (Orissa).	State Museum, Bhubaneswar; National Museum, New Delhi.
eighth–12th centuries	Pala	Nalanda and Paharpur (Bihar).	Site Museum, Nalanda.
11th–13th centuries	Senas		Ashutosh Museum, Calcutta; National Museum, New Delhi.
ninth–11th centuries	Pratihara	Kannauj (Uttar Pradesh), Osian, Kotah and Bikaner (Rajasthan).	National Museum, New Delhi; Museums in Bikaner, Kotah, Udaipur, etc.
ninth–12th centuries	Chola	Thanjavur, Gangai-kondacholapuram, Darasuram and Chidambaram (Tamil Nadu).	Government Museum, Chennai (Tamil Nadu); Thanjavur Art Gallery, Thanjavur (Tamil Nadu).
tenth–11th centuries	Chalukya	Somnath (Gujarat); Madurai (Tamil Nadu); Abu (Rajasthan); Gumla (Bihar).	

tenth–13th centuries	Chandella	Khajuraho (Madhya Pradesh).	Site Museum, Khajuraho; Indian Museum Calcutta; Bharat Kala Bhavan, Banaras (Uttar Pradesh);
12th–14th	Hoysala	Belur, Halebid and Somnathpur (Karnataka).	National Museum, New Delhi; Government Museum, Chennai (Tamil Nadu).
13th century	Slave Dynasty Marco Polo Visits south India	Qutb Minar complex, New Delhi.	
14th century	Khalji Tughlaqs	Tughlaqabad Fort (Delhi); Daulatabad Fort (Maharashtra).	
14th–16th centuries	Vijayanagar Sayyidi Lodis	Hampi (Karanataka).	Government Museum, Chennai; State Museum, Bangalore (Karanataka); Site Museum, Hampi.
15th century	Ahmad Shah	Monuments of Ahmedabad (Gujarat).	
	Rao Sodha Marwar	Fort of Jodhpur (Rajasthan).	Jodhpur Museum.
15th–17th centuries	Bahmanid Empire	Bijapur and Bidar (Karanataka); Golconda (Andhra Pradesh).	State Museums; British Museums, London. Salar Jung Museum, Hyderabad (Andhra Pradesh);
	Raja Man Singh	Gwalior Fort (Madhya Pradesh).	Gwalior State Museum.

1498	Vasco da Gama	Kozhikod (Kerala)	Archaeological Museum, Old Goa.
1510	Alfonso d'Albuquerque	(Goa).	Archaeological Museum, Old Goa.
16th century	Sultan of Mandi	Mandu (Madhya Pradesh).	Nimat Nama, National Museum.
1526	Mughals: Babur	Delhi.	National Museum, New Delhi.
1530–56	Humayun	Delhi.	
	Sher shah Suri	Delhi; (Bihar).	
1556–1605	Akbar	Agra and Fatehpur Sikri (Uttar Pradesh); Delhi.	National Museum, New Delhi; Prince of Wales Museum, Mumbai; Bharat Kala Bhavan, Banaras (Uttar Pradesh).
17th century	Basohli Punjab Hill State		National Museum, New Delhi; Chandigarh Museum, Chandigarh (Punjab); Prince of Wales Museum, Mumbai; Allahabad Museum (Uttar Pradesh); and others.
1605–27	Jahangir	Agra (Uttar Pradesh); Delhi; Lahore, Pakistan.	Prince of Wales Museum, Mumbai.
	Sir Thomas Roe from England		
	British rights to factories at Surat,		

	Ahmedabad and Cambay (Gujarat)		
1627–58	Shah Jahan	Agra (Uttar Pradesh); Delhi.	Prince of Wales Museum, Mumbai; National Museum, New Delhi; Victoria & Albert Museum, London.
1658–1704	Aurangzeb	Delhi, Aurangabad	
	French settlement at Pondicherry		
1691	Calcutta founded by Job Charnock		Victoria Memorial Museum, Calcutta.
18th century	Maharaja Jai Singh II	Building of Jaipur City, Observatories.	Maharaja Sawai Madho Singh Museum, Jaipur (Rajasthan).
	Nizam of Hyderabad	Hyderabad (Andhra Pradesh).	Salar Jung Museum, Hyderabad.
	Nadir Shah invades and sacks Delhi		
18th–19th centuries	Raja Sansar Chand, Kangra	Punjab Hills (Punjab).	Kangra Paintings, National Museum, New Delhi; Prince of Wales Museum, Mumbai; Bharat Kala Bhavan, Varanasi (Uttar Pradesh); Government Museum & Art Gallery, Chandigarh (Punjab); Allahabad Museum (Uttar Pradesh).

1784	Foundation of Asiatic Society		
18th–19th centuries	Visit of Thomas & William Daniell William Fraser		Victoria Memorial Museum, Calcutta. Fort St George, Chennai (Tamil Nadu).
1819		Ajanta caves (Maharashtra) are rediscovered.	
1837–58	Bahadur Shah II Last Mughal emperor exiled to Rangoon	Delhi.	National Museum, New Delhi; Victoria Memorial Museum, Calcutta.
1857	The Mutiny British Raj		
1858		Archaeological Survey of India formed.	
1862			Indian Museum, Calcutta, eastablished.
1877	Queen Victoria crowned Empress of India		Victoria Memorial Museum, Calcutta; Statues in Chennai, Bangalore, Delhi, etc; Prince of Wales Museum, Mumbai
	Independence Movement		
1913-31		New Delhi built as capital of British Raj in India.	Nehru Memorial Museum, Delhi; Gandhi Museum, etc.
1947	India gains Independence		

Recommended Reading

Ali, Salim *The Book of Indian Birds* (Bombay Natural History Society, Bombay, 1979)

Allchin, Raymond *The Rise of Civilization in India* (Cambridge University Press,
& Bridget Cambridge, 1982)
———, *The Birth of Indian Civilization* (Penguin India, New Delhi, 1993)
———, *Origins of a Civilization: The Prehistory and Early Archaeology
of South Asia* (Viking, New Delhi, 1997)

Anand, M R *The Hindu View of Art* (London, 1933)

Archer, W G *Indian Miniatures* (Victoria and Albert Museum, London, 1960)

Asher, Catherine B *Architecture of Mughal India* (Cambridge University Press, Cambridge, 1992)

Basham, A L *The Wonder That Was India* (Sidgwick & Jackson, London, 1954)
———, *The Origins and Development of Classical Hinduism* (OUP, New Delhi, 1990)
——— (ed), *A Cultural History of India* (Clarendon Press, Oxford, 1975)

Beach, Milo *Mughal and Rajput Painting* (Cambridge University Press, Cambridge,
Cleveland 1992)

Birwood, G C M *The Industrial Arts of India* 2 Vols (Chapman & Hall, London, 1880)

Brown, Percy *Indian Architecture* 2 Vols (Bombay, 1942)

Chattopadhyay, *Handicrafts of India* (ICCR, New Delhi, 1975)
Kamaladevi

Coomaraswamy, *The Dance of Shiva* (Dover, New York, reprint 1985)
Ananda Kentish
———, *History of India and Indonesian Art* (Dover, New York, reprint 1985)
Cooper Ilay, Gillow *Arts & Crafts of India* p160 (Thames and Hudson, London, 1996)
John

Davies, Philip *Monuments of India: Islamic, Rajput, European* Vol II (Viking, London, 1989)

Dange, Gouri (ed) *Mud Mirror and Thread Folk Traditions of Rural India* p22 (Mapin Publishing Pvt. Ltd. Chidambaram, Ahmedabad, India 1995 (reprint) 1993, 1st published)

Desmond, Ray *The European Discovery of Indian* (Flora OUP, Oxford, 1992)
Frater, Judy *Threads of Identity, Embroidery and Adornment of the Nomadic Rabaris* p203 (Mapin Publishers Pvt. Ltd, Chidambaram, Ahmedabad, India, 1995)

Gandhi, M K *My Experiments with Truth* (Harmondsworth: Penguin, 1982)

Gopinatha Rao, T A *Elements of Hindu Iconography* 2 vols (The Law Printing House, reprint, 1978)

Goswamy, B N *Essence of Indian Art Asian Arts Museum* (San Francisco, 1986)

Guy J and Swallow D (eds) — *Arts of India: 1550-1900* (Victoria and Albert Museum, London, 1990)

Harle, J C — *The Art and Architecture of the Indian Sub-continent* (Harmondsword: Penguin, 1986)

Jayakar, Pupul — *The Earth Mother: An Introduction to the Ritual Arts of Rural India* (Penguin, New Delhi, 1981)

Keay, John — *India Discovered* (Collins, London, 1988)

Kramrisch, Stella — *Indian Sculpture* (Calcutta, 1933)

——, — *The Hindu Temple* 2 vols (Calcutta, 1946)

Lanoy, Richard — *Speaking Tree* (Oxford University Press, New York, 1971)

Martand Singh, Rita Kapur (eds) — *Chishti Saris of India, Bihar & West Bengal* (Wiley Eastern Ltd, New Delhi, 1995)

Michell, George — *Monuments of India: Buddhist, Jain, Hindu* Vol I (Viking, London, 1989)

Nehru, Jawaharlal — *The Discovery of India* (Oxford University Press, New Delhi, 1916)

Patnaik, Naveen — *The Garden of Life. An introduction to the Healing Plants of India* (Doubleday, New York, 1993)

Punja, Shobita — *Great Monuments of India, Bhutan, Nepal, Pakistan and Sri Lanka* (Odyssey, Hong Kong, 1994)

Randhawa, Mohinder Singh and Doris Schreier — *Indian Sculpture: The Scene, Themes and Legends* (Abrams, Bombay, 1985)

Rowland, Benjamin — *The Art and Architecture of India* (Pelican History of Art) (Pelican, London, 1963)

Shah, Shampa (ed) — *Tribal Arts and Crafts of Madhya Pradesh* p136 (Mapin Publishing Pvt. Ltd, Ahmedabad and Vanya Prakashan, Bhopal, 1996)

Shivaramamurti, Calambur — *The Art of India* (Abrams, New York, 1974)

——, — *Nataraja in Art, Thought and Literature* (National Museum, New Delhi, 1974)

Stronge, Susan — *A Golden Treasury: Jewellery from the Indian Subcontinent* (Victoria and Albert Museum, London, 1988)

Spear, Percival — *A History of India* Vol II (Harmondsworth: Penguin, 1966)

Thapar, Romila — *A History of India* Vol I (Harmondsworth: Penguin, 1966)

Tillotson, G H R — *Mughal India* (Viking, London, 1990)

Vatsyayan, Kapila — *Classical Indian Dance in Literature and the Arts* (Sangeet Natak Akademi, New Delhi, 1968)

Wacjiarg, Francis, — Nath Amar   *Arts and Crafts of Rajasthan* p228 (Mapin Publishing Pvt Ltd Ahmedabad, 1994 reprint)

Index

Abhaya 84, 159, 235, 250
Abu 43
Adil Shahis 189
Adinatha Temple 209
Advent of the Rainy Season,
    painting of 106
Agra 66-9, 113, 143, 154, 156, 165
Ahichchhatra 85
Ahimsa 43
Ahmedabad (Gujarat) museums 17, 21,
    71, 170-9
Aihole, temple of 60, 86, 123-4, 129
Ajanta Caves 51, 57, 170, 175
Akbar 66-8, 94, 146, 156, 2188; period
    143, 253
Akbari style 253
Akbarnama, manuscript of 68
Akbar Hunting, painting of 94
Alasa Kanya, sculpture of 252
Allahabad Fort, painting of 154
Alwar (Rajasthan) museum 24, 178-80;
    school 180
Amaravati collection 45, 80, 141, 156-9,
    249
Anwar-I-Suhalli, illustrations of 127
Approaching Storm, painting of 254
Archaeological Museum: Goa 189-90;
    Khajuraho 209-14; New Delhi 113;
    Sanchi 231-3; Sarnath 50, 234-6
Archaeological Survey 20, 76, 113, 220,
    236
Architecture: Colonial 70-2, 103; Indo-
    European 72; Indo-Islamic 66-8;
    Islamic 64-8, 121, 202; Mughal 65-70,
    91, 121, 146, 202; temple 123, 209
Arms 69-70, 113 166-7, 180, 195-7,
    202, 204-5; Gallery 204-5; also see
    Daggers, Swords, Weapons
Armour 68, 132
Armoury 16, 24, 121-3
Artifacts 38, 68, 72, 76, 131, 135, 140,

146, 181, 195, 234
Ashoka tree 82
Ashutosh Museum, Calcutta 60, 73,
    144-9
Asiatic Society 20, 135, 156
Asian art 181
Ashoka, Emperor 49-50, 157, 217, 224,
    231, 234
Ashokan lion capital 50, 231, 234
Assam, kingdom in 60; State Museum
    42, 191-2;
Astasahasrika Prajnaparamita,
    manuscript of 90, 253
Aurangzeb 129-9, 197, 256
Aurangzeb Reading the Quran, painting
    of 129
Avalokitesvara, statuette of 131

Babur 65, 91, 127
Baburnama 66-7, 91, 127
Bacchanalian Figures 220
Badami, temple of 60, 86, 123, 189
Banks, Thomas 166
Baramasa series of paintings 206-7
Baroda Group 10
Baroda (Gujarat) museum 181-2
Basilica de Bom Jesus 189
Basohli region 94-5; School 11, 246-7,
    257, 284
Bathers, The 107
Bendre 110
Bengal school 105-6
Benzoni, G.B. 109
Bhagavad Gita 56, 215
Bhagavad Purana 95, 181, 246-7, 257,
    284
Bharat Bhavan, Bhopal 183
Bharat Kala Bhavan, Varanasi 46-7, 70,
    245
Bharhut Room 135-9, 273; site 45,
    135-9, 248-9

Bhikshatanamurti, sculpture of 241
Bhopal (Madhya Pradesh) museum 183
Bhu Varaha, sculpture of 212
Vhubaneswar museum 184-7; temple of 186
Bhumisparsa mudra 211
Bidri work 101, 131, 77, 195
Bijapur 189
Bikaner 86
Black Buck and Doe, painting of 123
Bodhisattva 5, 50, 123, 131, 181, 220, 225, 233, 235
Bodhi tree 134, 159, 273
Mumbai museum 121-33
Bombay Progressive Artists Group 108
Books 20, 72, 105, 107, 116, 151, 193-4, 205; Birdwood on textiles 147; Coomaraswamy 158, 161; palm-leaf 70, 90, 147; Randhawa on sculpture 135; sastras 32; Shivaramamurti 88-9, 161; zoological 143 book stands 70, 197-9;
Bose, Nandlal 106
Boxes 101, 123, 132, 177, 180, 197, 227-8; for gunpowder 197, 204-5
Brahma, 53, 86, 242; panel of 124; sculpture of 250
Brahmacharis, The 107
Brihadeswara Temple 239
British Museum, London 20, 45, 80, 136, 156, 218
British Raj 121, 150-5
Brocades 171, 194, 202; Benares, 256
Bronze galleries 88-90, 159-63, 225, 243; South Indian 161; sculpture 103, 156, 194, 241, 243
Buddha 17, 131, 141, 158-9, 211, 220, 225, 233-6; also see Bodhisattva; Bharhut Room
Buddha, figure of 84, 235
Buddha and Six Disciples from Miran, wall painting of 99
Buddha Taming the Mad Elephant, Nalagiri, sculpture of 249

Buddhism 40-53, 80, 137-40, 186, 219, 224, 234-5
Bundi, paintings from 130-1
Bust of the Devi, sculpture of 192
Bustan, manuscript of 91

Calcutta museums 135-55
Calico Museum of Textiles, ahmedabad 17, 21, 71, 170-5
Calligraphy 64, 90-1, 180, 253, 256
Camel Fight, painting of 58-9
Camel Flight, painting of 91
Carpets 199, 205
Chalcolithic period 37, 78
Chalukyas 57, 60, 86, 123, 159, 189
Chamunda, sculptures of 86-7
Chand 94
Chandellas 60, 62, 142, 208-9, 212, 25-2, 287
Chanhu-daro 37, 76
Chardin 199
Chariot festival 62; wooden chariots 62, 244; also see Palanquins
Chaundhury, D.P. Roy 103
Chauhan kingdom 60, 86
Chavda 110
Chera kingdom 60
Chidambaram, temples of 57
Chitragupta Temple 209
Cholas 60-1, 89, 159, 160-1, 163, 200-1, 239, 241, 243, 270
Chugtai, A.R. 107
Cire perdue 161, 241
Citrakathi paintings 228-9
Claude Martin with His Friends, painting of 154
Cock on a Tree, ivory work of 132
Cloisonne 132
Coins 48, 72, 140-1, 166-7, 190, 217, 219, 231; gold 48, 141
Colonial period 36, 70-2, 144, 150, 155, 166, 193, 195
Colour symbolism 32; festivals and seasons 170; the blue gold' 32

Company school 103, 105
Constable 132, 199
Copper 78, 86, 177; also see Cire perdue
Crafts Collection, Calcutta 146-9
Crafts Museum, New Delhi 73, 110-3
Curzon, Lord 21, 150

da Gama, Vasco 189-90
Daggers 113, 123, 180, 193, 195-7, 204-5
Daimabad 80
Dalliance of Krishna, painting of 131
Damaged Stucco Horse, sculpture of 99
Dance of Creation, sculptures of 161
Dancing Ganesh, sculptures of 208, 210, 252
Dancing Girl, sculpture of 74, 78
Daniell, Thomas and William 103, 105, 154, 166-7
Dara Shikoh 94, 128
Dara Shikoh, painting of 128
Davis, Samuel 154
De Albuquerque, Afonso 189-90
De, Sailendranath 106
Deccani school 70, 129-30, 198-9, 206
Deogarh 84
Devi 17, 20, 191-2, 211, 242, 270, 275
Dhamekh stupa at Sarnath 234-5
Dhananjaya 187
Dharma 50, 234; dharma chakra 235
Documents 72, 116, 155, 166-7, 238; farmans 113
Dream of Buddha's Mother, Maya, sculptured panel of 158
Durga 87, 149, 250

Eastern Gangas 60-1
Elephant see Nalagiri
Ellora Caves 57, 170
Embassy of Haider Beg to Calcutta, painting of 154
Embroidery 194, 203, 256
Emperor Jahangir Holding a Picture of the Madonna, painting of 94

Empress, sculpture of the 150
European art 132, 181, 199; engravings 154
Everyday life, arts of 226-9; also see Household objects, Kitsch

Falcon, The 91
Fall of Tipu and the Imprisonment of His Children, painting of 238
Flight, painting of 110
Flying Gandharvas, sculpture of 86
Fort paintings 105, 154, 253; prints 167
Fort, Red: Agra 66, 69; Delhi 69, 113-5, 256
Fort St George Museum, Madras 17, 72, 105, 155, 163-7
Fatehpur Sikri 66, 156
Fraser's drawings of the Himalayas 154

Gandhara region 53, 219; art of 48, 99, 123; school 51, 250; sculpture 48, 50, 81-4, 123, 139-400, 220, 249-50
Gandhi Memorial Museum, New Delhi 73, 116-8
Ganesh 96, 124, 210-1, 226, 233; also see Dancing Ganesh
Ganga 41, 49, 205, 242, 245; figure of 85
Gangaikondacholapuram temple 239
Gardens 65, 68-9, 72, 102-3, 120-1, 150, 170, 181, 190, 218, 234, 237-8, 243; in art 91, 99, 128, 130, 180, 186, 194, 203, 206, 218
Garuda 88, 277
Gateway of India 121
Gautama 41
Gesture No. 2, painting of The 110
Ghulam Ali Khan, portrait of 103
Girl Praying Near Fire, painting of 105
Gita Govinda, manuscript of 126-7, 186-7, 215
Galss 16, 72, 111, 132, 194, 199, 204; paintings on 239
Goa Archaeological Museum 189-90

Goat and Coolie from Shillong, painting of 106
Gold: book stands 70; coins 48, 141; inlaid with 123, 180, 204; jewellery 38, 68, 78; religious items 189; swords 197; thread 101, 171-4, 194, 202-3, 256; also see Bidri work, Cire perdue
Goli stupa 159
Govardhana 252-3
Graeco-Roman influence 51, 81, 217, 220, 249
Gulistan, manuscript of 180
Gunpowder boxes/containers 197, 204-5
Gupta period 82-5, 191, 218, 220, 235; sculpture 235-6; terracotta 225
Guwahati (Assam) museum 191-2
Gwalior (Madhya Pradesh) museum 72, 280

Halder, Asit Kumar 106
Hampi 64
Hamzanama, manuscript of 253
Handicrafts and Handlooms Museum, New Delhi 73, 110-3
Hara Gauri, sculpture of 250
Harappa 37, 75-6
Harappan Civilization 37-8, 75=80, 171; also see Indus Valley
Hari Hara, figure of 211
Haudahs 205
Head of Shiva, painting of 106; terracotta figurine of 248
Head Study, painting of 107
Hebbar 110
Hinayana period 157, 159, 219, 231; school 51, 139
Hinduism 40, 53, 56, 85, 186, 189
Himalayas, Fraser's drawings of 154
History of museums 20-4
Hodges, william 103, 151, 154
Holi Festival, painting of 128
Household objects 70, 72, 151, 166-7; also see Everyday life, arts of; Kitsch

Hoysala kingdom 60-1; period 88, 159
Humayun 65-8
Hussain, M.F. 108-10
Hyderabad (Andhra Pradesh) museum 193-9

Independence movement 72-3
Indian Museum, Calcutta 16-7, 21, 36, 45, 48, 62, 134-43, 152-3, 156, 218, 248, 273
Indian royality 103, 180-1
Indo-European architecture 72
Indo-Islamic architecture 66-8
Indra 40, 42, 96, 252-3
Indus Valley Civilization 37-8, 800, 101-2, 121, 126, 170, 175; Gallery of 75-80; terracottas of 245, 248 Iron Age 38-40
Islamic architecture 64-8, 121, 202; Ivory 101, 126, 132, 180-1, 205; Room 195

Jade 69-70, 123, 131-2, 180, 193, 195, 204; Room 197-8
Jahangir 68, 148, 165, 197-9, 206; paintings of 94, 128, 206
Jahangir and His courtiers, painting of 206
Jahangir with His Attendants in a Garden, painting of 128
Jahangirnama, manuscript of 91
Jain palm-leaf miniatures 198; rock-hewn architecture 57; sculpture 210, 214, 217; temples 43, 62, 209
Jainism 40-4, 53, 186, 189
Jaipur House, New Delhi 102, 110
Jaipur (Rajasthan) museum 202-7
Jataka tales 45, 249
Jayadeva 95, 186, 215
Jewellery 16, 37-8, 68-9, 77-8, 82, 101, 126, 131, 160, 203; boxes 177; appearing in paintings 70, 95, 103, 105, 128, 143, 186, 239; appearing in sculpture 61, 84, 88, 124, 139, 162-3,

186, 210, 213, 224-5, 233, 241, 243, 248-9, 251
Journey I, painting of 110

Kailash Temple 57; Mountain 209, 250
Kailashnath Temple, Kanchipuram 57
Kalamkari 173, 194
Kali 150
Kalibangam 37
Kalikacharyakatha, manuscript of 126
Kaliya 88-90
Kaliya Krishna, sculpture of 88
Kaliya Mardan Krishna, bronze of 89-90
Kalki 211
Kalpasutra, manuscript of 126, 147
Kalyanasundaramurti, sculpture of 241
Kamakhya Devi temple 191
Kanchipuram, temples of 56-7, 86, 159; silk 173
Kandariya Mahadeo Temple 209
Kangra 92-3, 95, 152-3
Kanishka 51; statue of Emperor 217; also see King Kanishka
Kantha 149
Karnataka, temples in 123, 129
Karttikeya 96, 162; sculpture of 252
Kashmir 60, 64; bronzes 88; paper 180; rumals 101; shawls 101, 143, 174, 194, 256
Kerala uruli 175
Kettle, Tilly 154
Khadi 171
Khajuraho (Madhya Pradesh) museum 208-14, 287; temples of 142, 209
Khakar, Bhupen 110
Khaljis 64
King Kanishka, figure of 219
King Vima Kadphises, figure of 218
Kirtan, painting of 108
Kishangarh style 98
Kitsch 24, 72, 143, 228; also see Everyday life, arts of; Household objects
Konarak, Sun Temple at 61-2, 186;

sculptures from 32, 86, 186
Kotah 98
Krishna 11, 32, 56, 88-90, 95-6, 98-9, 108, 127-8, 131, 152-3, 187, 215, 217-8, 252-4, 256-7. 284
Krishna and Balarama, painting of 108
Krishna Holding Mount Goverdhana, statue of 25
Krishna Installing the Parijata Celestial Tree in His Palace in Dwaraka, painting of 96
Krishna Making Love to Gopies, painting of 96
Krishna Making Love to Gopies, painting of 95
Krishna Steals the Gopies' Clothes, painting of 92-3, 95
Krishna Sitting with His Beloved, painting of 131
Krishna with the Cow Herds, painting of 128
Kula hut 111
Kumar, Ram 110
Kurma Avatar
Kushana coins 217; empire 45, 51, 217; sculpture 82, 218-9, 249

Ladies in the Garden, painting of 99
Lady Dorabji Tata, portrait of 132
Lady Looking in a Mirror, painting of 130
Lady on a Swing, painting of 99
Lady Dorabji Tata, portrait of 132
Lady Looking in a Mirror, painting of 130
Lady on a Swing, painting of 206
Lady Ratan Tata, portrait of 132
Lady Riding a Griffon, sculpture of 249
Lady with a Crane, painting of 207
Lady with an Attendant and a Peacock, painting of 129
Lady Writing a Love Letter, Sculpture of 142
Ladhore (Pakistan) 48, 107, 140

Laila, painting of 107
Laila and Majnu, painting of 199
Lakshmana 55, 84-5, 163; temple 209;
Lakshmi 131, 220, 226-7, 233
Lakshmi and Narayana, sculpture of 88,
131, 213-4
Lamps 226-7
Landscape, pastel of 106
Lapwing, drawing of 127
Lion capital 50, 231, 234
Literature 26-9 also see Manuscripts,
Poems, Poetry
Locks 227
Lodi Sultanate 64
Lothal 37, 76
Lotus flower 26, 29, 35, 82, 121, 124,
130-1, 139, 159, 163, 186, 211-3,
231, 233-4, 249; position 159
Lovers at Night, painting of 205
Lumbini 82

Mabarak Mahal 202
Madhubani 111
Madonna and Child, painting of 198
Madonna with Her Child, painting of
The 206
Madras museums 21, 36, 45, 156-67,
200-1, 258-9, 275
Madurai, temples of 57; museum in 116
Magician, painting of 107
Mahabalipuram, temples at 56-7, 86, 159
Mahabharata 40, 55-6, 85, 215, 228
Mahakapi Jataka 137
Mahaparinirvana of Buddha, manuscript
art of 90
Maharaja Sawai Madho Singh Museum,
Jaipur 202-7
Mahavira 43, 97
Mahayana period 140, 157, 231
Mahishasuramardini, painting of 96
Mahishasuramardini, sculpture of 87,
186, 233
Mahishasuramardini Durga, sculpture of
250

Maitreya, sculpture of 123
Majnu in the Company of Wild Animals,
painting of 99
Majumdar, Kshitindranath 106
Man II, painting of 110
Man with a Bunch of Plastic Flowers,
painting of 110
Mandu 90
Mandu Kalpasutra, manuscript of 90, 97
Manuscripts 9, 180-1, 199, 253; Gallery
of 90-9; palm-leaf 62, 70, 87, 90, 126-
7, 147, 184-6, 205
Marriage of Dara Shikoh, painting of
The 94
Marshall, Sir John 21, 76, 231
Mataji, painting of 110
Mathura 45, 80-2, 884, 105, 249, 253
Mathura (Uttar Pradesh) museum 45,
51-215-21
Mauryan period 45, 49-51, 75, 80, 121,
189, 216-7, 220, 224-5, 231, 24, 245
Maya's dream 158
Meeting at the Staircase, painting of 107
Meeting of Sufis, painting of The 94
Mehta, Tyeb 110
Menon, Anjoli Ela 110
Menon, Anjoli Ela 110
Metal, images in 101, 131
Metalware 193, 195, 227
Mineralogy gallery 135
Miniature painting 70, 121, 130, 132,
143, 170, 187, 194, 198-9, 257
Modern Art Gallery, New Delhi 73, 102-
10
Mohenjo-daro 37-9, 75-6, 78, 80
Mohini, sculpture of 88
Mother and Child, figure of 101
Mother and Child Lying on a Bed,
sculpture of 142
Mughal 65-70, 85, 101, 113, 121-3,
127-9, 141, 146, 156, 165, 192, 197-8,
202, 205, 218, 224, 245, 256; school
of painting 58-9, 67, 91-4, 99, 105,
123, 127-9, 143, 180, 205-6, 253-4

Mukherjee, Binodi Behari 107
Music 25
Musicians, painting of 30-1, 107; sculpture of 88

Naga, Nagadeva 221, 251
Naga Queen of the Serpents, bust of a 221
Nagarjunakonda stupa 159
Nalagiri 158, 249
Nalanda, ancient university of 53, 144
Nanda 249-50
Narasimha, King 86; sculptures of 87
Narayana see Lakshmi
Nari Kunjam, painting of 206
Nataraja or Natesa, sculptures of 89, 160-1, 243, 280
National Gallery of Modern Art, new Delhi 73, 102-10
National Museum, New Delhi 9, 22-3, 39, 45, 67, 74-102
Natural History 132-3; also see Zoological Section
Nature, love for 170; respect for 28-9
Nayak period 239
Nayika in Agony, painting of 130
Nehru Memorial Museum and Library, New Delhi 73, 118-20
Nehru Planetarium 118
Nepal 41, 51, 60, 82, 90, 131, 199, 224
Nepal and Tibet gallery, Mumbai 121, 131
New Delhi museums 75-120
Niravana 41, 159, 245
Nutcrackers 177, 227-8

Observatory at Benares, watercolour of
Omar Khayam, painting of 107
Orissa, architecture of 61-2
Orissa State Museum 184-7

Padmapani, figure of 5, 233
Pahari school 46-7, 128, 246-7, 257; Pahari-Guler school 254

Paintings: from Bundi 130-1; Citrakathi 228-9; on cloth 173, 194; National Museum Gallery of 90-9; glass paintings of Tanjore 239; Modern Art 103-10; wall paintings 99, 111; also see Baramasa, Chardin, Constable, Daniell, Davis, Deccani school, Pahari school, Pahari-Guler school, Portraits, Royal Gallery, Turner, Zoffany
Pala period 60, manuscript of 90; sculpture of 87, 142, 144-6, 192
Palace museums: alwar 180; Baroda 181; Hyderabad 193-9; Jaipur 202-7; Summer Palace, Srirangapatnam 237-8
Palanquins 160, 205
Pallava period 159, 161, 239-40; school 163
Palm-leaf manuscripts 147, 184-7, 205; miniatures 198
Pandya kingdom 60, 239
Parsvanatha Temple 209
Part of the Fort at Vellore, watercolour of 105
Parvati 96, 124, 128, 162, 241, 250-2
Pataliputra 49, 224-5
Patna (Bihar) museum 5, 51, 224-5
Patachitra 146-7, 94
Pattadakal, temple of 60, 86, 123
Photographs 119, 151, 194
Pipal tree 139, 211
Pithawala, M.F. 105
Playing cards 147
Poems 40, 84, 127, 186; also see Gita Govinda, Mahabharata, Ramayana
Poetry 26-8, 32, 62-4, 72, 130, 136, 142, 147, 161, 170, 183
Pondicherry 48, 71-2, 165-6
Porcelain 132, 165, 167, 199
Portrait of Daniyal, painting of 123
Portraits 70, 87, 94, 96, 103, 107, 119, 128, 132, 151, 154, 166, 180-1, 190, 196, 206, 228, 238; Gallery 151, 166; Tilly Kettle's 154
Post-Mughal style 103

Pottery 37-40, 48, 76-7, 111-2, 126, 181, 225, 231, 245
Pratihara period 60, 251-2
Pratiksha, painting of 106
Prehistoric artifacts 181
Prince and the Hawk, painting of The 198
Prince of Wales Museum, Mumbai 21, 25, 33, 36, 39, 58-9, 69, 121-33, 164
Princess and Musicians, painting of 206
Princess on the Terrace, painting of 206
Pune (Maharashtra) museum 226-9
Punjab school 103; museum 50, 284-5
Purana Qila 111
Puri, chariot festival at 62; temple at 61-2

Queen Alexandra and King Edward VII, portrait of 103
Quilting 149
Quran 90
Qutb Minar 64

Radha 127-8, 187, 215; paintings of 11, 95, 98-9, 152-3, 254
Radha and Krishna Sheltering from the Rain, painting of 95
Radha Offering Flowers to Yogi Krishna, painting of 98-9
Raga Balwant Deva with his Berber, painting of 129
Raga Megha Malhat, painting of 98
Ragamala series of paintings 180-1
Ragini series of paintings 206
Rasika 32-4
Raja Dinkar Kelkar Museum 226-9
Raja Medini Pal of Basohli, painting of 94
Raja Sansar Chand of Kangra, painting of 94
Rajasthani school 199
Rajput kingdom 60, 204, 224
Rama 55, 84-5, 163
Rama, Sita and Lakshmana, figure of 163, 200-1

Ramayana 40, 30-1, 46-7, 54-6, 84, 147, 228, 278
Ramkinkar 106
Rasa 33-4, 130
Rastrakuta period 57, 60
Ravana 55, 84-5, 250-1
Ravana Nugraha Murti, sculpture of 250
Raza 110
Red Fort see Fort
Roe, Sir Thomas 94, 165
Roy, Jamini 108
Royal Gallery 151; household objects 70, 72, 151
Rumals 101, 174, 256
Rupar 76

Salar Jung Museum 71, 193-9
Sanchi (Madhya Pradesh) museum 231-3, 288
Sanganer, fabrics from 203
Saraswati, sculpture of 86
Saris 148, 171
Sarnath Archaeological Museum 234-6
Sastras 29, 32
Satavahana period 45, 80, 189
Sati stones 190
Satyabhama 96
Sawai Madho Singh I on a Boat, painting of 206
Scene of an Assault on a Fort, painting of 253
Screens 194
Scroll 108, 146-7, 180, 194, 205; paintings 228
Sculpture: Buddhist, Hindu and Jain 17, 54, 123-4, 131, 139, 141, 144-6, 190-2, 210-4, 219-21, 233, 235-6, 241-3, 248-52; from Java and Cambodia 143; Medieval Gallery 85-8; stone 239, 248; also see Armaravati collection, Ashokan lion capital, Bharut Room, Bronze, Gandhara, Konark, Kushana, Pala,

Sena, Terracotta, Western Art Section, Wood figures
Seascape, painting of 106
Self Portrait, Shergil's 107
Sena period 60, 87; sculpture of 144-6
Sesanaga 33
Sesha 124
Shah Jahan 68-70, 94, 113, 128, 218, 253, 256
Shakti worship 192
Shawls of Kashmir 101, 143, 174, 194, 256
Sheik, Gulam Mohammed 110
Sherbati fabrics 170
Shergil, amrita 107
Shikaras 57, 61
Sikhism 70
Silk 148, 171, 173, 202, 245, 256
Silver: decorative arts 126, 131; dining table 180; inlaid with 180, 204; large jars 205; jewellery 78, 139, 224; religious items 167, 189; also see Bidri work, Cire perdue
Sita 55, 84-5, 163
Shiva 53, 55, 96, 124, 128, 162, 240-3, 250-2; Gallery 210; sculptures of 161-3, 241, 251
Shiva and Parvati, paintings of 128; sculpture of 251
Shiva's Family and banasura, painting of 96-8
Shiva Purana 162
Skanda 162
Somaskanda figures 162
Souza 110
Srirangapatnam (Karnataka) museum 237-8
St Cajetan, church of 189
St Francis of Assisi, convent of 190
St Mary's Church 166
Stone Age 37, 191
Storming of Srirangapatnam, painting of The 238

Stupas 45, 51, 80-1, 131, 135-6, 140-1, 156-7, 159, 217, 219, 221, 224, 226, 231-5, 248-9
Sumair, portrait of 107
Sun god 62, 213, 221, 250; also see Surya
Sun Temple of Konark 62, 87, 186
Sundaram, Vivan 110
Sunga period 45, 80, 217, 220, 245
Surasundaris, sculpture of 213
Surat 165
Surpanakha being punished by Lakshmana, panel of 83-4
Surya, sculptures of 213, 221, 250
Surya Mandir 87
Swaminathan 110
Swords 113, 180, 193, 195-7

Tagore, abanindranath 105
Tagore, Gaganendranath 107
Tagore, Rabindranath 104, 106
Taj Mahal 68-9, 150, 256
Taming of the Elephant Nalagiri, circular panel of 158
Tanjore (Tamil Nadu) gallery 239-42
Tara, statuette of 131
Taxila (Pakistan) 48, 53, 81, 140
Temple Door, painting of 107
Temples 44, 52, 146, 159, 191, 268
Terracotta 51, 54, 85, 121, 140, 183, 191, 216, 219-20, 224-5, 236, 245, 248
Textiles 147-9, 170-5, 193-4, 256-7; Gallery 202-4; Museum 170-5; wood-block printed cloth 203; also see Shawls of Kashmir,
Thanjavur Art Gallery 163, 239-42, 270
Thankas 131
Tibet 60, 144, 191, 199
Tibet (Nepal and) gallery, Mumbai 121, 131
Tiger Hunt, painting of 154
Timingila Jataka, stone panel of 249

Tipu Sultan Museum 237-8
Tirthankaras, sculpture of 214
Toilet Bearer, sculpture of 249
Toys 24, 38, 77, 102, 108, 111, 146, 183, 199, 225-7, 248
Tribal art 101, 183
Tripurnataka, sculpture of 86
Triumph of Labour, sculpture of 103
Tiruvananthapuram (Kerala) museum 243-4
Tughlaqs 64
Turner 199
Tutinama 91
Twilight, painting of 106
Two Women 107

Uma-Mahesa, sculpture of 190
Uma-Mahesvara, panel of 124, 129
Uma Worshipping Shiva, painting of 128
Universal themes 34
Utensils Museum, Ahmedabad 17, 175-7

Vaishnava Gallery 210
Vajrapani, figure of 233
Vamana 211
Varaha 212-3, 285
Varanasi (Uttar Pradesh) museums 245-57
Varma, Ravi 105
Vedit Literature 38-40
Veiled Lady, painting of 107
Veiled Rebecca, sculpture of 199
Venkatappa 106
Victoria and albert Museum, London 20, 68-9
Victoria Memorial Museum, Calcutta 72, 105, 150-5, 167
View of the fort at Trichinopoly, watercolour of 105
View of Mathura on the River Yamuna, watercolour of 105
Vijayanagar empire 64, 189
Vishabhantika with the Devi, sculputre of 242
Vishapaharana, sculpture of 163
Vishnu 33, 53, 84, 87-8, 90, 124, 180, 210-3, 215, 233, 285, 287
Vishnu, sculpture of 84, 287
Vishnu and his Consorts sculpture of 87
Vishnu on the sesha, sculpture of 124
Vishnu Srinivasa, sculputre of 243
Vishnudharmottaram 26
Vishnupur region, temples in 146
Visvanatha Temple 209

Wall paintings 99, 111
Weapons 38, 72, 167, 193, 195, 204-5; also see Arms
Weaving 101, 148, 172-4; silk 148, 173, 202, 245
Western Art Section 199
Western Chalukyas 60
Wood 28, 34, 73, 111, 126, 226-7, 244; blocks 173; covers 90, 147, 250; figures 101, 140, 181, 189, 191; kitsch 143; lacquered 132; also see Boxes, chariots
Wood-cock, drawing of 127
Woman Holding Fruit, painting of 105
Woman in Moonlight, painting of 105

Yakshi figures 138, 142, 217, 233, 248, 288
Yakshi from Didarganj, sculpture of 224
Yamuna 68, 85, 105, 215
Yashoda and Krishna, painting of 108

Zamin, painting of 108
Zari work 194, 203
Zoffany, Johann 154
Zoological Section 143; garden 243; also see Natural History